D1327447

THE CYCLE OF WATER

To Camille, my parents, Mammy.
To Sophie, Hugo (AKA Joe), and Heloise.
Special thanks to Eric Chevalier for his
invaluable help with dialogue.

— Hub

PLAINFIELD PUBLIC LIBRARY
15025 S. Illinois Street
Plainfield, IL 60544

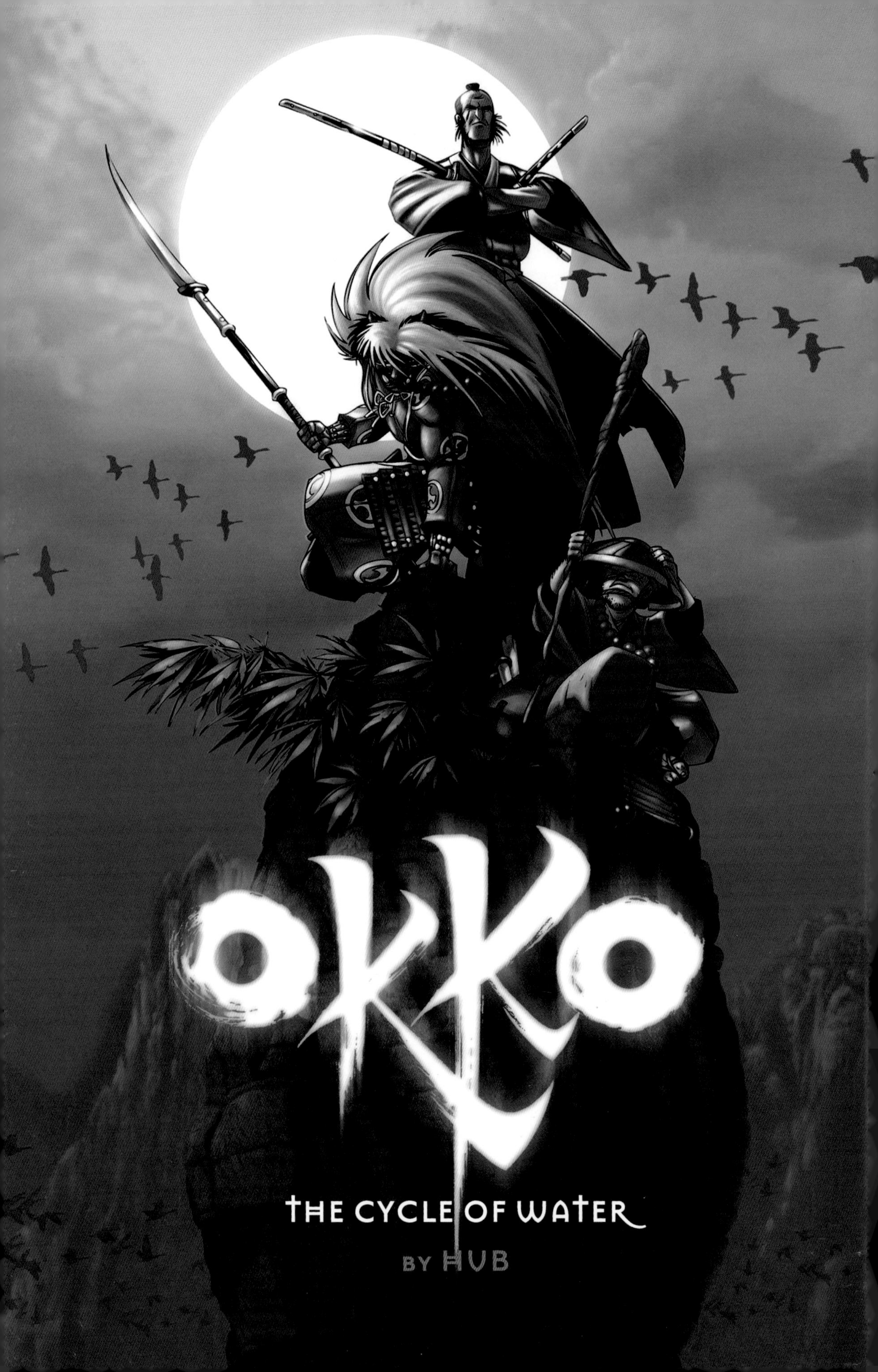
OKKO
THE CYCLE OF WATER
BY HUB

ARCHAIA

OKKO
THE CYCLE OF WATER

Written and Illustrated by HUB
Colors by HUB and
STEPHAN PECAYO
Translated by EDWARD GAUVIN

Published in the US by **Archaia**

PJ Bickett, *President*
Mark Smylie, *Publisher*
Stephen Christy III, *Director of Development*
Mel Caylo, *Marketing Manager*
Brian Torney, *Associate Director, Creative Services*

Archaia Entertainment LLC
1680 Vine Street, Suite 912
Los Angeles, California, 90028
www.archaia.com

Originally published
in France by
DELCOURT

Okko: The Cycle of Water
ISBN 1-932386-45-9
ISBN 13: 978-1-932386-45-5

10 9 8 7 6 5 4 3 2

OKKO™ is © and TM 2005
Guy Delcourt Productions.
The Archaia™ Logo is TM 2009
Archaia Entertainment LLC.
All rights reserved. No unauthorized
reproductions permitted, except for review
purposes. Any similarity to persons
alive or dead is purely coincidental.

Printed in China.

3 1907 00285 6754

THE CYCLE OF WATER

BOOK ONE

WRITTEN & ILLUSTRATED BY
HUB

COLORS BY
HUB & STEPHAN PELAYO

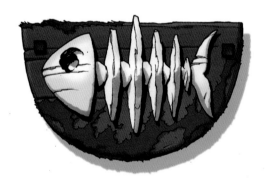

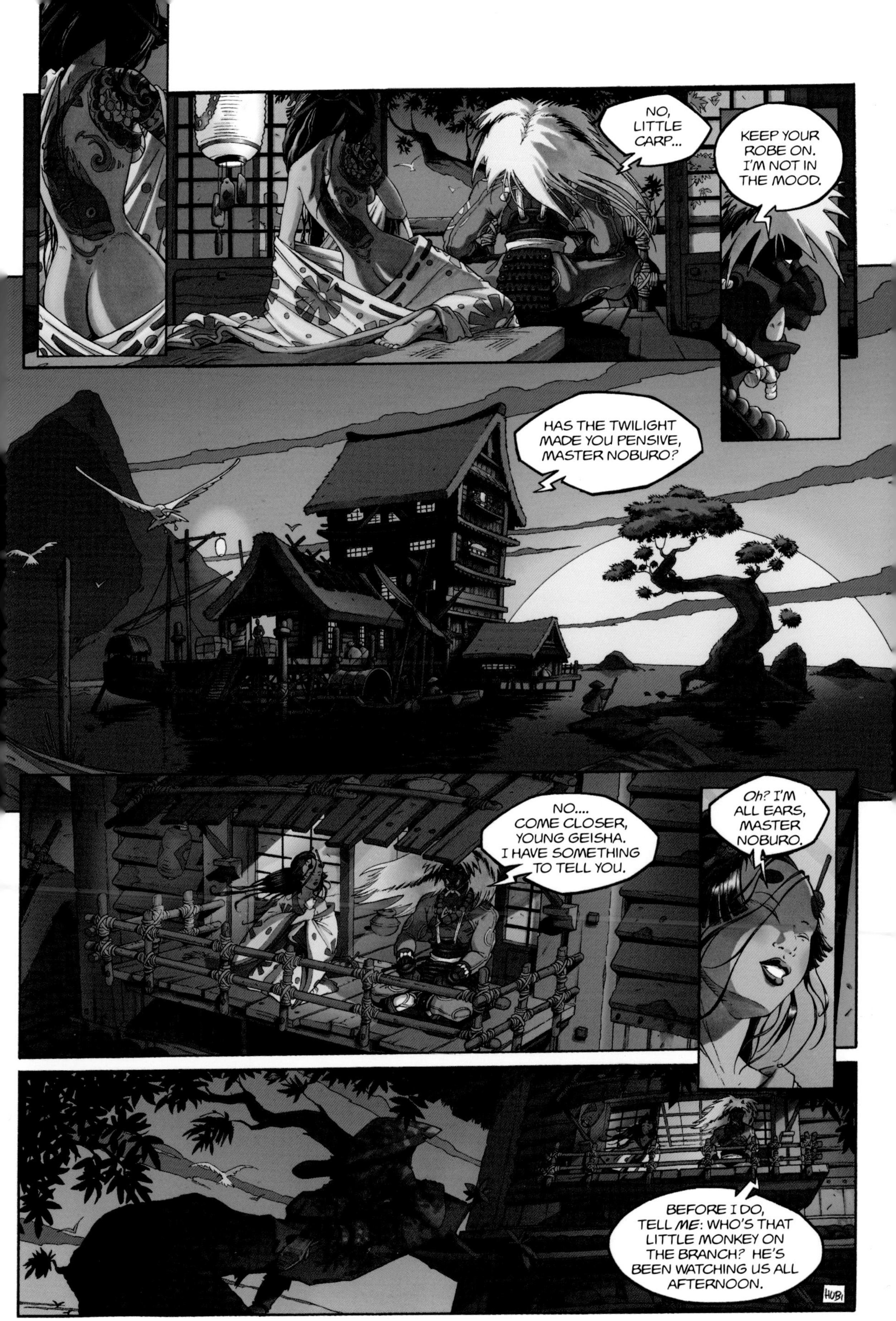
NO, LITTLE CARP...
KEEP YOUR ROBE ON. I'M NOT IN THE MOOD.
HAS THE TWILIGHT MADE YOU PENSIVE, MASTER NOBURO?
NO.... COME CLOSER, YOUNG GEISHA. I HAVE SOMETHING TO TELL YOU.
Oh? I'M ALL EARS, MASTER NOBURO.
BEFORE I DO, TELL *ME*: WHO'S THAT LITTLE MONKEY ON THE BRANCH? HE'S BEEN WATCHING US ALL AFTERNOON.
HUBi

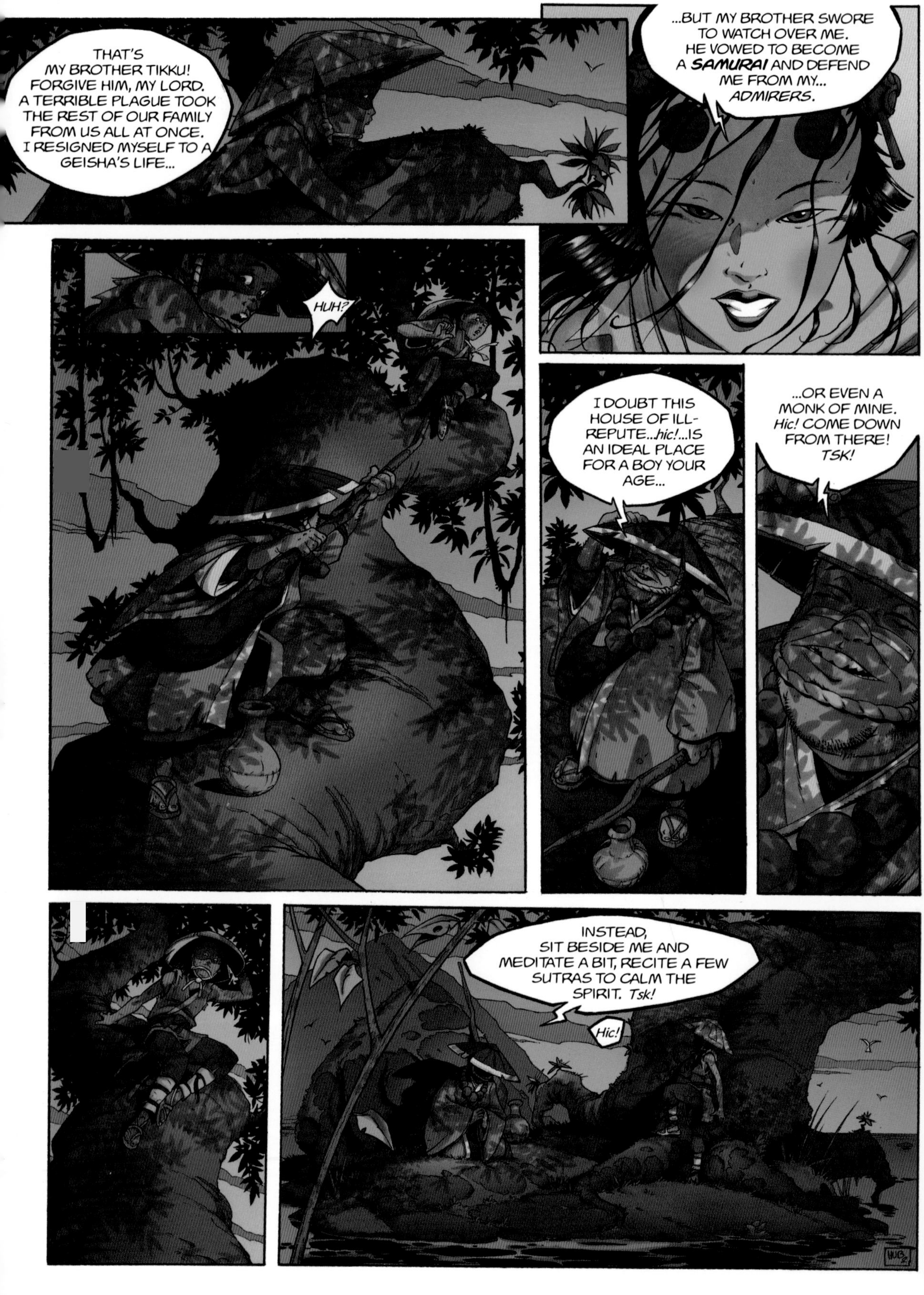
THAT'S MY BROTHER TIKKU! FORGIVE HIM, MY LORD. A TERRIBLE PLAGUE TOOK THE REST OF OUR FAMILY FROM US ALL AT ONCE. I RESIGNED MYSELF TO A GEISHA'S LIFE...
...BUT MY BROTHER SWORE TO WATCH OVER ME. HE VOWED TO BECOME A SAMURAI AND DEFEND ME FROM MY... ADMIRERS.
HUH?
I DOUBT THIS HOUSE OF ILL-REPUTE...hic!...IS AN IDEAL PLACE FOR A BOY YOUR AGE...
...OR EVEN A MONK OF MINE. Hic! COME DOWN FROM THERE! TSK!
INSTEAD, SIT BESIDE ME AND MEDITATE A BIT, RECITE A FEW SUTRAS TO CALM THE SPIRIT. Tsk!
Hic!

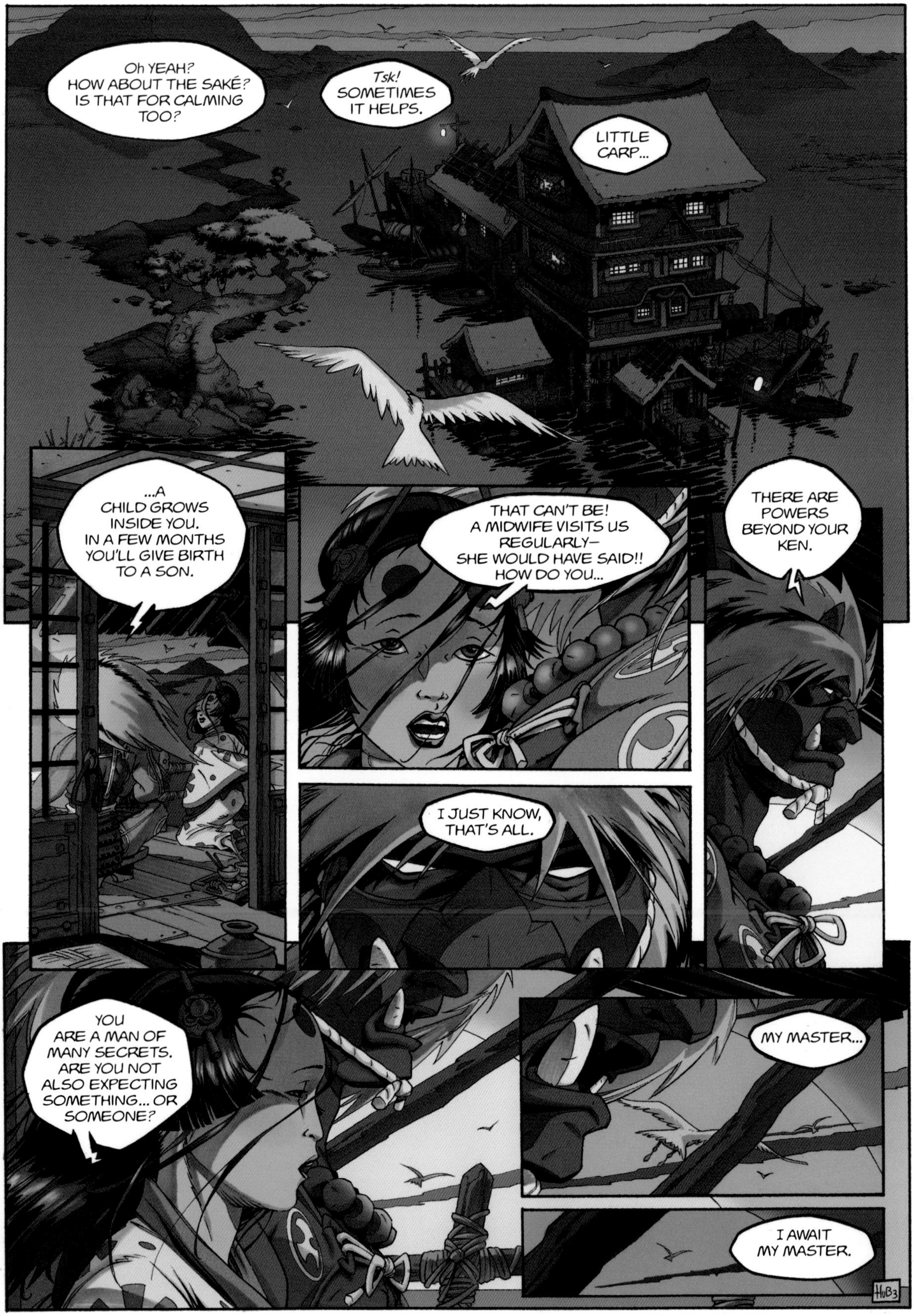
Oh YEAH? HOW ABOUT THE SAKÉ? IS THAT FOR CALMING TOO?
Tsk! SOMETIMES IT HELPS.
LITTLE CARP...
...A CHILD GROWS INSIDE YOU. IN A FEW MONTHS YOU'LL GIVE BIRTH TO A SON.
THAT CAN'T BE! A MIDWIFE VISITS US REGULARLY— SHE WOULD HAVE SAID!! HOW DO YOU...
THERE ARE POWERS BEYOND YOUR KEN.
I JUST KNOW, THAT'S ALL.
YOU ARE A MAN OF MANY SECRETS. ARE YOU NOT ALSO EXPECTING SOMETHING... OR SOMEONE?
MY MASTER...
I AWAIT MY MASTER.
HuB3

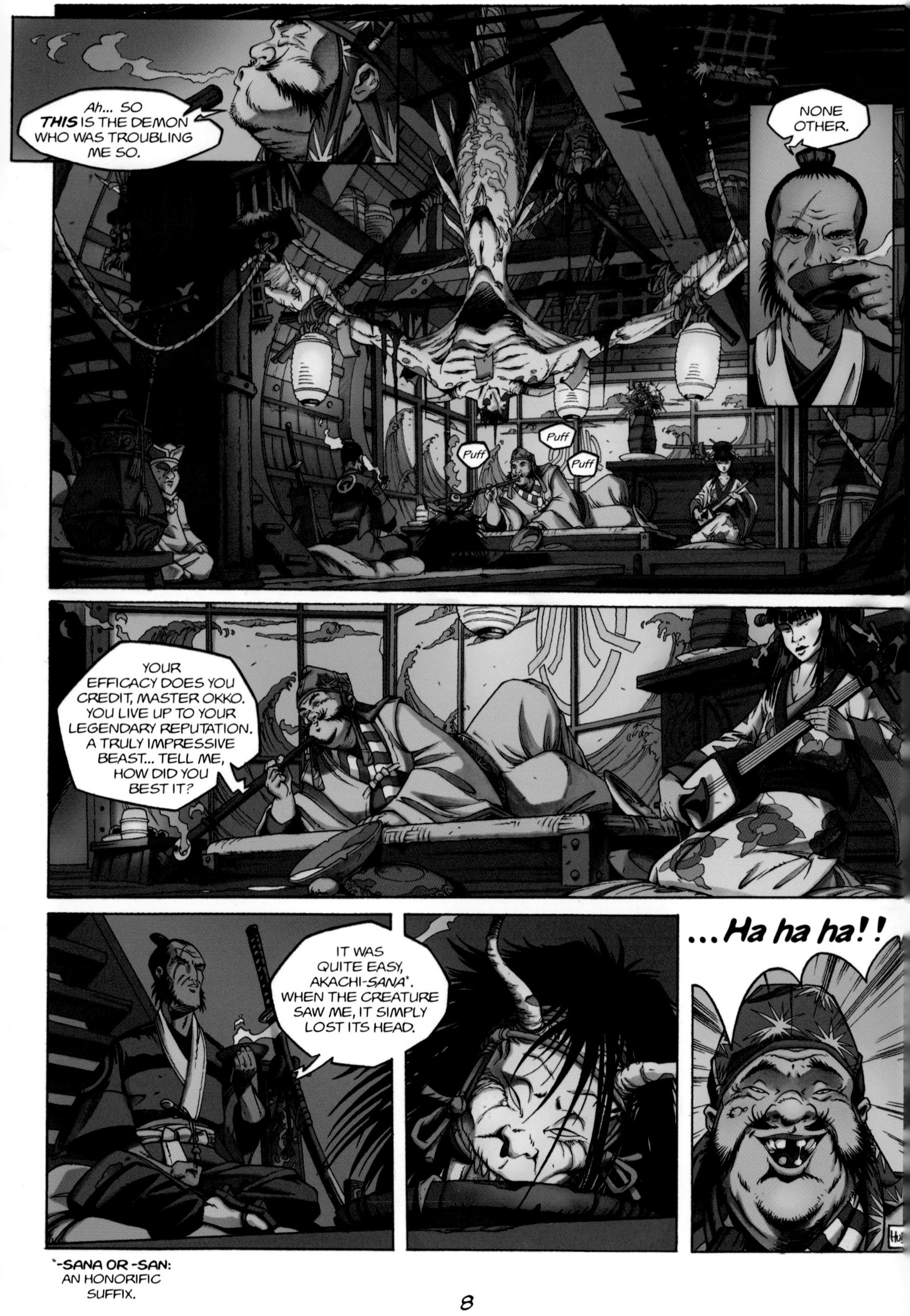

Ah... SO THIS IS THE DEMON WHO WAS TROUBLING ME SO.
NONE OTHER.
Puff
Puff
Puff
YOUR EFFICACY DOES YOU CREDIT, MASTER OKKO. YOU LIVE UP TO YOUR LEGENDARY REPUTATION. A TRULY IMPRESSIVE BEAST... TELL ME, HOW DID YOU BEST IT?
IT WAS QUITE EASY, AKACHI-SANA*. WHEN THE CREATURE SAW ME, IT SIMPLY LOST ITS HEAD.
...Ha ha ha!!

*-SANA OR -SAN: AN HONORIFIC SUFFIX.

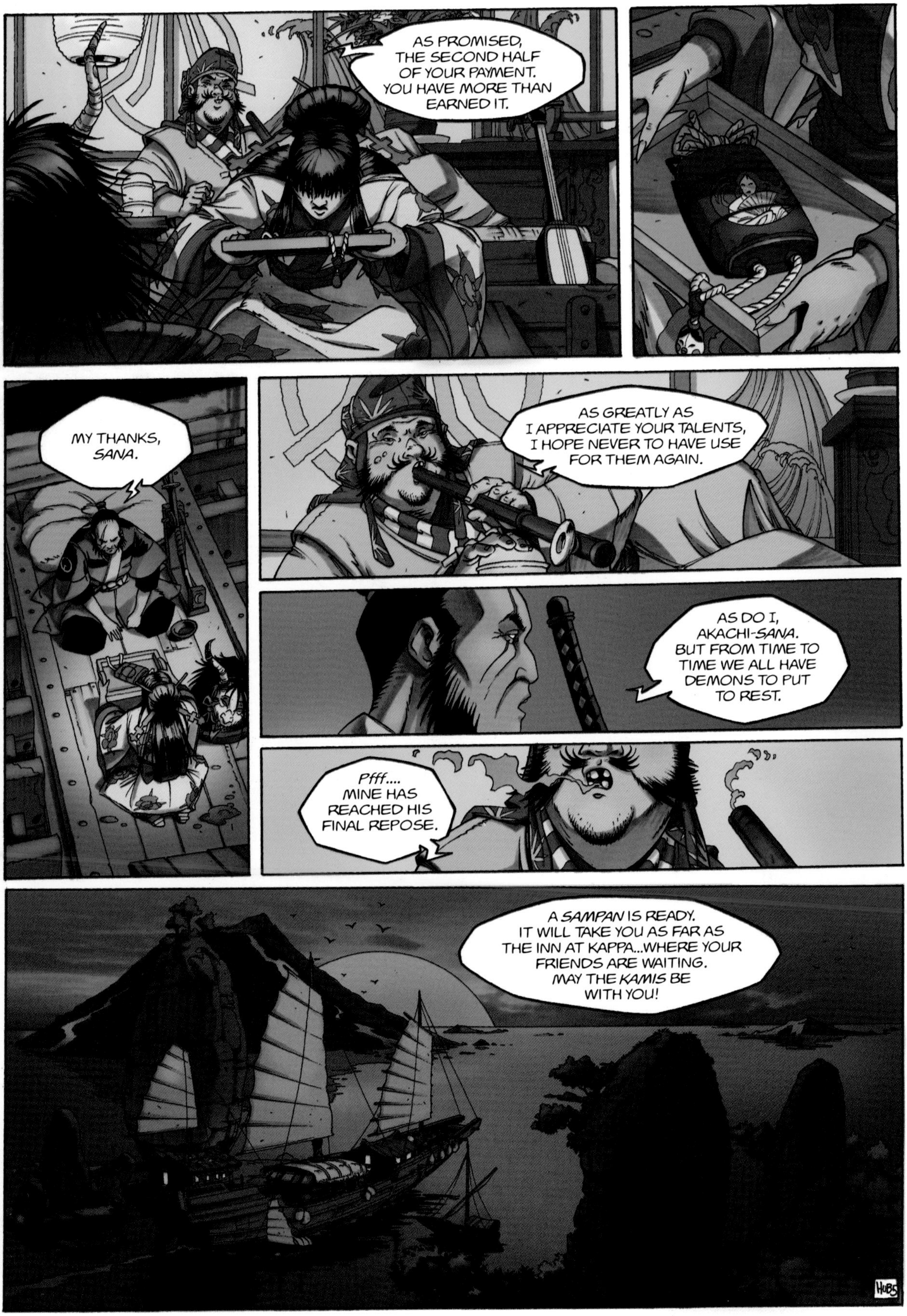
AS PROMISED, THE SECOND HALF OF YOUR PAYMENT. YOU HAVE MORE THAN EARNED IT.
MY THANKS, SANA.
AS GREATLY AS I APPRECIATE YOUR TALENTS, I HOPE NEVER TO HAVE USE FOR THEM AGAIN.
AS DO I, AKACHI-SANA. BUT FROM TIME TO TIME WE ALL HAVE DEMONS TO PUT TO REST.
Pfff.... MINE HAS REACHED HIS FINAL REPOSE.
A SAMPAN IS READY. IT WILL TAKE YOU AS FAR AS THE INN AT KAPPA...WHERE YOUR FRIENDS ARE WAITING. MAY THE KAMIS BE WITH YOU!
HUBS

TWO SOUTH WINDS AND A RISING TSUNAMI?!

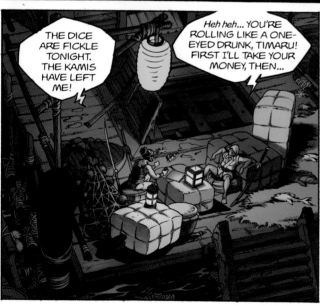

THE DICE ARE FICKLE TONIGHT. THE KAMIS HAVE LEFT ME!

Heh heh... YOU'RE ROLLING LIKE A ONE-EYED DRUNK, TIMARU! FIRST I'LL TAKE YOUR MONEY, THEN...

Huh?

Sshh!

WHO GOES THERE?

NO ONE. COME BACK AND LOSE SOME MORE.

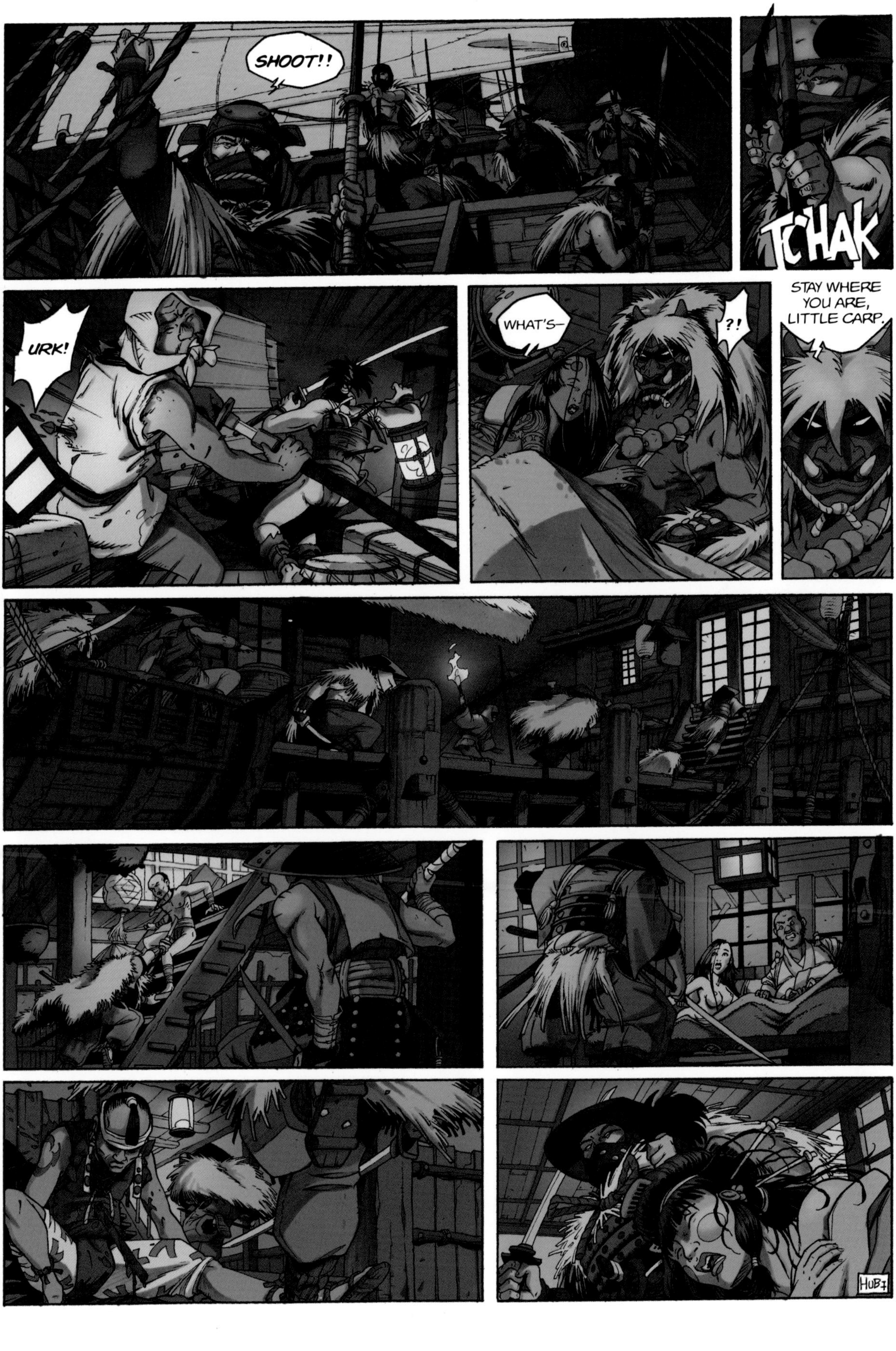
SHOOT!!
TCHAK
URK!
WHAT'S—
?!
STAY WHERE YOU ARE, LITTLE CARP.
HUB

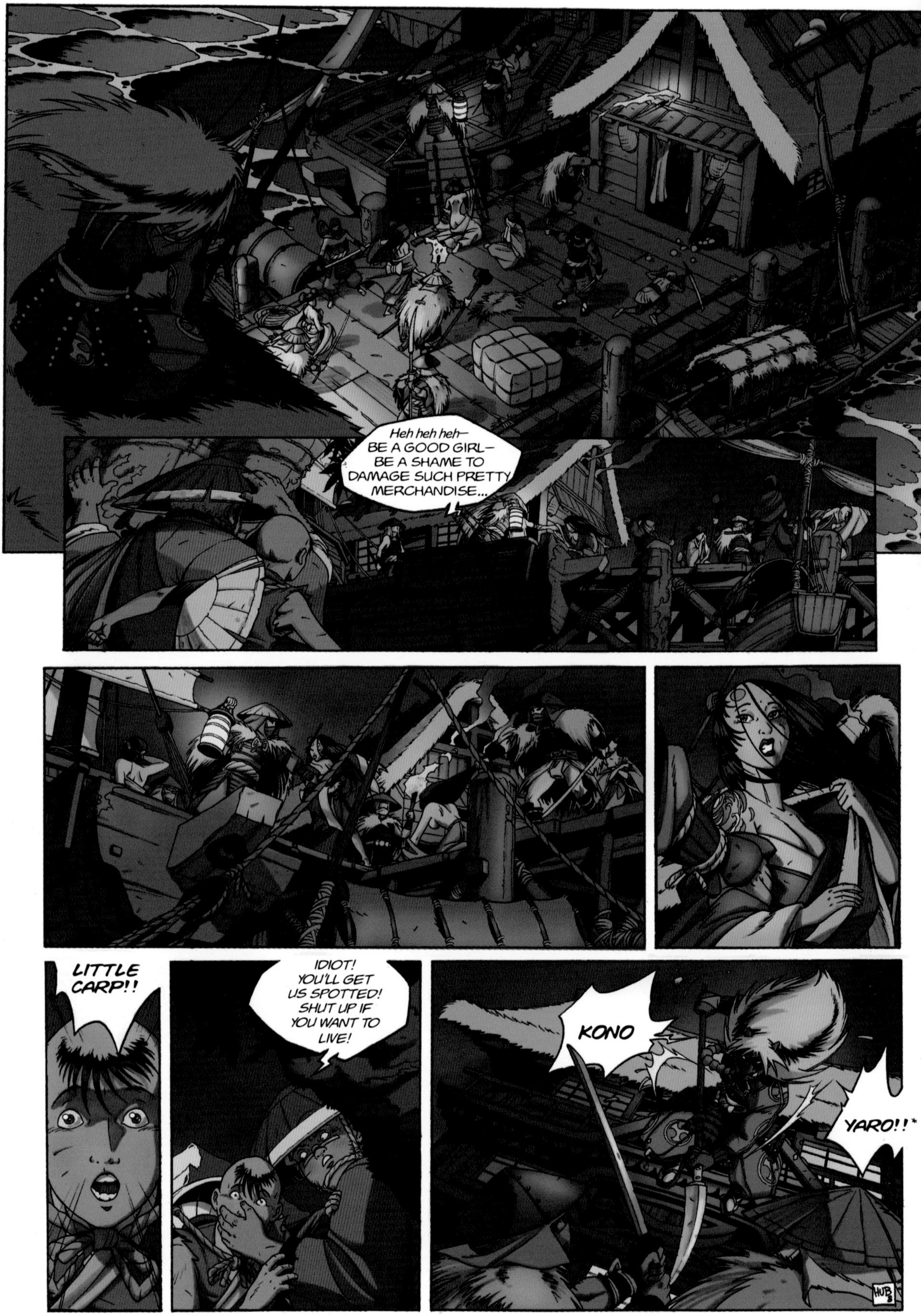
Heh heh heh—
BE A GOOD GIRL—
BE A SHAME TO
DAMAGE SUCH PRETTY
MERCHANDISE...
LITTLE CARP!!
IDIOT! YOU'LL GET US SPOTTED! SHUT UP IF YOU WANT TO LIVE!
KONO
YARO!!*
HUB

*ROUGHLY:
YOU BASTARDS!

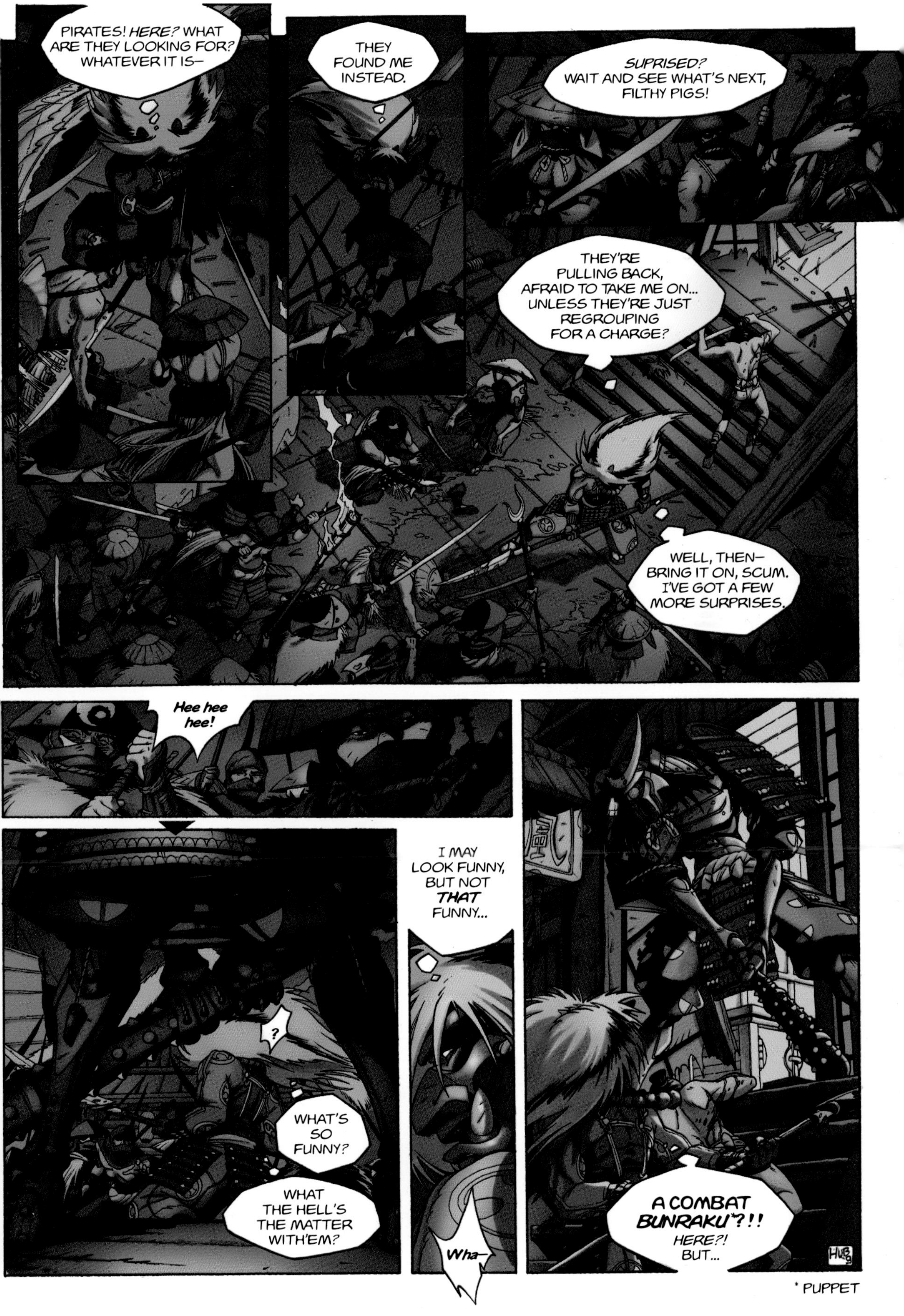
PIRATES! HERE? WHAT ARE THEY LOOKING FOR? WHATEVER IT IS—
THEY FOUND ME INSTEAD.
SUPRISED? WAIT AND SEE WHAT'S NEXT, FILTHY PIGS!
THEY'RE PULLING BACK, AFRAID TO TAKE ME ON... UNLESS THEY'RE JUST REGROUPING FOR A CHARGE?
WELL, THEN— BRING IT ON, SCUM. I'VE GOT A FEW MORE SURPRISES.
Hee hee hee!
?
WHAT'S SO FUNNY?
WHAT THE HELL'S THE MATTER WITH'EM?
I MAY LOOK FUNNY, BUT NOT THAT FUNNY...
Wha—
A COMBAT BUNRAKU*?!! HERE?! BUT...

* PUPPET

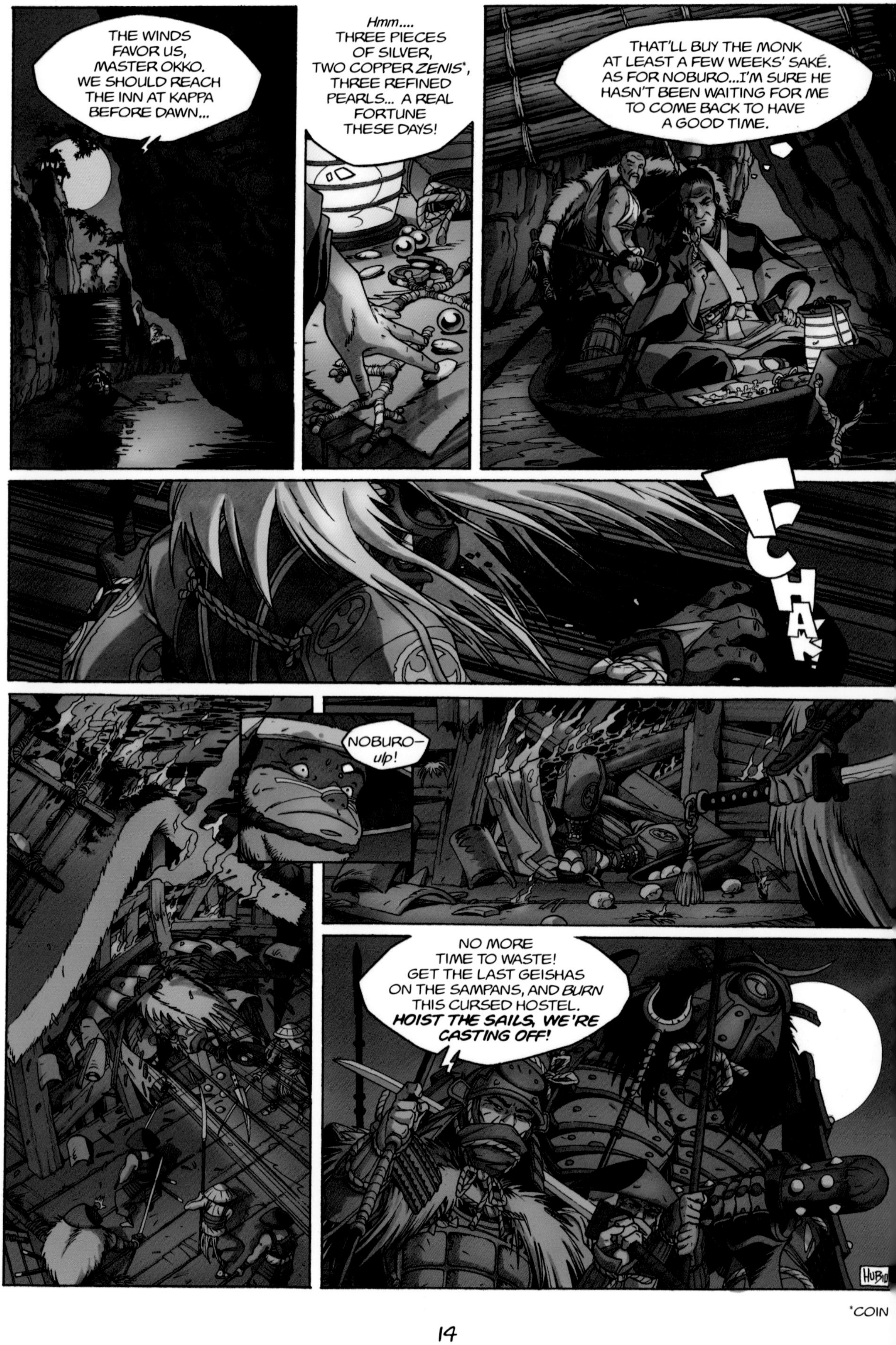
THE WINDS FAVOR US, MASTER OKKO. WE SHOULD REACH THE INN AT KAPPA BEFORE DAWN...
Hmm.... THREE PIECES OF SILVER, TWO COPPER ZENIS*, THREE REFINED PEARLS... A REAL FORTUNE THESE DAYS!
THAT'LL BUY THE MONK AT LEAST A FEW WEEKS' SAKÉ. AS FOR NOBURO...I'M SURE HE HASN'T BEEN WAITING FOR ME TO COME BACK TO HAVE A GOOD TIME.
TCHAK!
NOBURO— ulp!
NO MORE TIME TO WASTE! GET THE LAST GEISHAS ON THE SAMPANS, AND BURN THIS CURSED HOSTEL. HOIST THE SAILS, WE'RE CASTING OFF!
HUB

*COIN

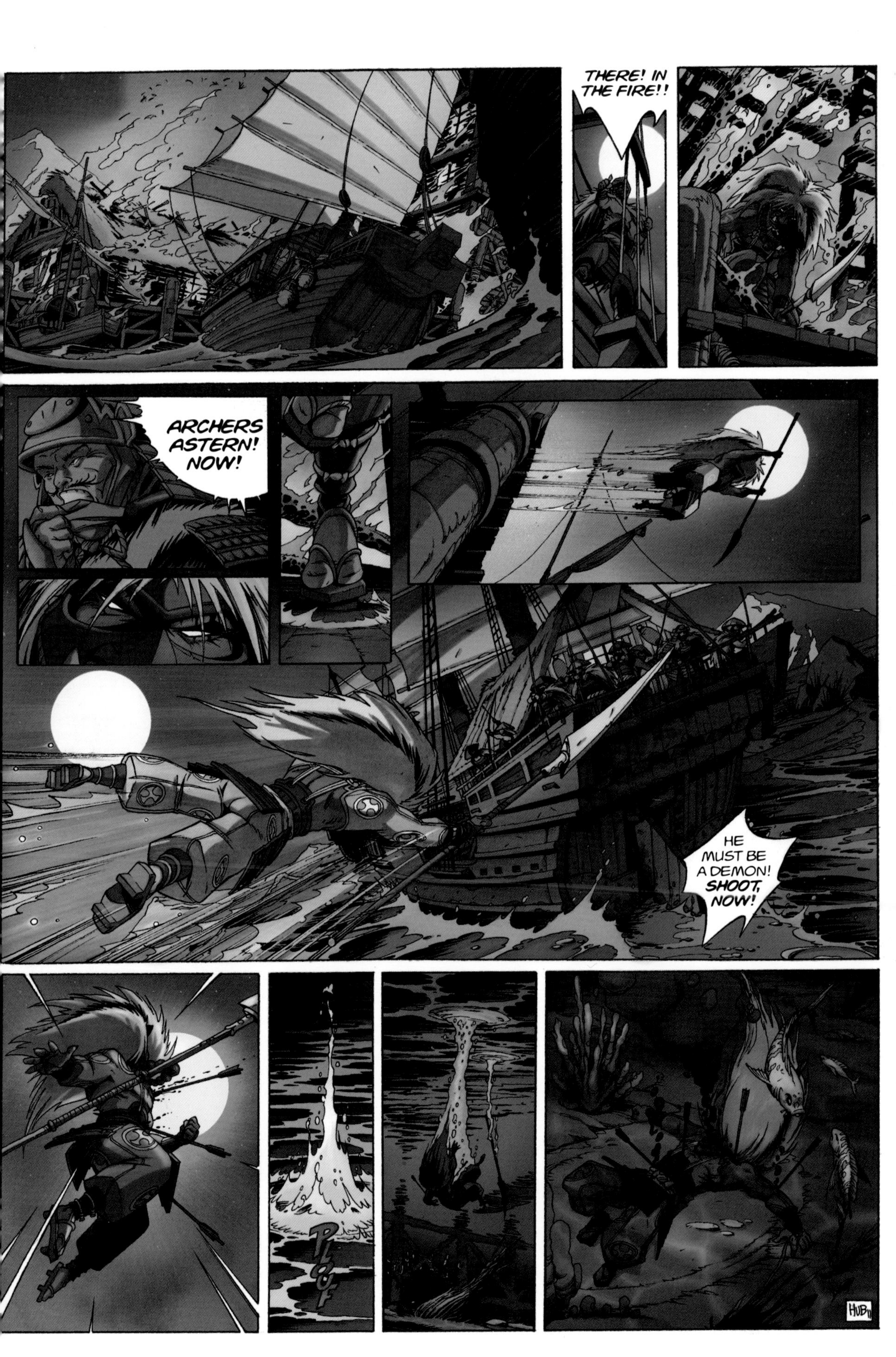
THERE! IN THE FIRE!!
ARCHERS ASTERN! NOW!
HE MUST BE A DEMON! SHOOT, NOW!
PLOUF
HUB

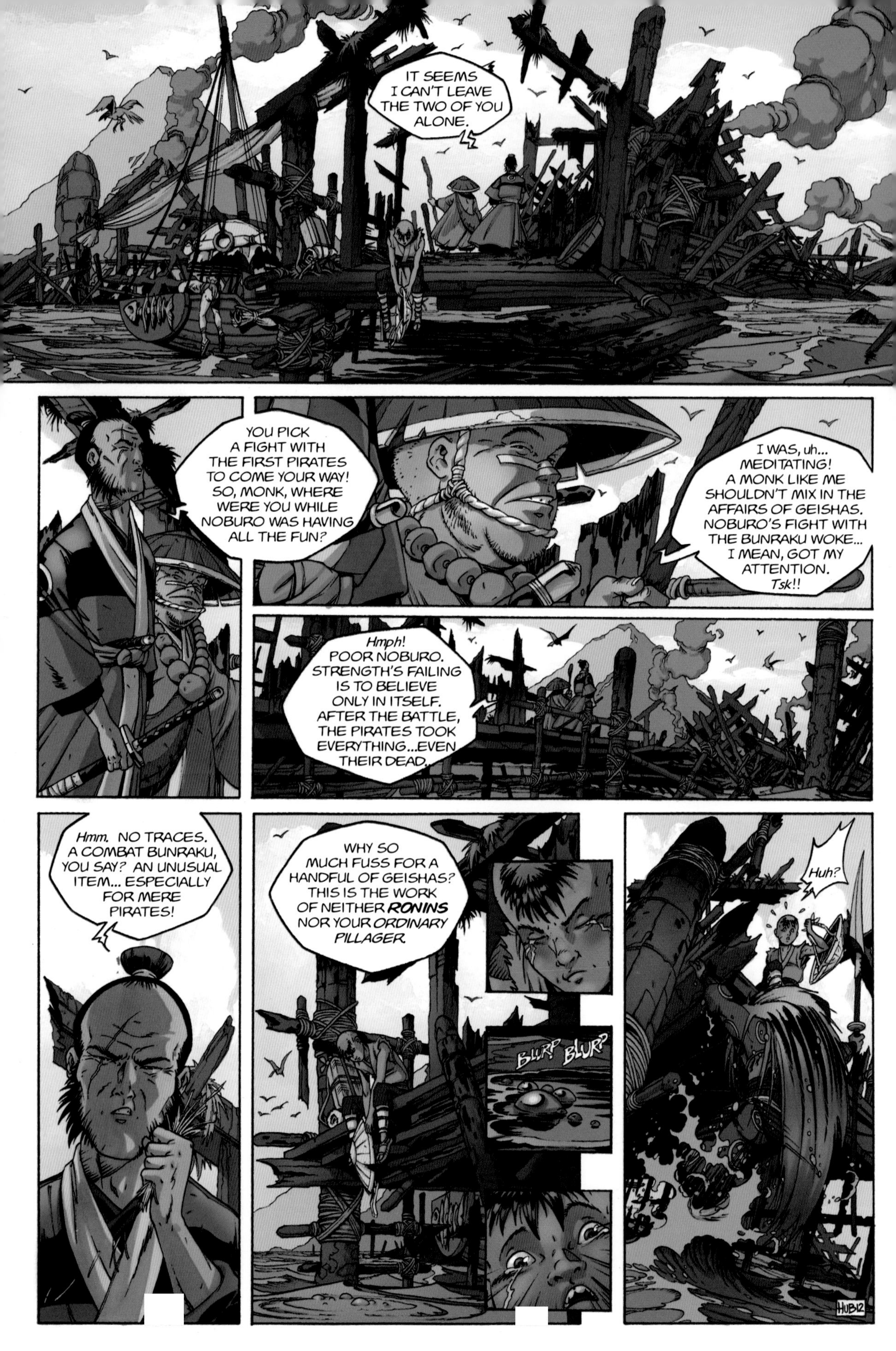
IT SEEMS I CAN'T LEAVE THE TWO OF YOU ALONE.
YOU PICK A FIGHT WITH THE FIRST PIRATES TO COME YOUR WAY! SO, MONK, WHERE WERE YOU WHILE NOBURO WAS HAVING ALL THE FUN?
I WAS, uh... MEDITATING! A MONK LIKE ME SHOULDN'T MIX IN THE AFFAIRS OF GEISHAS. NOBURO'S FIGHT WITH THE BUNRAKU WOKE... I MEAN, GOT MY ATTENTION. Tsk!!
Hmph! POOR NOBURO. STRENGTH'S FAILING IS TO BELIEVE ONLY IN ITSELF. AFTER THE BATTLE, THE PIRATES TOOK EVERYTHING...EVEN THEIR DEAD...
Hmm. NO TRACES. A COMBAT BUNRAKU, YOU SAY? AN UNUSUAL ITEM... ESPECIALLY FOR MERE PIRATES!
WHY SO MUCH FUSS FOR A HANDFUL OF GEISHAS? THIS IS THE WORK OF NEITHER RONINS NOR YOUR ORDINARY PILLAGER.
BLURP BLURP
Huh?
HUB12

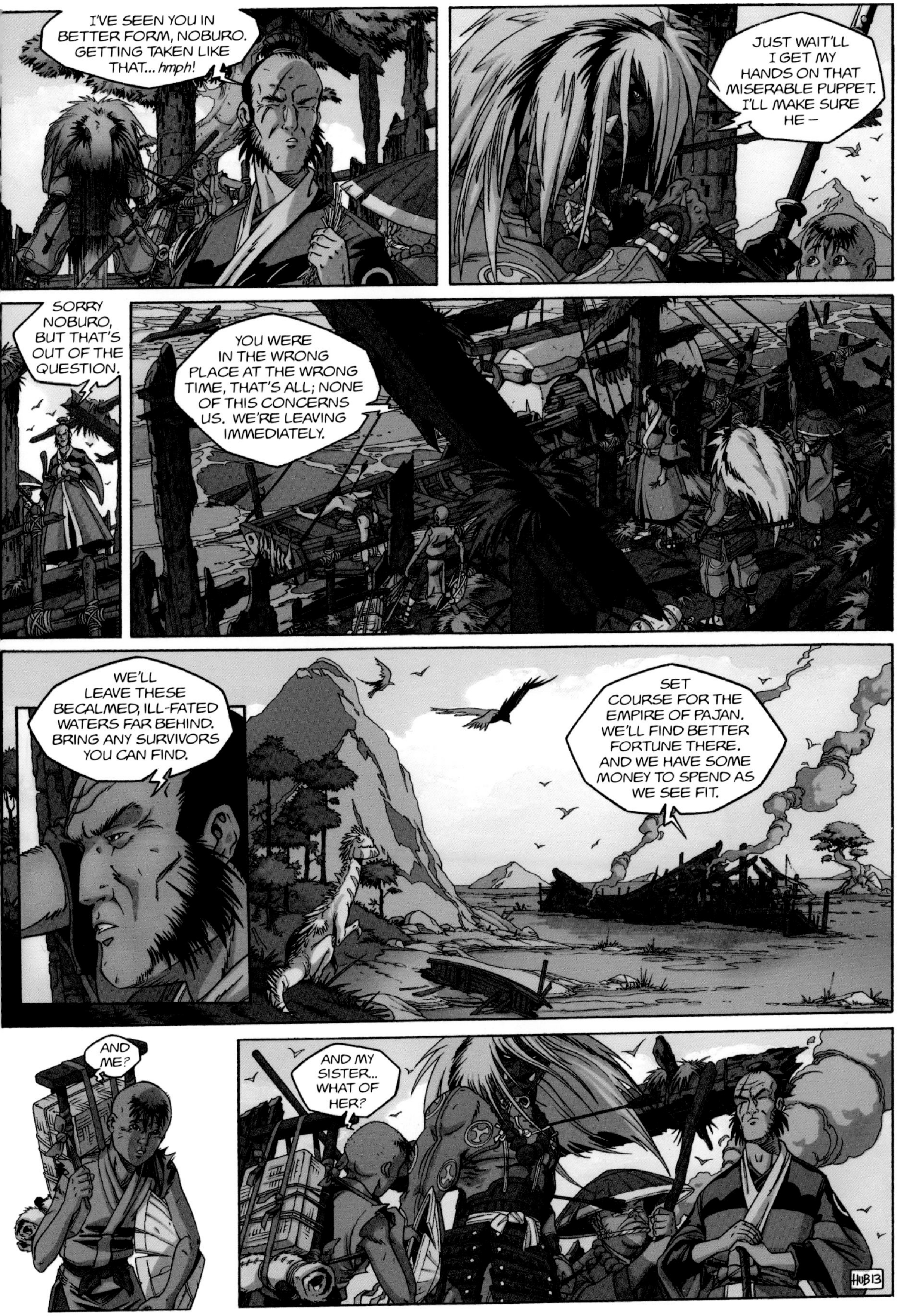
I'VE SEEN YOU IN BETTER FORM, NOBURO. GETTING TAKEN LIKE THAT... *hmph*!
JUST WAIT'LL I GET MY HANDS ON THAT MISERABLE PUPPET. I'LL MAKE SURE HE –
SORRY NOBURO, BUT THAT'S OUT OF THE QUESTION.
YOU WERE IN THE WRONG PLACE AT THE WRONG TIME, THAT'S ALL; NONE OF THIS CONCERNS US. WE'RE LEAVING IMMEDIATELY.
WE'LL LEAVE THESE BECALMED, ILL-FATED WATERS FAR BEHIND. BRING ANY SURVIVORS YOU CAN FIND.
SET COURSE FOR THE EMPIRE OF PAJAN. WE'LL FIND BETTER FORTUNE THERE. AND WE HAVE SOME MONEY TO SPEND AS WE SEE FIT.
AND ME?
AND MY SISTER... WHAT OF HER?
HUB 13

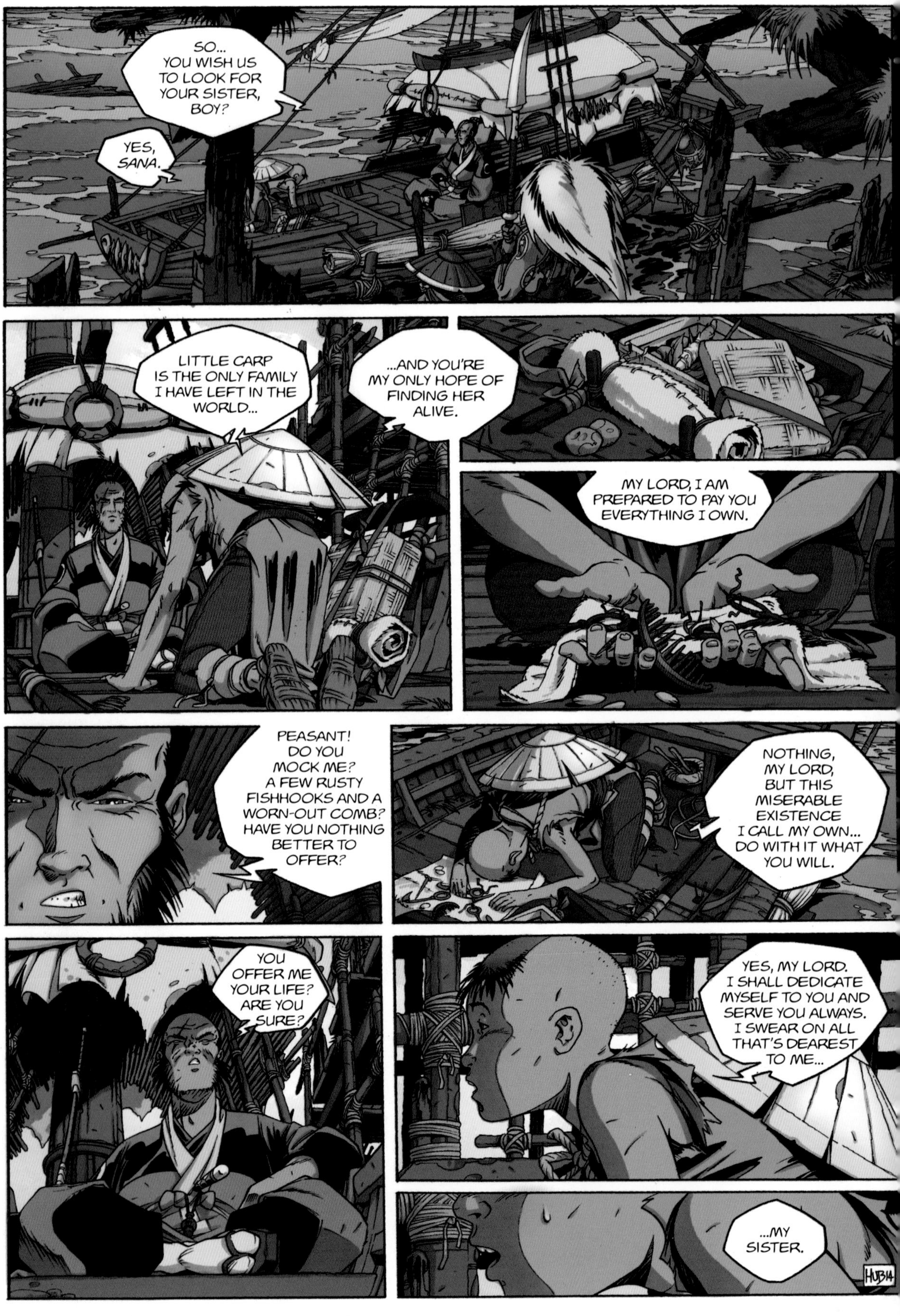
SO... YOU WISH US TO LOOK FOR YOUR SISTER, BOY?
YES, SANA.
LITTLE CARP IS THE ONLY FAMILY I HAVE LEFT IN THE WORLD...
...AND YOU'RE MY ONLY HOPE OF FINDING HER ALIVE.
MY LORD, I AM PREPARED TO PAY YOU EVERYTHING I OWN.
PEASANT! DO YOU MOCK ME? A FEW RUSTY FISHHOOKS AND A WORN-OUT COMB? HAVE YOU NOTHING BETTER TO OFFER?
NOTHING, MY LORD, BUT THIS MISERABLE EXISTENCE I CALL MY OWN... DO WITH IT WHAT YOU WILL.
YOU OFFER ME YOUR LIFE? ARE YOU SURE?
YES, MY LORD. I SHALL DEDICATE MYSELF TO YOU AND SERVE YOU ALWAYS. I SWEAR ON ALL THAT'S DEAREST TO ME...
...MY SISTER.
HUB14

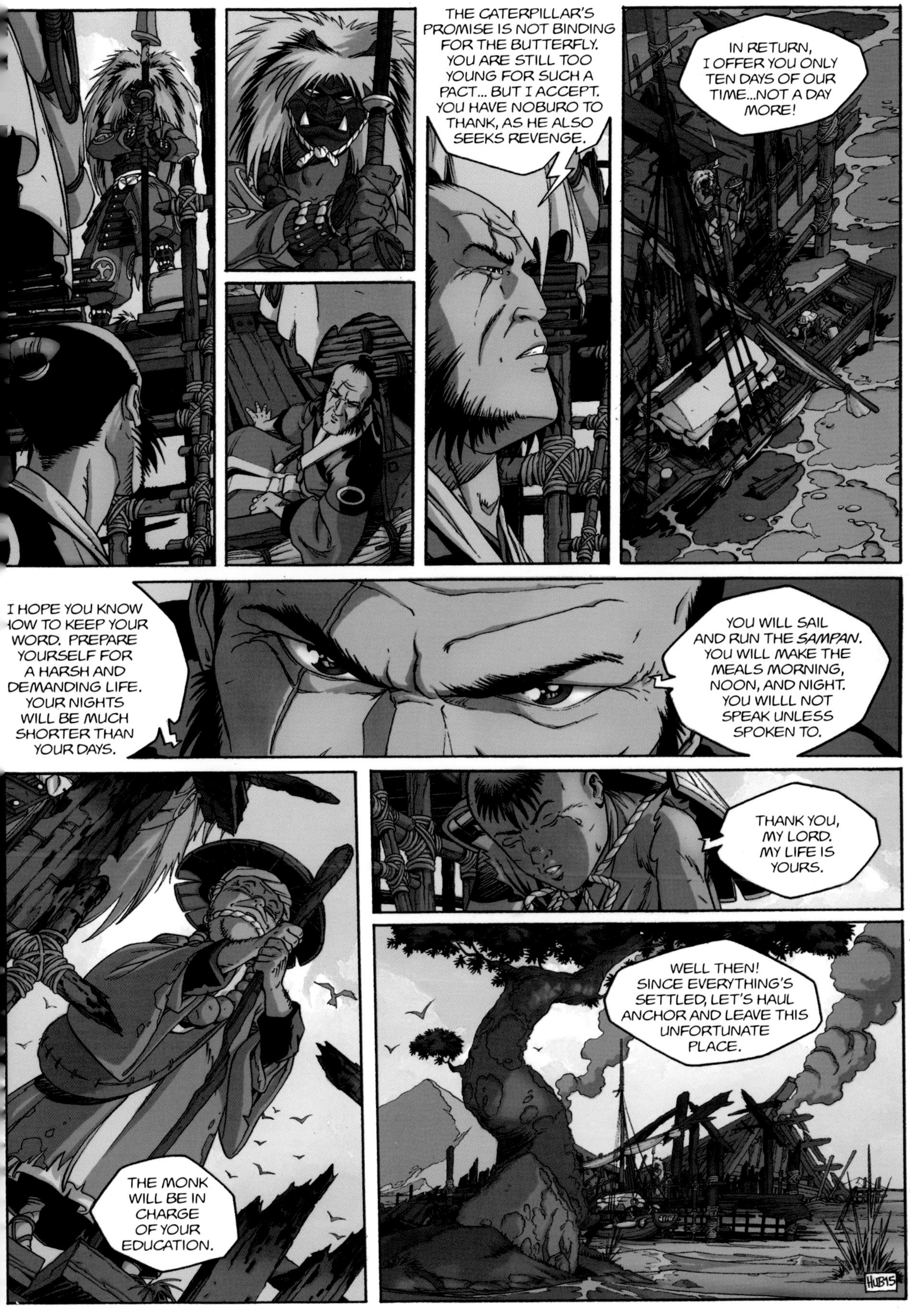
THE CATERPILLAR'S PROMISE IS NOT BINDING FOR THE BUTTERFLY. YOU ARE STILL TOO YOUNG FOR SUCH A PACT... BUT I ACCEPT. YOU HAVE NOBURO TO THANK, AS HE ALSO SEEKS REVENGE.
IN RETURN, I OFFER YOU ONLY TEN DAYS OF OUR TIME...NOT A DAY MORE!
I HOPE YOU KNOW HOW TO KEEP YOUR WORD. PREPARE YOURSELF FOR A HARSH AND DEMANDING LIFE. YOUR NIGHTS WILL BE MUCH SHORTER THAN YOUR DAYS.
YOU WILL SAIL AND RUN THE SAMPAN. YOU WILL MAKE THE MEALS MORNING, NOON, AND NIGHT. YOU WILLL NOT SPEAK UNLESS SPOKEN TO.
THANK YOU, MY LORD. MY LIFE IS YOURS.
THE MONK WILL BE IN CHARGE OF YOUR EDUCATION.
WELL THEN! SINCE EVERYTHING'S SETTLED, LET'S HAUL ANCHOR AND LEAVE THIS UNFORTUNATE PLACE.
HUB'15

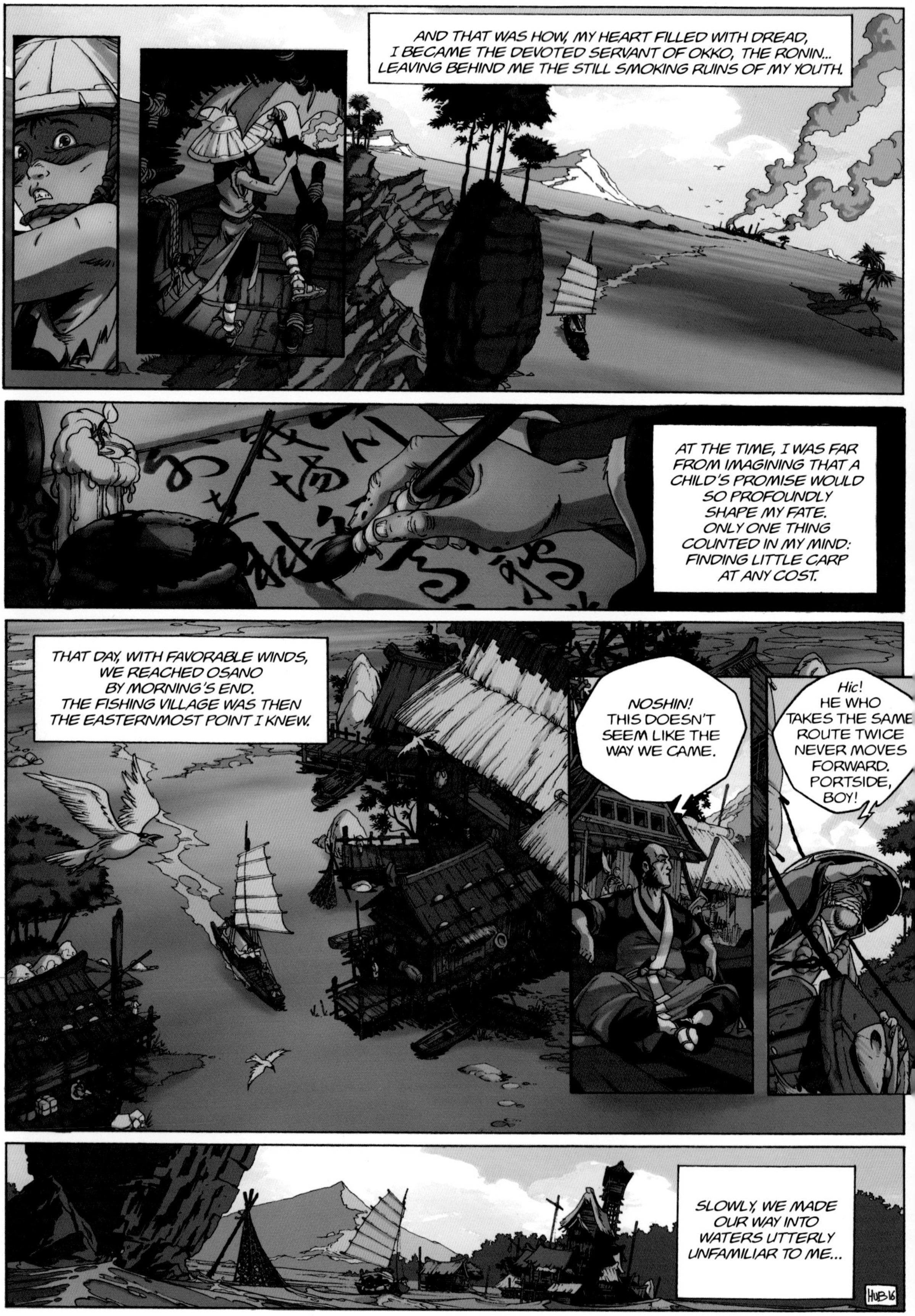
AND THAT WAS HOW, MY HEART FILLED WITH DREAD, I BECAME THE DEVOTED SERVANT OF OKKO, THE RONIN... LEAVING BEHIND ME THE STILL SMOKING RUINS OF MY YOUTH.
AT THE TIME, I WAS FAR FROM IMAGINING THAT A CHILD'S PROMISE WOULD SO PROFOUNDLY SHAPE MY FATE. ONLY ONE THING COUNTED IN MY MIND: FINDING LITTLE CARP AT ANY COST.
THAT DAY, WITH FAVORABLE WINDS, WE REACHED OSANO BY MORNING'S END. THE FISHING VILLAGE WAS THEN THE EASTERNMOST POINT I KNEW.
NOSHIN! THIS DOESN'T SEEM LIKE THE WAY WE CAME.
Hic! HE WHO TAKES THE SAME ROUTE TWICE NEVER MOVES FORWARD. PORTSIDE, BOY!
SLOWLY, WE MADE OUR WAY INTO WATERS UTTERLY UNFAMILIAR TO ME...
HUB 16

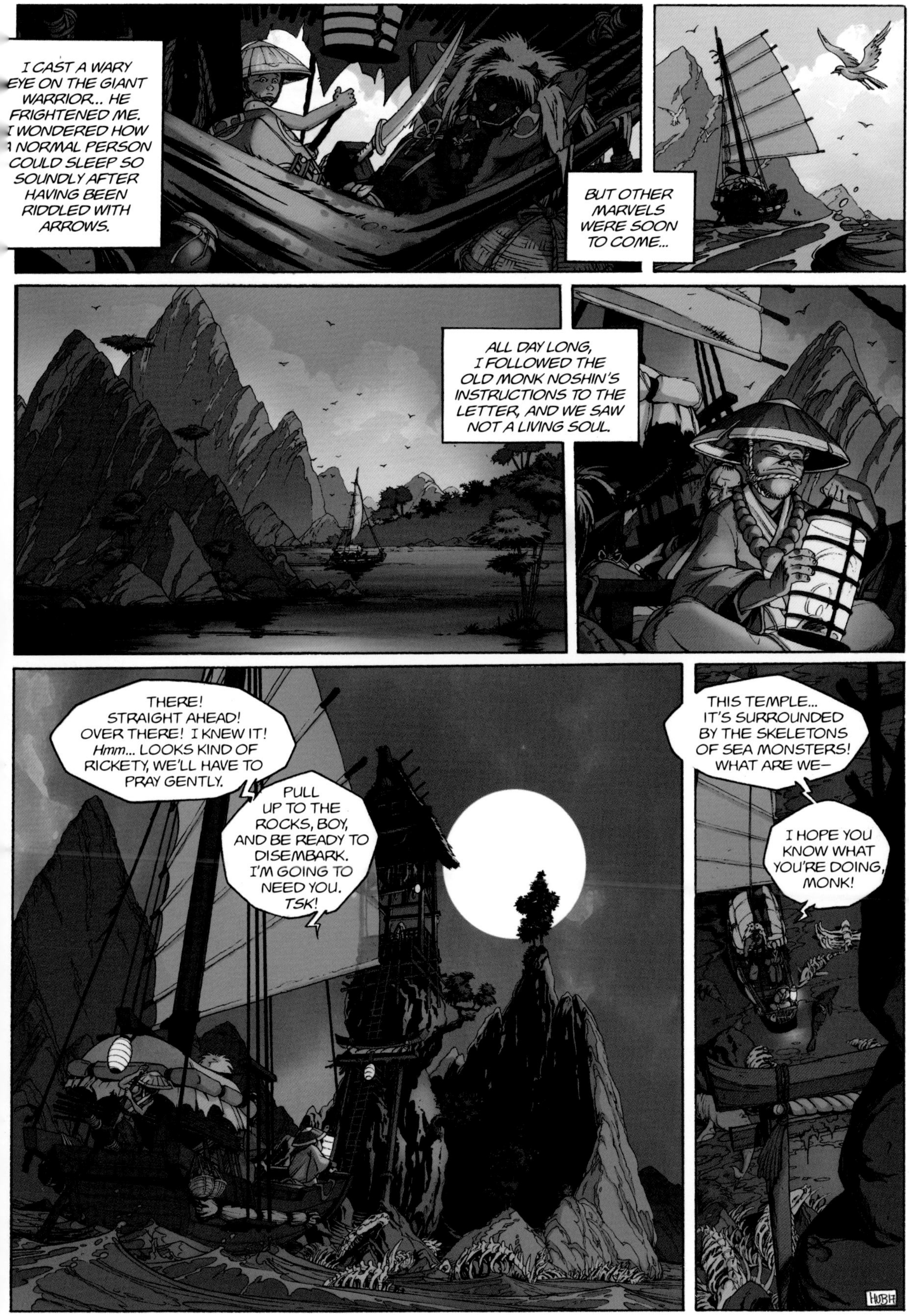
I CAST A WARY EYE ON THE GIANT WARRIOR... HE FRIGHTENED ME. I WONDERED HOW A NORMAL PERSON COULD SLEEP SO SOUNDLY AFTER HAVING BEEN RIDDLED WITH ARROWS.
BUT OTHER MARVELS WERE SOON TO COME...
ALL DAY LONG, I FOLLOWED THE OLD MONK NOSHIN'S INSTRUCTIONS TO THE LETTER, AND WE SAW NOT A LIVING SOUL.
THERE! STRAIGHT AHEAD! OVER THERE! I KNEW IT! Hmm... LOOKS KIND OF RICKETY, WE'LL HAVE TO PRAY GENTLY.
PULL UP TO THE ROCKS, BOY, AND BE READY TO DISEMBARK. I'M GOING TO NEED YOU. TSK!
THIS TEMPLE... IT'S SURROUNDED BY THE SKELETONS OF SEA MONSTERS! WHAT ARE WE–
I HOPE YOU KNOW WHAT YOU'RE DOING, MONK!
HUB

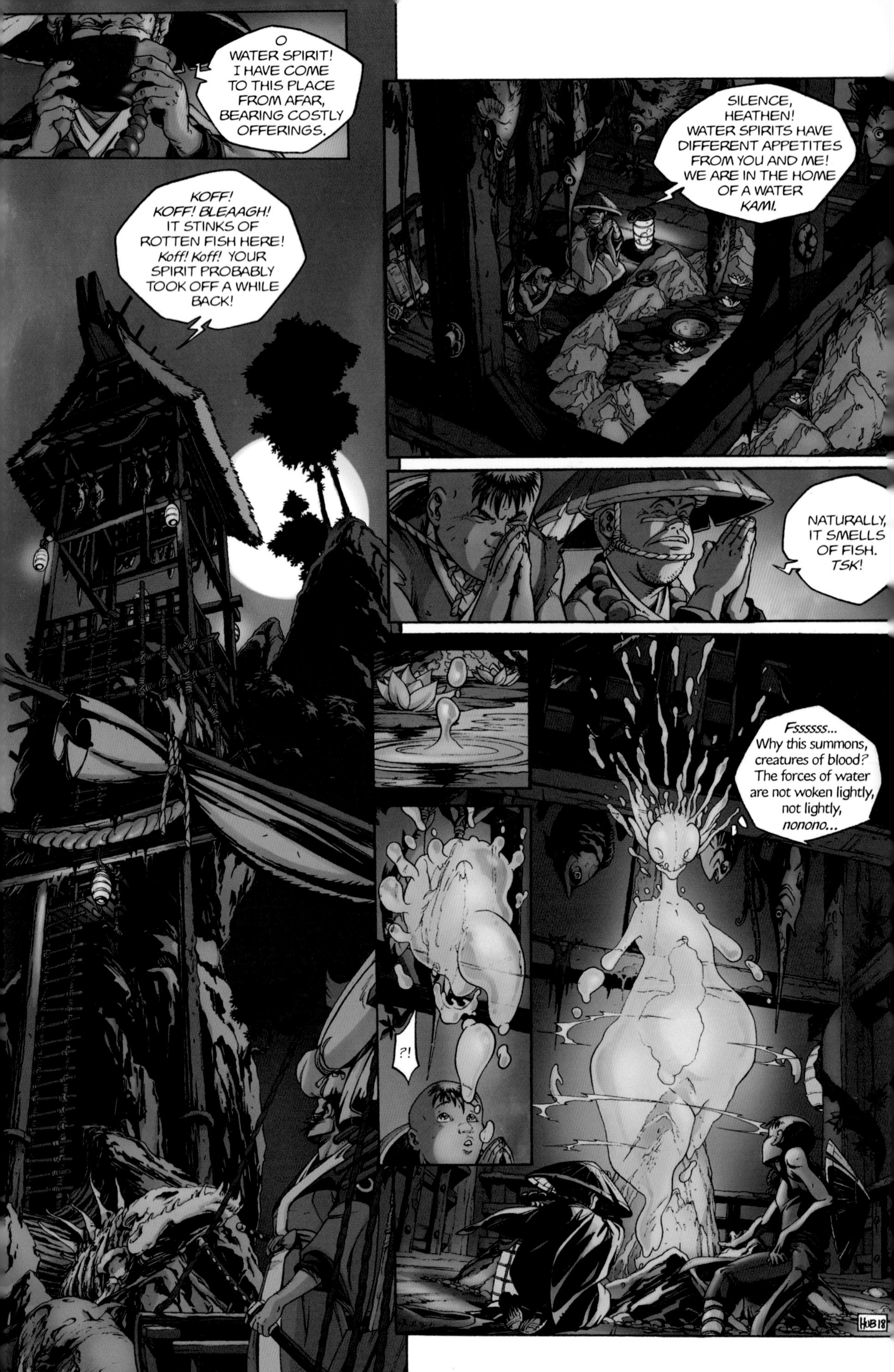
O WATER SPIRIT! I HAVE COME TO THIS PLACE FROM AFAR, BEARING COSTLY OFFERINGS.
SILENCE, HEATHEN! WATER SPIRITS HAVE DIFFERENT APPETITES FROM YOU AND ME! WE ARE IN THE HOME OF A WATER *KAMI.*
KOFF! KOFF! BLEAAGH! IT STINKS OF ROTTEN FISH HERE! *Koff! Koff!* YOUR SPIRIT PROBABLY TOOK OFF A WHILE BACK!
NATURALLY, IT SMELLS OF FISH. *TSK!*
Fssssss... Why this summons, *creatures of blood?* The forces of water are not woken lightly, not lightly, *nonono...*
?!
HUB 18

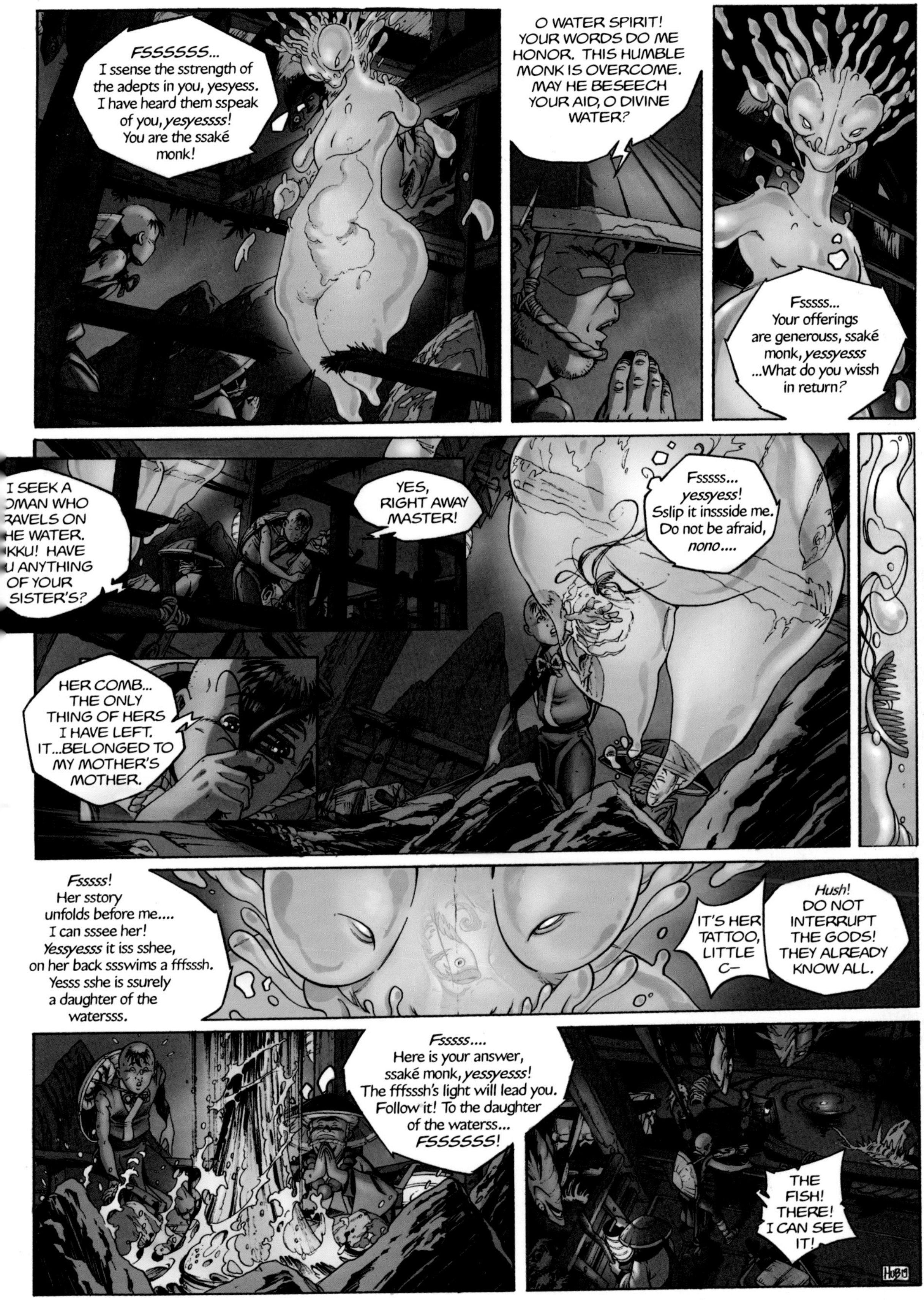
FSSSSSS...
I ssense the sstrength of the adepts in you, yesyess. I have heard them sspeak of you, yesyessss! You are the ssaké monk!
O WATER SPIRIT! YOUR WORDS DO ME HONOR. THIS HUMBLE MONK IS OVERCOME. MAY HE BESEECH YOUR AID, O DIVINE WATER?
Fsssss... Your offerings are generouss, ssaké monk, yessyesss ...What do you wissh in return?
I SEEK A OMAN WHO RAVELS ON HE WATER. KKU! HAVE U ANYTHING OF YOUR SISTER'S?
YES, RIGHT AWAY MASTER!
HER COMB... THE ONLY THING OF HERS I HAVE LEFT. IT...BELONGED TO MY MOTHER'S MOTHER.
Fsssss... yessyess! Sslip it inssside me. Do not be afraid, nono....
Fsssss! Her sstory unfolds before me.... I can sssee her! Yessyesss it iss sshee, on her back ssswims a fffsssh. Yesss sshe is ssurely a daughter of the watersss.
IT'S HER TATTOO, LITTLE C–
Hush! DO NOT INTERRUPT THE GODS! THEY ALREADY KNOW ALL.
Fsssss.... Here is your answer, ssaké monk, yessyesss! The fffsssh's light will lead you. Follow it! To the daughter of the waterss... FSSSSSS!
THE FISH! THERE! I CAN SEE IT!
HUB

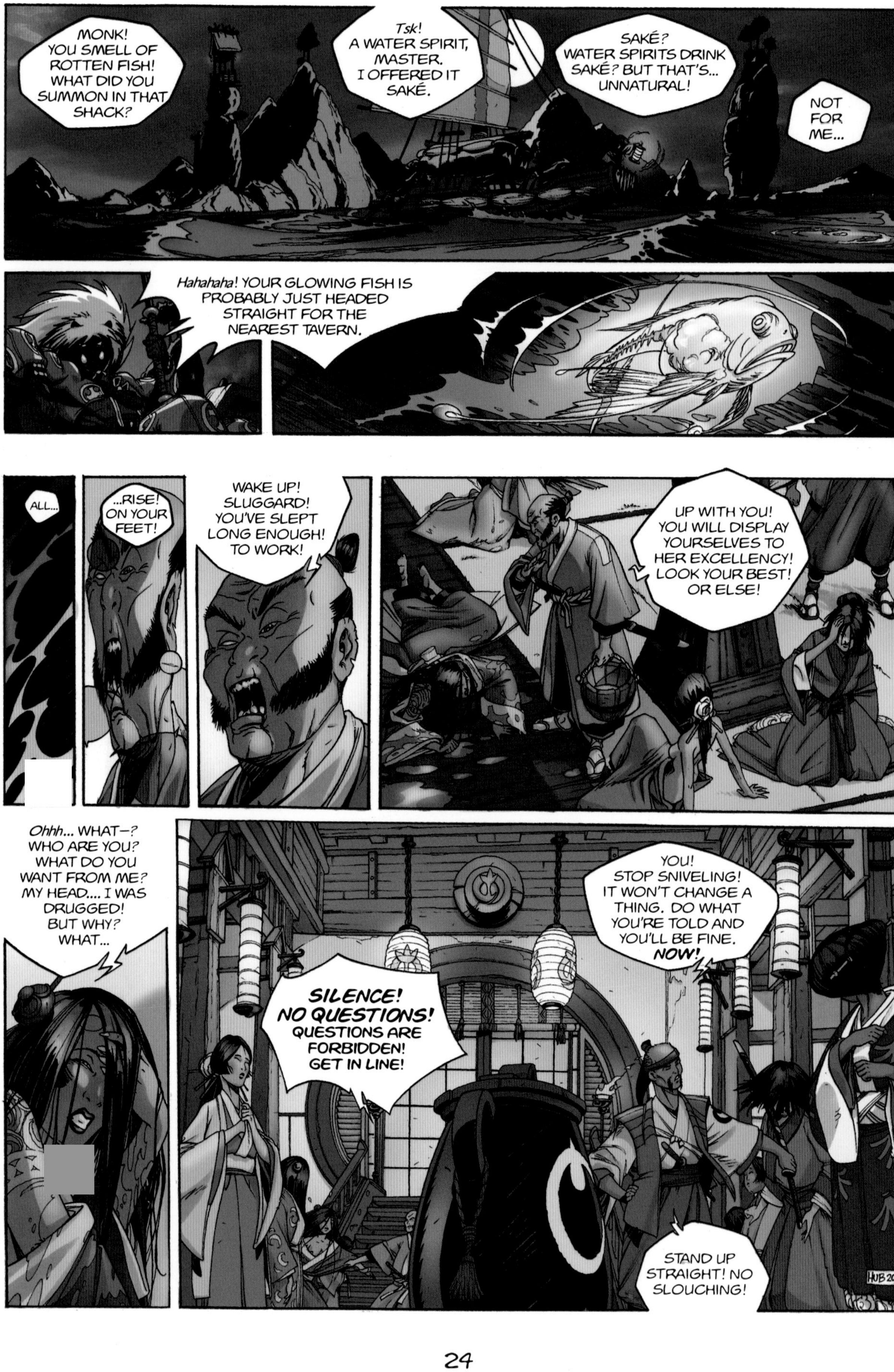
MONK! YOU SMELL OF ROTTEN FISH! WHAT DID YOU SUMMON IN THAT SHACK?
Tsk! A WATER SPIRIT, MASTER. I OFFERED IT SAKÉ.
SAKÉ? WATER SPIRITS DRINK SAKÉ? BUT THAT'S... UNNATURAL!
NOT FOR ME...
Hahahaha! YOUR GLOWING FISH IS PROBABLY JUST HEADED STRAIGHT FOR THE NEAREST TAVERN.
ALL...
...RISE! ON YOUR FEET!
WAKE UP! SLUGGARD! YOU'VE SLEPT LONG ENOUGH! TO WORK!
UP WITH YOU! YOU WILL DISPLAY YOURSELVES TO HER EXCELLENCY! LOOK YOUR BEST! OR ELSE!
Ohhh... WHAT—? WHO ARE YOU? WHAT DO YOU WANT FROM ME? MY HEAD.... I WAS DRUGGED! BUT WHY? WHAT...
SILENCE! NO QUESTIONS! QUESTIONS ARE FORBIDDEN! GET IN LINE!
YOU! STOP SNIVELING! IT WON'T CHANGE A THING. DO WHAT YOU'RE TOLD AND YOU'LL BE FINE. ***NOW!***
STAND UP STRAIGHT! NO SLOUCHING!
HUB 20

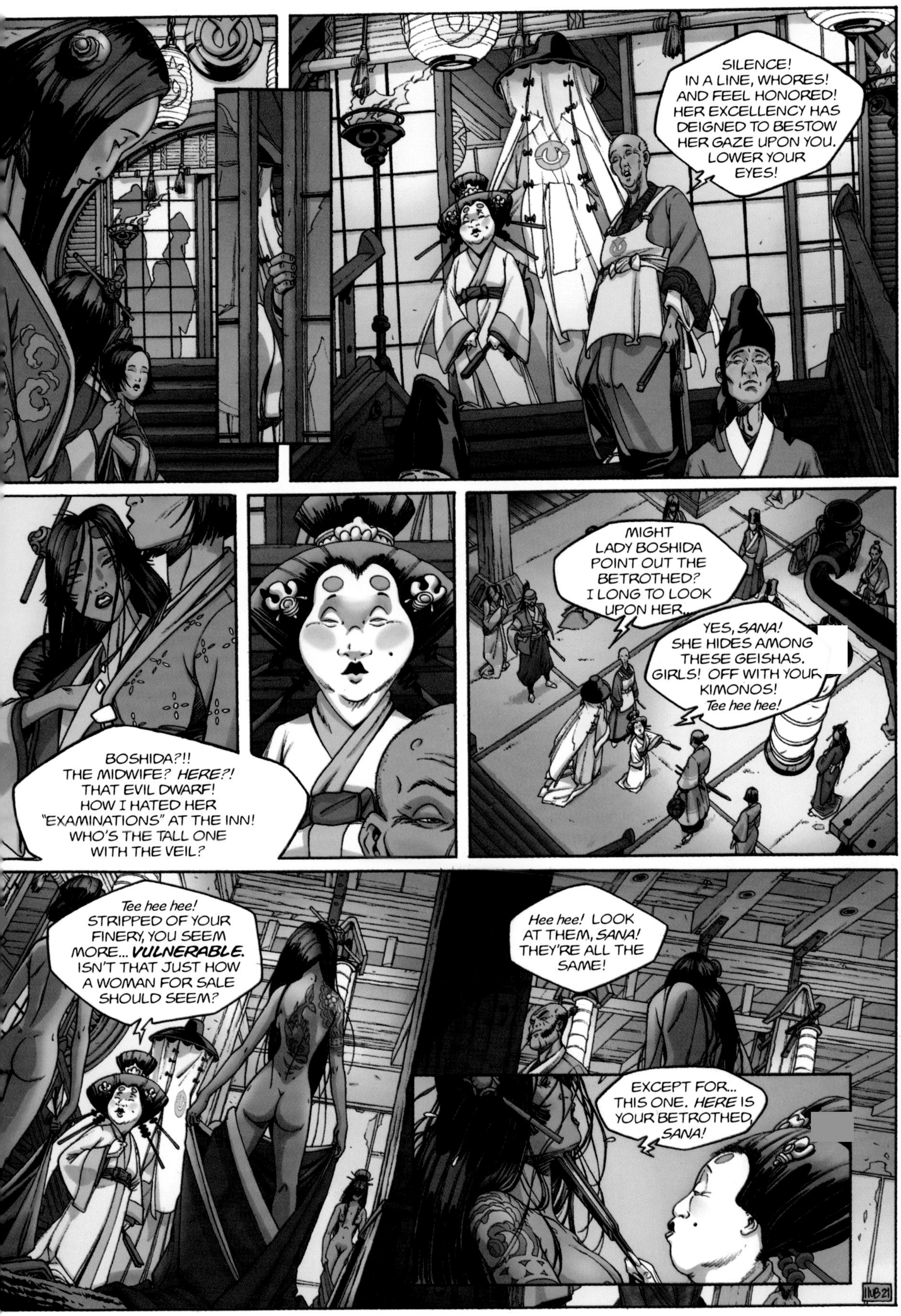
SILENCE! IN A LINE, WHORES! AND FEEL HONORED! HER EXCELLENCY HAS DEIGNED TO BESTOW HER GAZE UPON YOU. LOWER YOUR EYES!
BOSHIDA?!! THE MIDWIFE? HERE?! THAT EVIL DWARF! HOW I HATED HER "EXAMINATIONS" AT THE INN! WHO'S THE TALL ONE WITH THE VEIL?
MIGHT LADY BOSHIDA POINT OUT THE BETROTHED? I LONG TO LOOK UPON HER...
YES, SANA! SHE HIDES AMONG THESE GEISHAS. GIRLS! OFF WITH YOUR KIMONOS! Tee hee hee!
Tee hee hee! STRIPPED OF YOUR FINERY, YOU SEEM MORE... VULNERABLE. ISN'T THAT JUST HOW A WOMAN FOR SALE SHOULD SEEM?
Hee hee! LOOK AT THEM, SANA! THEY'RE ALL THE SAME!
EXCEPT FOR... THIS ONE. HERE IS YOUR BETROTHED, SANA!
HUB 21

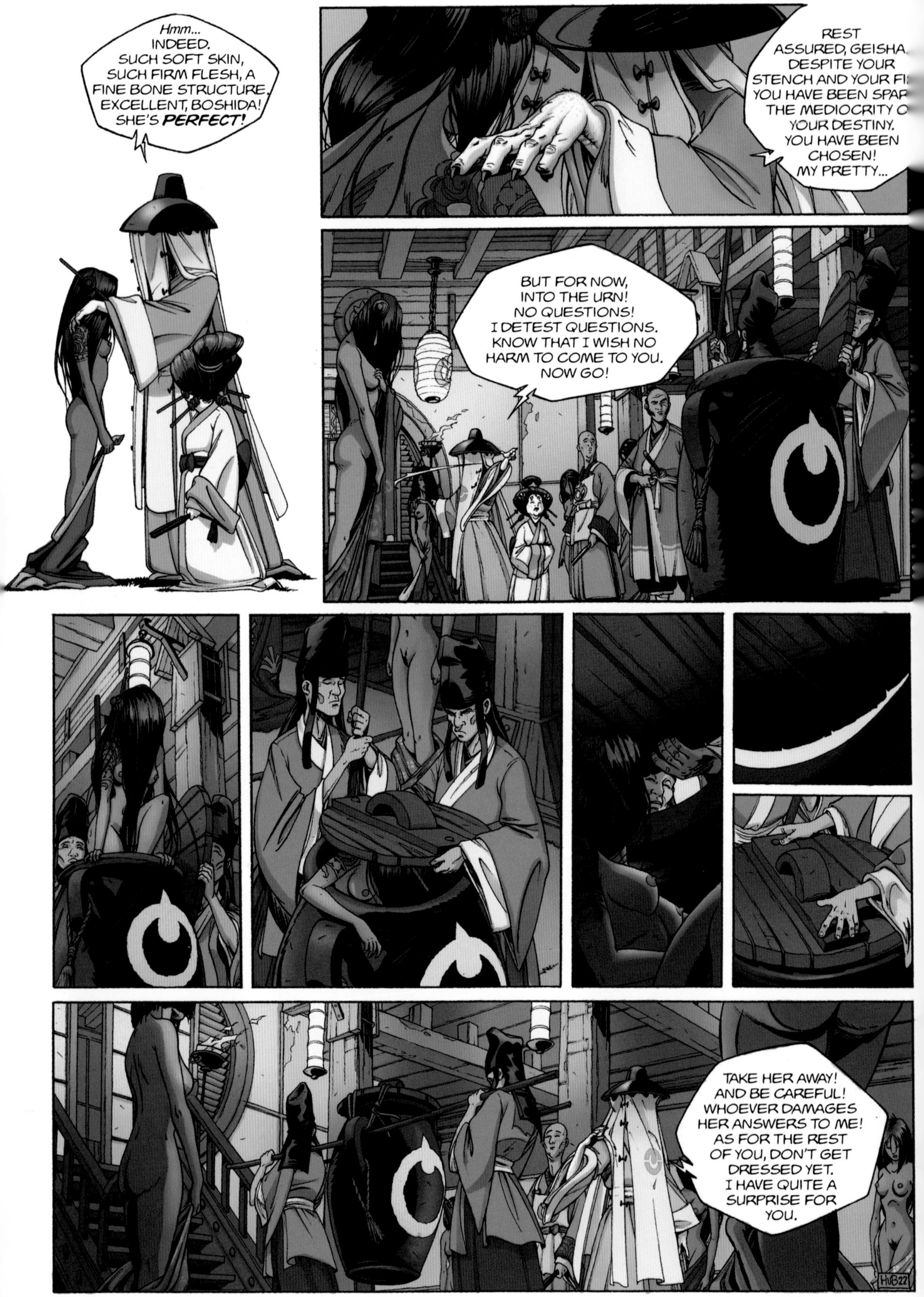
Hmm... INDEED. SUCH SOFT SKIN, SUCH FIRM FLESH, A FINE BONE STRUCTURE. EXCELLENT, BOSHIDA! SHE'S PERFECT!
REST ASSURED, GEISHA. DESPITE YOUR STENCH AND YOUR FI YOU HAVE BEEN SPAR THE MEDIOCRITY O YOUR DESTINY. YOU HAVE BEEN CHOSEN! MY PRETTY...
BUT FOR NOW, INTO THE URN! NO QUESTIONS! I DETEST QUESTIONS. KNOW THAT I WISH NO HARM TO COME TO YOU. NOW GO!
TAKE HER AWAY! AND BE CAREFUL! WHOEVER DAMAGES HER ANSWERS TO ME! AS FOR THE REST OF YOU, DON'T GET DRESSED YET. I HAVE QUITE A SURPRISE FOR YOU.
HUB22

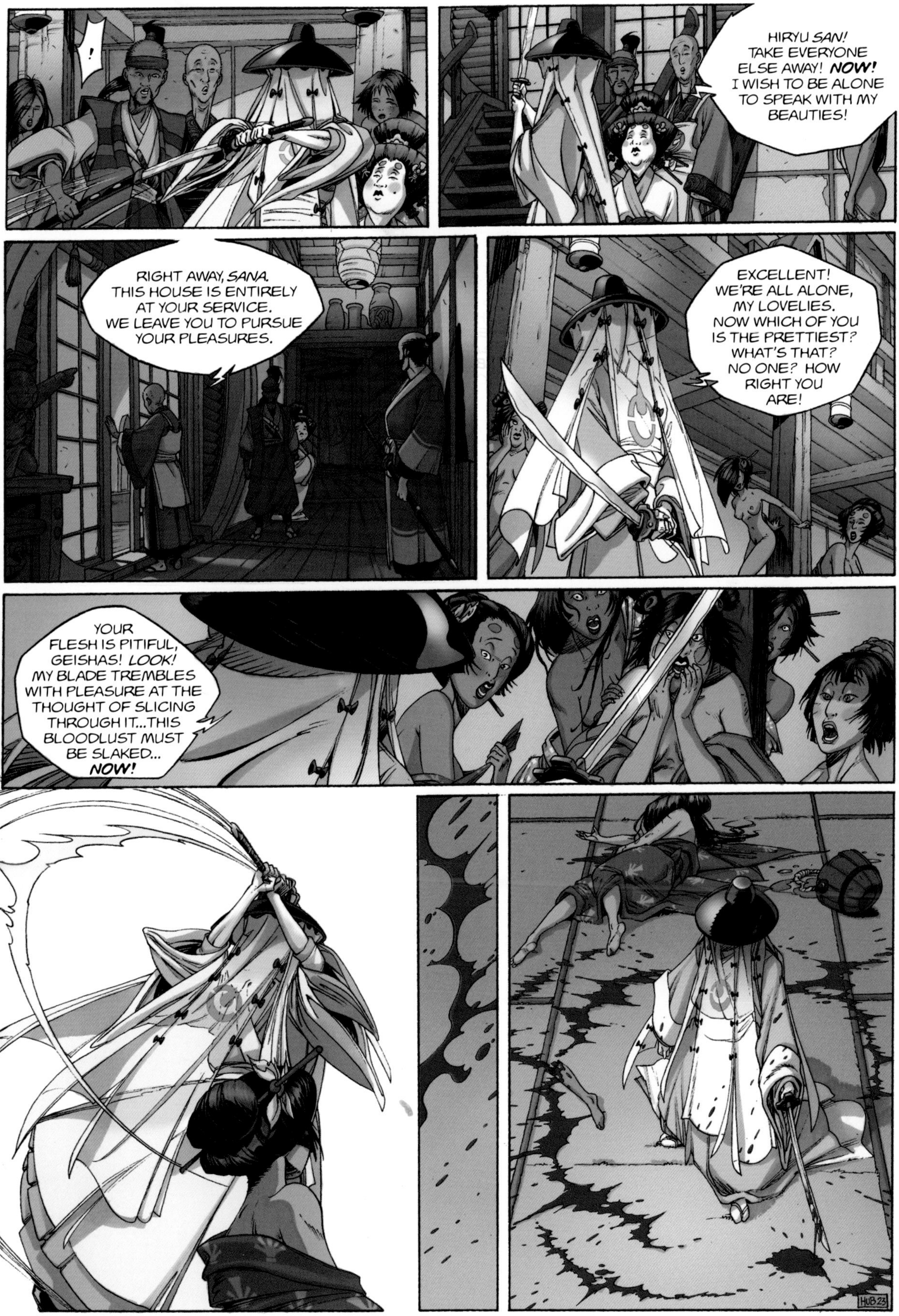
!
HIRYU SAN! TAKE EVERYONE ELSE AWAY! NOW! I WISH TO BE ALONE TO SPEAK WITH MY BEAUTIES!
RIGHT AWAY, SANA. THIS HOUSE IS ENTIRELY AT YOUR SERVICE. WE LEAVE YOU TO PURSUE YOUR PLEASURES.
EXCELLENT! WE'RE ALL ALONE, MY LOVELIES. NOW WHICH OF YOU IS THE PRETTIEST? WHAT'S THAT? NO ONE? HOW RIGHT YOU ARE!
YOUR FLESH IS PITIFUL, GEISHAS! LOOK! MY BLADE TREMBLES WITH PLEASURE AT THE THOUGHT OF SLICING THROUGH IT...THIS BLOODLUST MUST BE SLAKED... NOW!
HUB 23

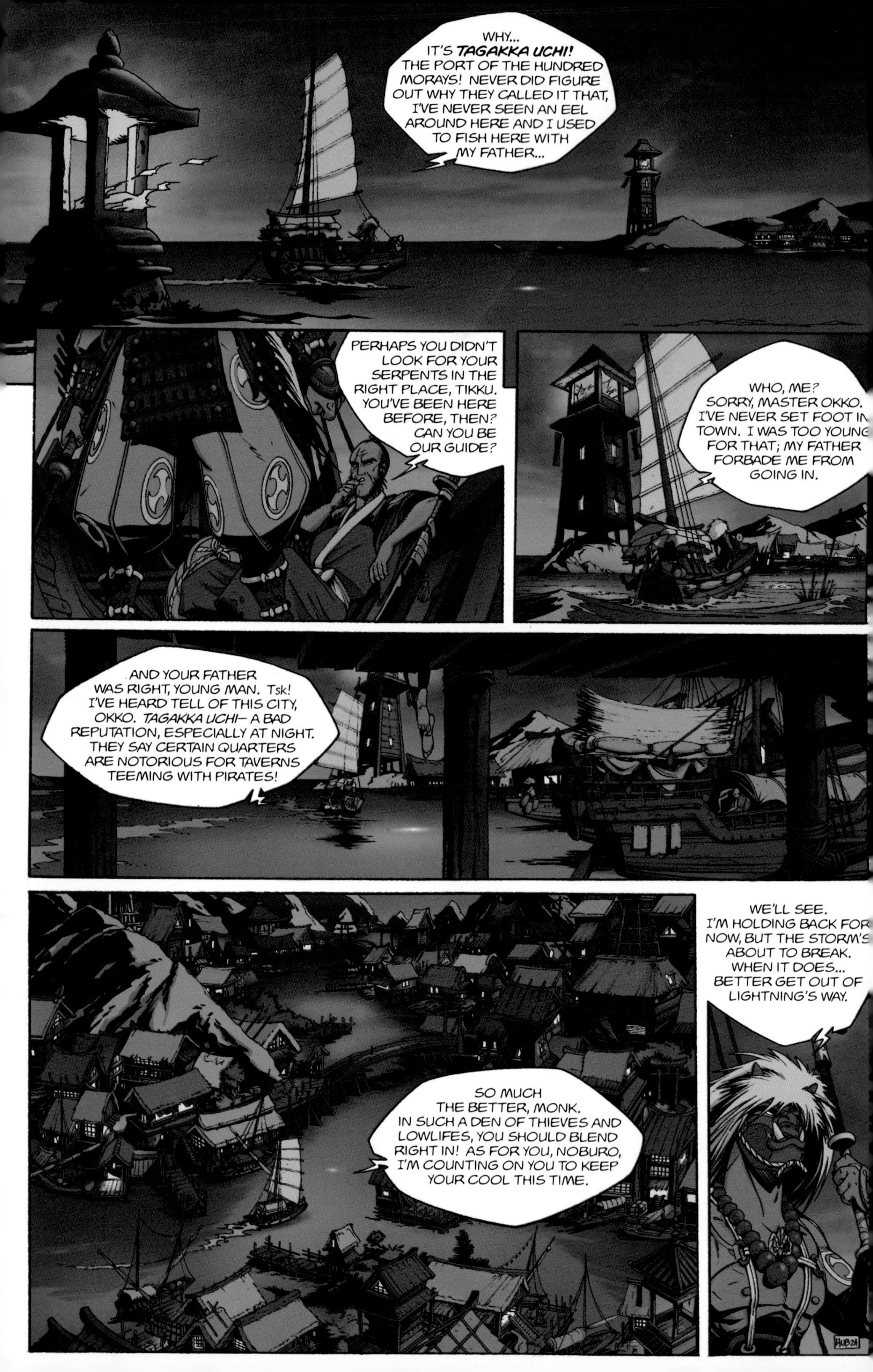
WHY... IT'S *TAGAKKA UCHI!* THE PORT OF THE HUNDRED MORAYS! NEVER DID FIGURE OUT WHY THEY CALLED IT THAT, I'VE NEVER SEEN AN EEL AROUND HERE AND I USED TO FISH HERE WITH MY FATHER...
PERHAPS YOU DIDN'T LOOK FOR YOUR SERPENTS IN THE RIGHT PLACE, TIKKU. YOU'VE BEEN HERE BEFORE, THEN? CAN YOU BE OUR GUIDE?
WHO, ME? SORRY, MASTER OKKO. I'VE NEVER SET FOOT IN TOWN. I WAS TOO YOUNG FOR THAT; MY FATHER FORBADE ME FROM GOING IN.
AND YOUR FATHER WAS RIGHT, YOUNG MAN. Tsk! I'VE HEARD TELL OF THIS CITY, OKKO. *TAGAKKA UCHI*– A BAD REPUTATION, ESPECIALLY AT NIGHT. THEY SAY CERTAIN QUARTERS ARE NOTORIOUS FOR TAVERNS TEEMING WITH PIRATES!
SO MUCH THE BETTER, MONK. IN SUCH A DEN OF THIEVES AND LOWLIFES, YOU SHOULD BLEND RIGHT IN! AS FOR YOU, NOBURO, I'M COUNTING ON YOU TO KEEP YOUR COOL THIS TIME.
WE'LL SEE. I'M HOLDING BACK FOR NOW, BUT THE STORM'S ABOUT TO BREAK. WHEN IT DOES... BETTER GET OUT OF LIGHTNING'S WAY.
HUB 24

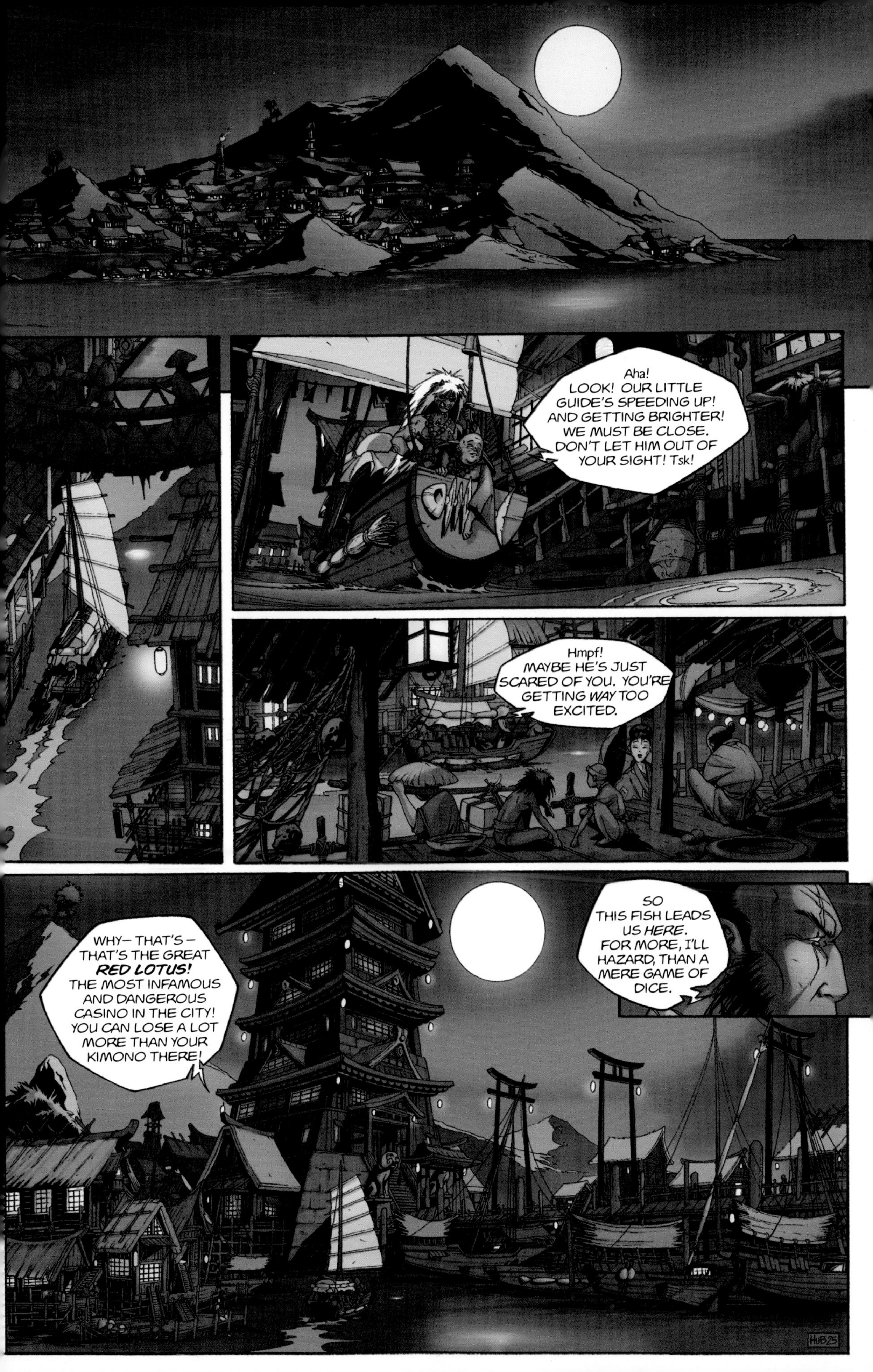
Aha!
LOOK! OUR LITTLE GUIDE'S SPEEDING UP! AND GETTING BRIGHTER! WE MUST BE CLOSE. DON'T LET HIM OUT OF YOUR SIGHT! Tsk!
Hmpf! MAYBE HE'S JUST SCARED OF YOU. YOU'RE GETTING *WAY* TOO EXCITED.
WHY– THAT'S– THAT'S THE GREAT ***RED LOTUS!*** THE MOST INFAMOUS AND DANGEROUS CASINO IN THE CITY! YOU CAN LOSE A LOT MORE THAN YOUR KIMONO THERE!
SO THIS FISH LEADS US *HERE*. FOR MORE, I'LL HAZARD, THAN A MERE GAME OF DICE.
HuB 25

Hmm; TWO MUSCLEBOUND GOONS AT THE TOP OF THE STEPS.

I HOPE YOUR EXCELLENCY WAS PLEASED WITH HER STAY. IT IS ALWAYS AN HONOR TO RECEIVE YOU IN MY HUMBLE ABODE.

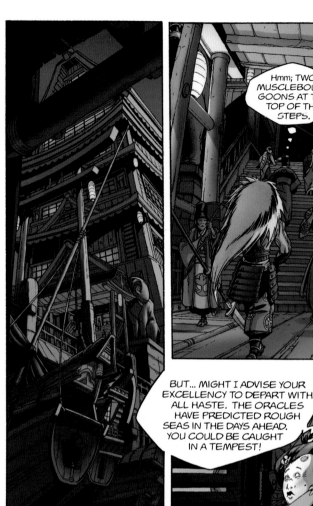

BUT... MIGHT I ADVISE YOUR EXCELLENCY TO DEPART WITH ALL HASTE. THE ORACLES HAVE PREDICTED ROUGH SEAS IN THE DAYS AHEAD. YOU COULD BE CAUGHT IN A TEMPEST!

STEP LIVELY, NOBURO. NO TIME FOR DALLYING. IT'S LATE.

Hmmm.... COMING, MASTER, COMING.

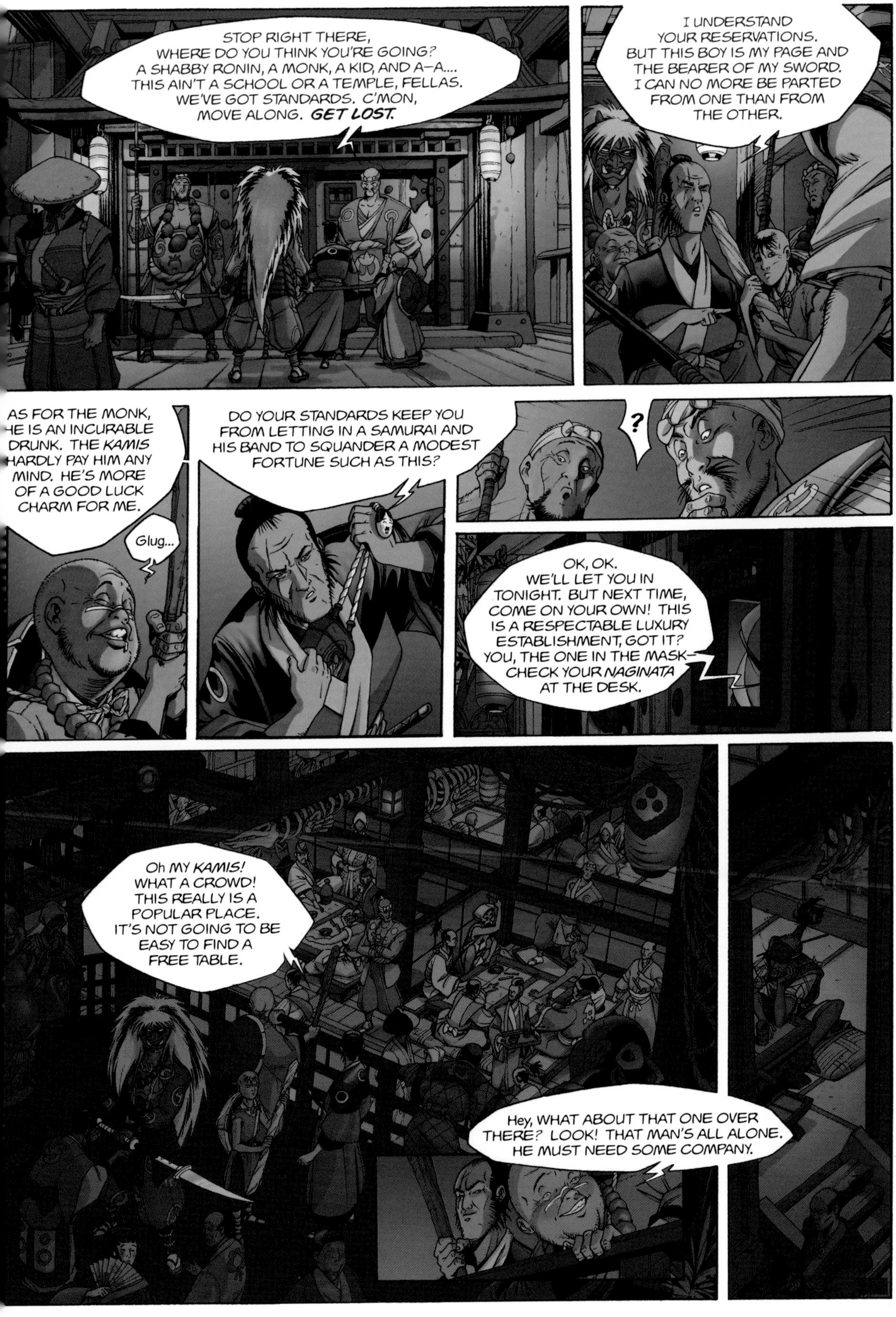
STOP RIGHT THERE, WHERE DO YOU THINK YOU'RE GOING? A SHABBY RONIN, A MONK, A KID, AND A–A.... THIS AIN'T A SCHOOL OR A TEMPLE, FELLAS. WE'VE GOT STANDARDS. C'MON, MOVE ALONG. GET LOST.
I UNDERSTAND YOUR RESERVATIONS. BUT THIS BOY IS MY PAGE AND THE BEARER OF MY SWORD. I CAN NO MORE BE PARTED FROM ONE THAN FROM THE OTHER.
AS FOR THE MONK, HE IS AN INCURABLE DRUNK. THE KAMIS HARDLY PAY HIM ANY MIND. HE'S MORE OF A GOOD LUCK CHARM FOR ME.
Glug...
DO YOUR STANDARDS KEEP YOU FROM LETTING IN A SAMURAI AND HIS BAND TO SQUANDER A MODEST FORTUNE SUCH AS THIS?
?
OK, OK. WE'LL LET YOU IN TONIGHT. BUT NEXT TIME, COME ON YOUR OWN! THIS IS A RESPECTABLE LUXURY ESTABLISHMENT, GOT IT? YOU, THE ONE IN THE MASK– CHECK YOUR NAGINATA AT THE DESK.
Oh MY KAMIS! WHAT A CROWD! THIS REALLY IS A POPULAR PLACE. IT'S NOT GOING TO BE EASY TO FIND A FREE TABLE.
Hey, WHAT ABOUT THAT ONE OVER THERE? LOOK! THAT MAN'S ALL ALONE. HE MUST NEED SOME COMPANY.

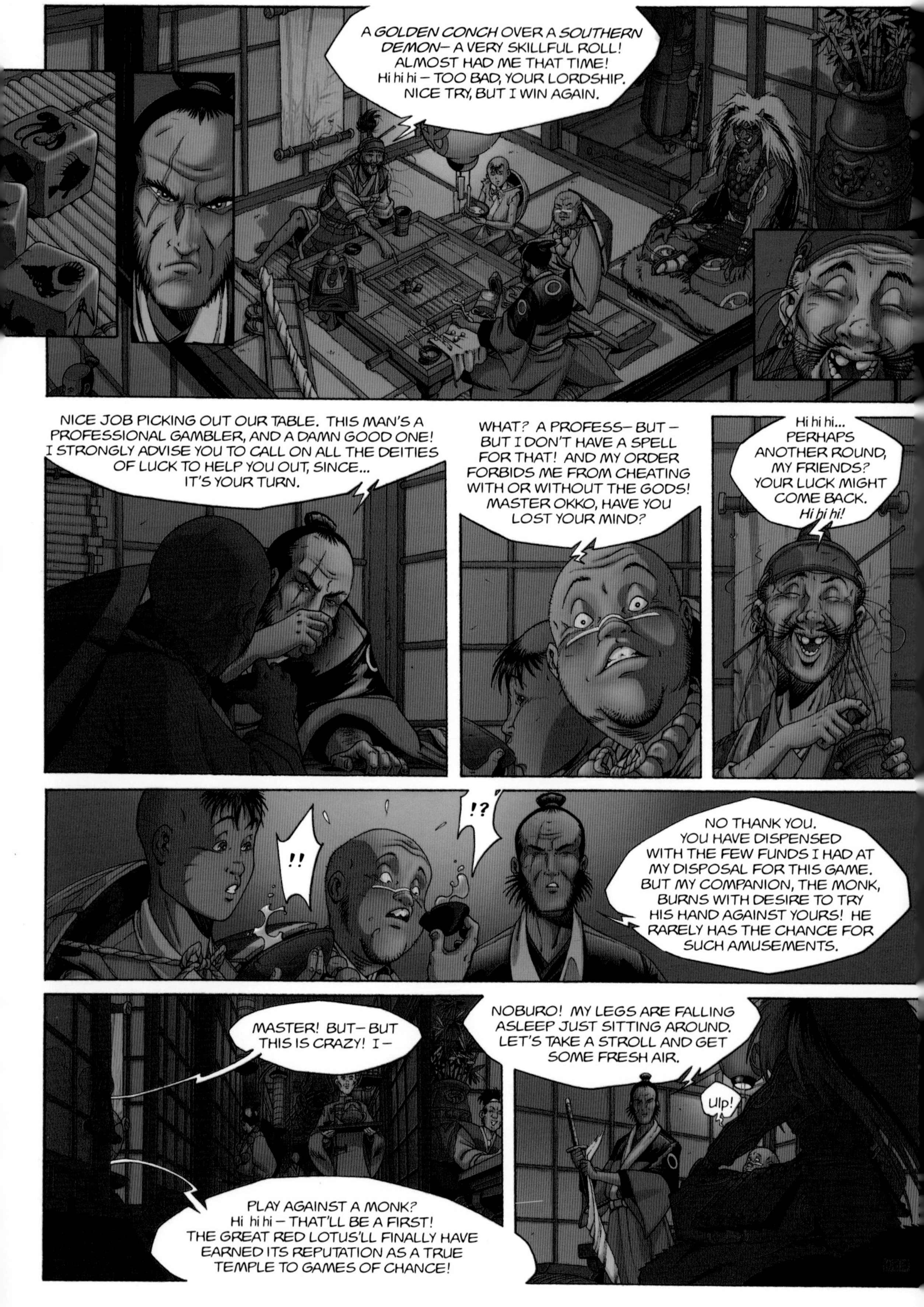
A GOLDEN CONCH OVER A SOUTHERN DEMON– A VERY SKILLFUL ROLL! ALMOST HAD ME THAT TIME! Hi hi hi – TOO BAD, YOUR LORDSHIP. NICE TRY, BUT I WIN AGAIN.
NICE JOB PICKING OUT OUR TABLE. THIS MAN'S A PROFESSIONAL GAMBLER, AND A DAMN GOOD ONE! I STRONGLY ADVISE YOU TO CALL ON ALL THE DEITIES OF LUCK TO HELP YOU OUT, SINCE... IT'S YOUR TURN.
WHAT? A PROFESS– BUT – BUT I DON'T HAVE A SPELL FOR THAT! AND MY ORDER FORBIDS ME FROM CHEATING WITH OR WITHOUT THE GODS! MASTER OKKO, HAVE YOU LOST YOUR MIND?
Hi hi hi... PERHAPS ANOTHER ROUND, MY FRIENDS? YOUR LUCK MIGHT COME BACK. Hi hi hi!
!!
!?
NO THANK YOU. YOU HAVE DISPENSED WITH THE FEW FUNDS I HAD AT MY DISPOSAL FOR THIS GAME. BUT MY COMPANION, THE MONK, BURNS WITH DESIRE TO TRY HIS HAND AGAINST YOURS! HE RARELY HAS THE CHANCE FOR SUCH AMUSEMENTS.
MASTER! BUT– BUT THIS IS CRAZY! I–
PLAY AGAINST A MONK? Hi hi hi – THAT'LL BE A FIRST! THE GREAT RED LOTUS'LL FINALLY HAVE EARNED ITS REPUTATION AS A TRUE TEMPLE TO GAMES OF CHANCE!
NOBURO! MY LEGS ARE FALLING ASLEEP JUST SITTING AROUND. LET'S TAKE A STROLL AND GET SOME FRESH AIR.
Ulp!

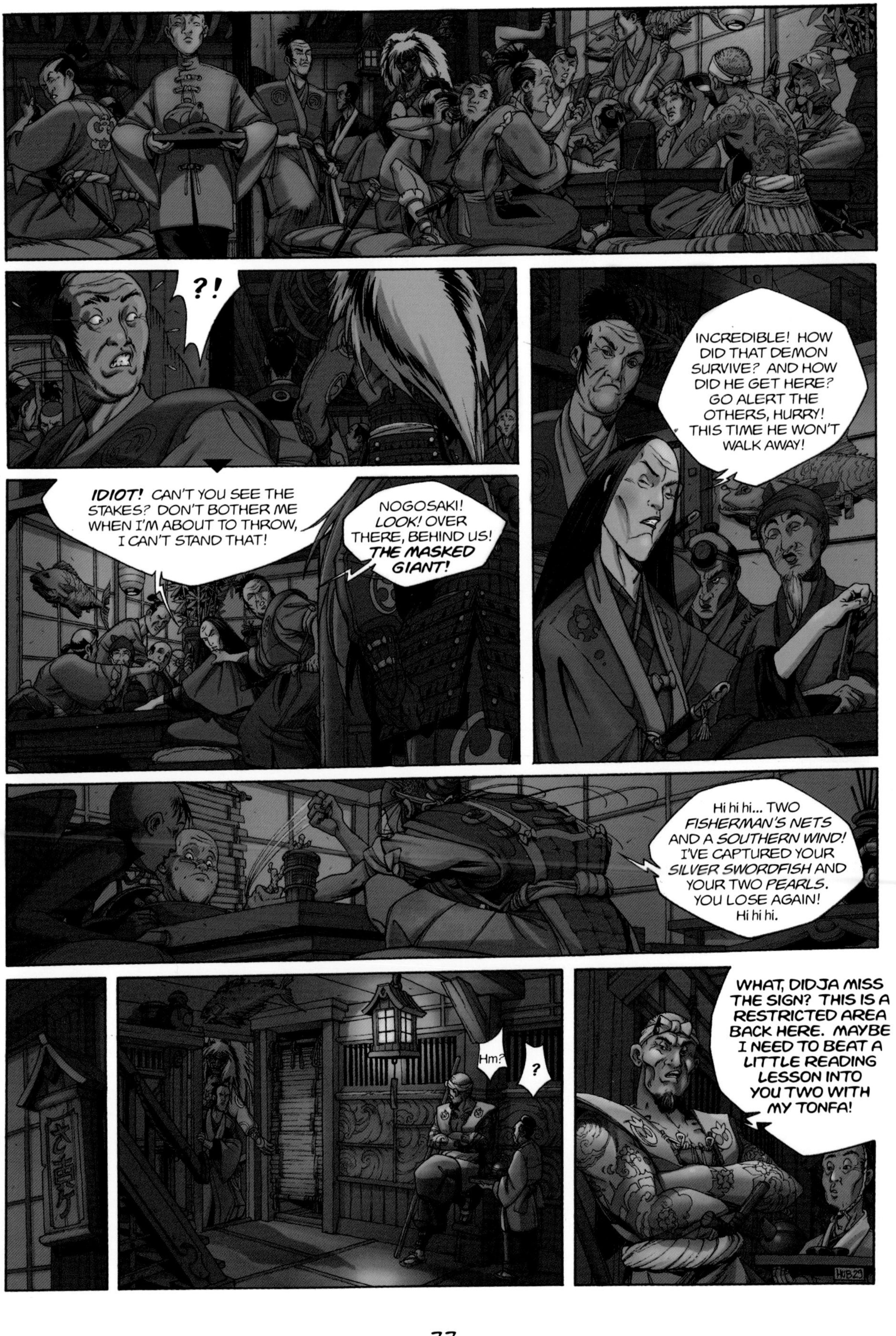
?!
INCREDIBLE! HOW DID THAT DEMON SURVIVE? AND HOW DID HE GET HERE? GO ALERT THE OTHERS, HURRY! THIS TIME HE WON'T WALK AWAY!
IDIOT! CAN'T YOU SEE THE STAKES? DON'T BOTHER ME WHEN I'M ABOUT TO THROW, I CAN'T STAND THAT!
NOGOSAKI! LOOK! OVER THERE, BEHIND US! THE MASKED GIANT!
Hi hi hi... TWO FISHERMAN'S NETS AND A SOUTHERN WIND! I'VE CAPTURED YOUR SILVER SWORDFISH AND YOUR TWO PEARLS. YOU LOSE AGAIN! Hi hi hi.
Hm?
?
WHAT, DIDJA MISS THE SIGN? THIS IS A RESTRICTED AREA BACK HERE. MAYBE I NEED TO BEAT A LITTLE READING LESSON INTO YOU TWO WITH MY TONFA!
HUB

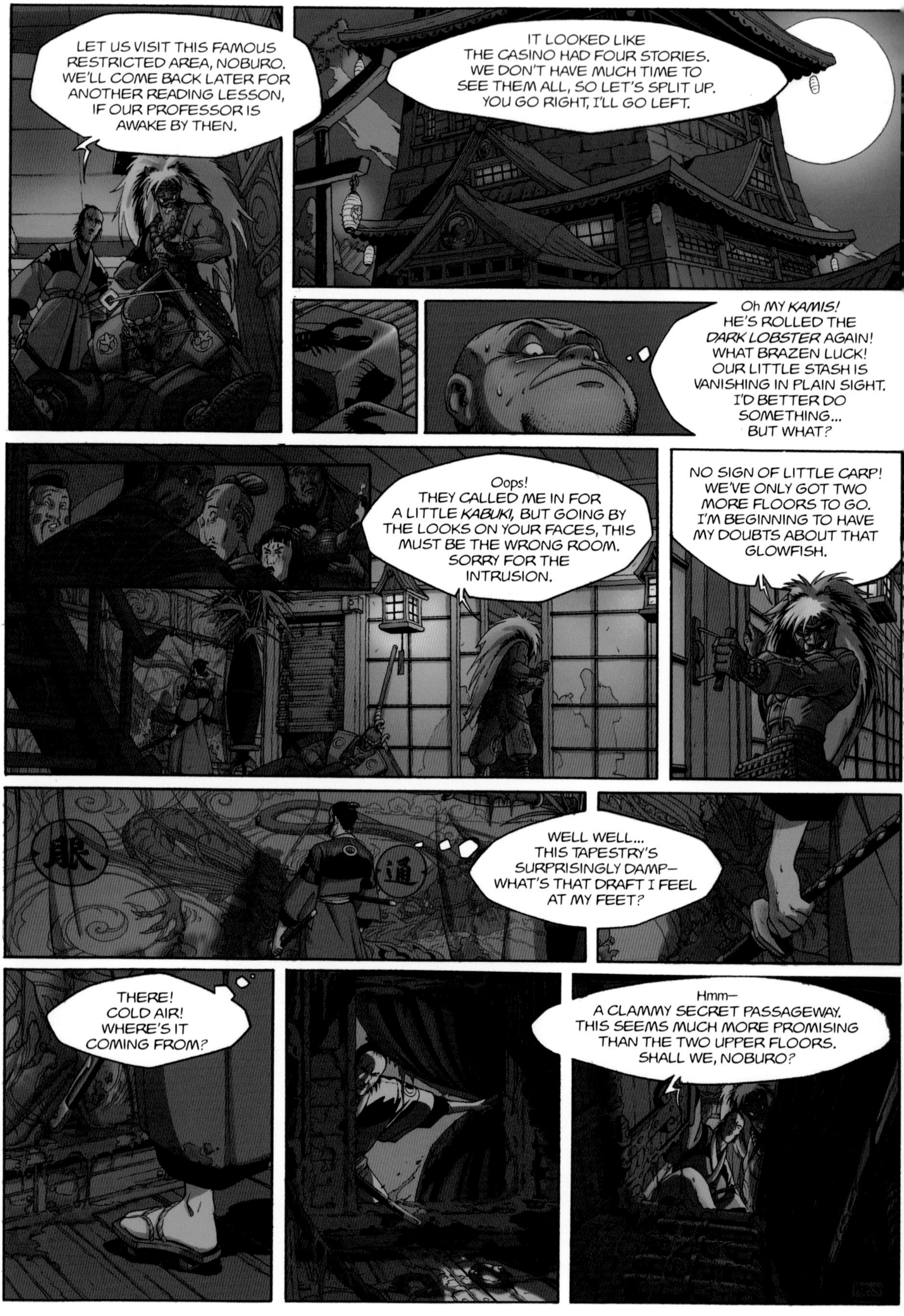
LET US VISIT THIS FAMOUS RESTRICTED AREA, NOBURO. WE'LL COME BACK LATER FOR ANOTHER READING LESSON, IF OUR PROFESSOR IS AWAKE BY THEN.
IT LOOKED LIKE THE CASINO HAD FOUR STORIES. WE DON'T HAVE MUCH TIME TO SEE THEM ALL, SO LET'S SPLIT UP. YOU GO RIGHT, I'LL GO LEFT.
Oh MY *KAMIS!* HE'S ROLLED THE *DARK LOBSTER* AGAIN! WHAT BRAZEN LUCK! OUR LITTLE STASH IS VANISHING IN PLAIN SIGHT. I'D BETTER DO SOMETHING... BUT WHAT?
Oops! THEY CALLED ME IN FOR A LITTLE *KABUKI,* BUT GOING BY THE LOOKS ON YOUR FACES, THIS MUST BE THE WRONG ROOM. SORRY FOR THE INTRUSION.
NO SIGN OF LITTLE CARP! WE'VE ONLY GOT TWO MORE FLOORS TO GO. I'M BEGINNING TO HAVE MY DOUBTS ABOUT THAT GLOWFISH.
WELL WELL... THIS TAPESTRY'S SURPRISINGLY DAMP— WHAT'S THAT DRAFT I FEEL AT MY FEET?
THERE! COLD AIR! WHERE'S IT COMING FROM?
Hmm— A CLAMMY SECRET PASSAGEWAY. THIS SEEMS MUCH MORE PROMISING THAN THE TWO UPPER FLOORS. SHALL WE, NOBURO?

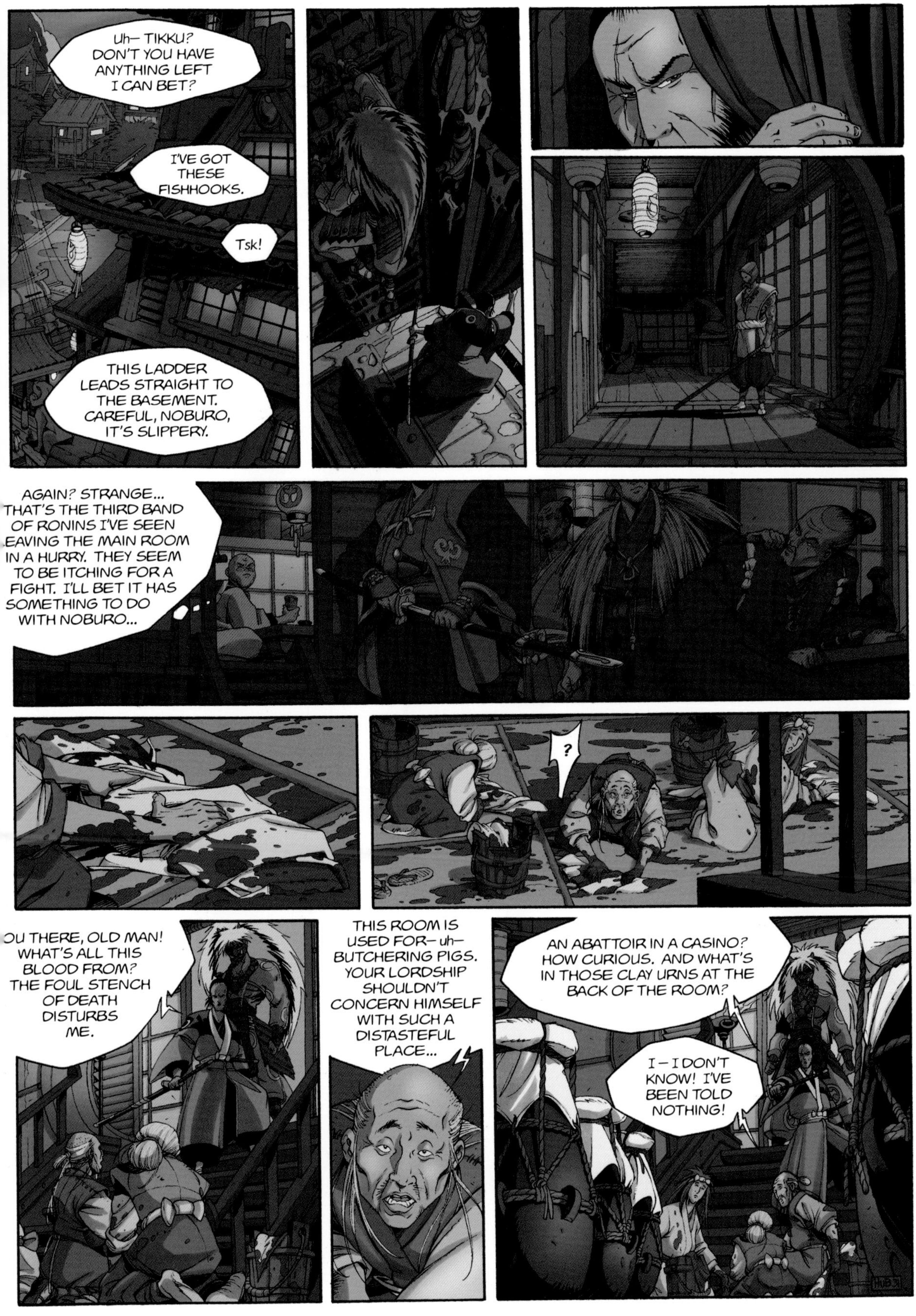
Uh– TIKKU? DON'T YOU HAVE ANYTHING LEFT I CAN BET?
I'VE GOT THESE FISHHOOKS.
Tsk!
THIS LADDER LEADS STRAIGHT TO THE BASEMENT. CAREFUL, NOBURO, IT'S SLIPPERY.
AGAIN? STRANGE... THAT'S THE THIRD BAND OF RONINS I'VE SEEN LEAVING THE MAIN ROOM IN A HURRY. THEY SEEM TO BE ITCHING FOR A FIGHT. I'LL BET IT HAS SOMETHING TO DO WITH NOBURO...
?
YOU THERE, OLD MAN! WHAT'S ALL THIS BLOOD FROM? THE FOUL STENCH OF DEATH DISTURBS ME.
THIS ROOM IS USED FOR– uh– BUTCHERING PIGS. YOUR LORDSHIP SHOULDN'T CONCERN HIMSELF WITH SUCH A DISTASTEFUL PLACE...
AN ABATTOIR IN A CASINO? HOW CURIOUS. AND WHAT'S IN THOSE CLAY URNS AT THE BACK OF THE ROOM?
I– I DON'T KNOW! I'VE BEEN TOLD NOTHING!

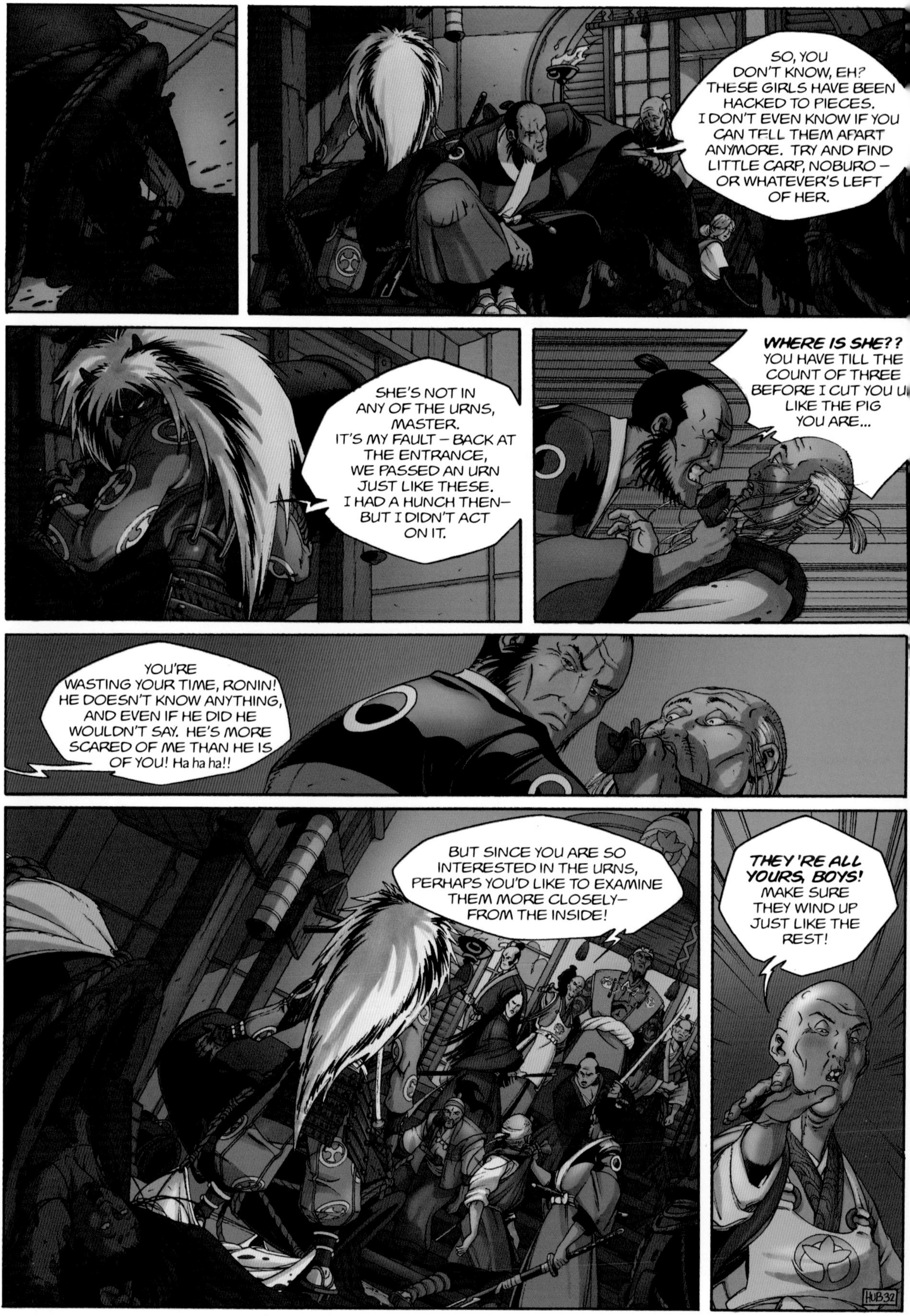
SO, YOU DON'T KNOW, EH? THESE GIRLS HAVE BEEN HACKED TO PIECES. I DON'T EVEN KNOW IF YOU CAN TELL THEM APART ANYMORE. TRY AND FIND LITTLE CARP, NOBURO — OR WHATEVER'S LEFT OF HER.
SHE'S NOT IN ANY OF THE URNS, MASTER. IT'S MY FAULT — BACK AT THE ENTRANCE, WE PASSED AN URN JUST LIKE THESE. I HAD A HUNCH THEN— BUT I DIDN'T ACT ON IT.
WHERE IS SHE?? YOU HAVE TILL THE COUNT OF THREE BEFORE I CUT YOU U LIKE THE PIG YOU ARE...
YOU'RE WASTING YOUR TIME, RONIN! HE DOESN'T KNOW ANYTHING, AND EVEN IF HE DID HE WOULDN'T SAY. HE'S MORE SCARED OF ME THAN HE IS OF YOU! Ha ha ha!!
BUT SINCE YOU ARE SO INTERESTED IN THE URNS, PERHAPS YOU'D LIKE TO EXAMINE THEM MORE CLOSELY— FROM THE INSIDE!
THEY'RE ALL YOURS, BOYS! MAKE SURE THEY WIND UP JUST LIKE THE REST!
HUB 32

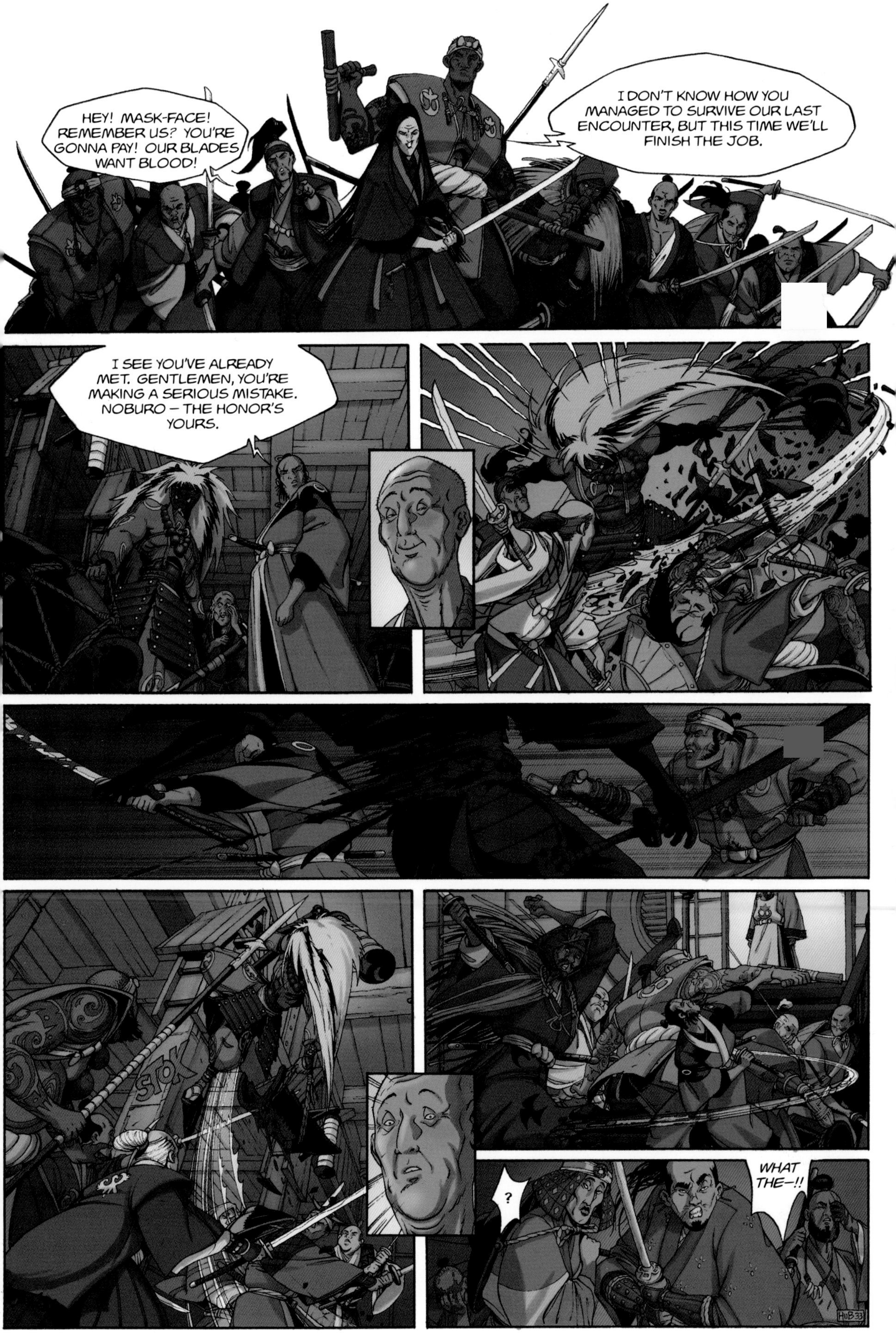
HEY! MASK-FACE! REMEMBER US? YOU'RE GONNA PAY! OUR BLADES WANT BLOOD!
I DON'T KNOW HOW YOU MANAGED TO SURVIVE OUR LAST ENCOUNTER, BUT THIS TIME WE'LL FINISH THE JOB.
I SEE YOU'VE ALREADY MET. GENTLEMEN, YOU'RE MAKING A SERIOUS MISTAKE. NOBURO – THE HONOR'S YOURS.
STOK
?
WHAT THE–!!
HUB 33

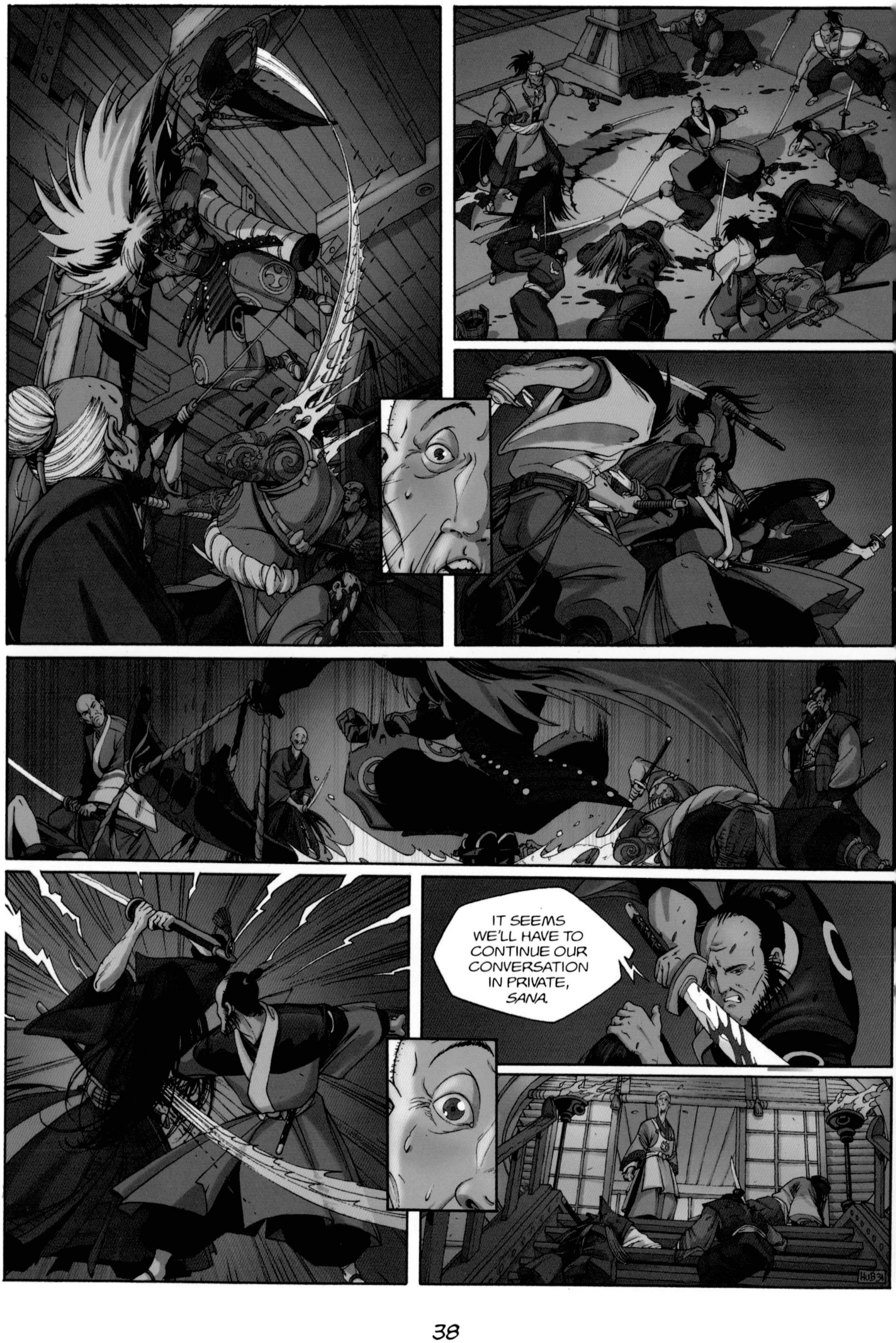
IT SEEMS WE'LL HAVE TO CONTINUE OUR CONVERSATION IN PRIVATE, SANA.

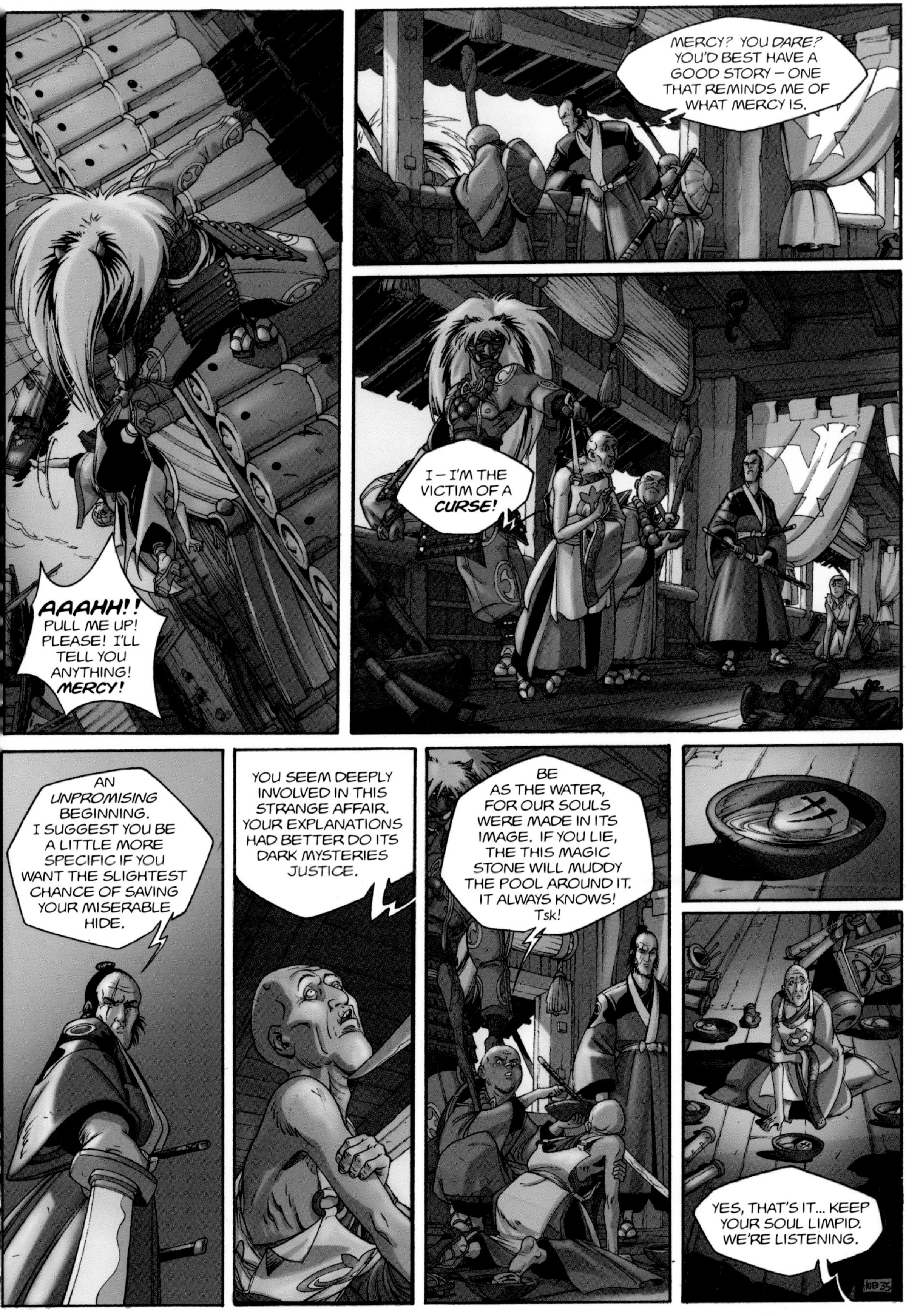

AAAHH!! PULL ME UP! PLEASE! I'LL TELL YOU ANYTHING! MERCY!
MERCY? YOU DARE? YOU'D BEST HAVE A GOOD STORY – ONE THAT REMINDS ME OF WHAT MERCY IS.
I – I'M THE VICTIM OF A CURSE!
AN UNPROMISING BEGINNING. I SUGGEST YOU BE A LITTLE MORE SPECIFIC IF YOU WANT THE SLIGHTEST CHANCE OF SAVING YOUR MISERABLE HIDE.
YOU SEEM DEEPLY INVOLVED IN THIS STRANGE AFFAIR. YOUR EXPLANATIONS HAD BETTER DO ITS DARK MYSTERIES JUSTICE.
BE AS THE WATER, FOR OUR SOULS WERE MADE IN ITS IMAGE. IF YOU LIE, THE THIS MAGIC STONE WILL MUDDY THE POOL AROUND IT. IT ALWAYS KNOWS! Tsk!
YES, THAT'S IT... KEEP YOUR SOUL LIMPID. WE'RE LISTENING.
HUB 35

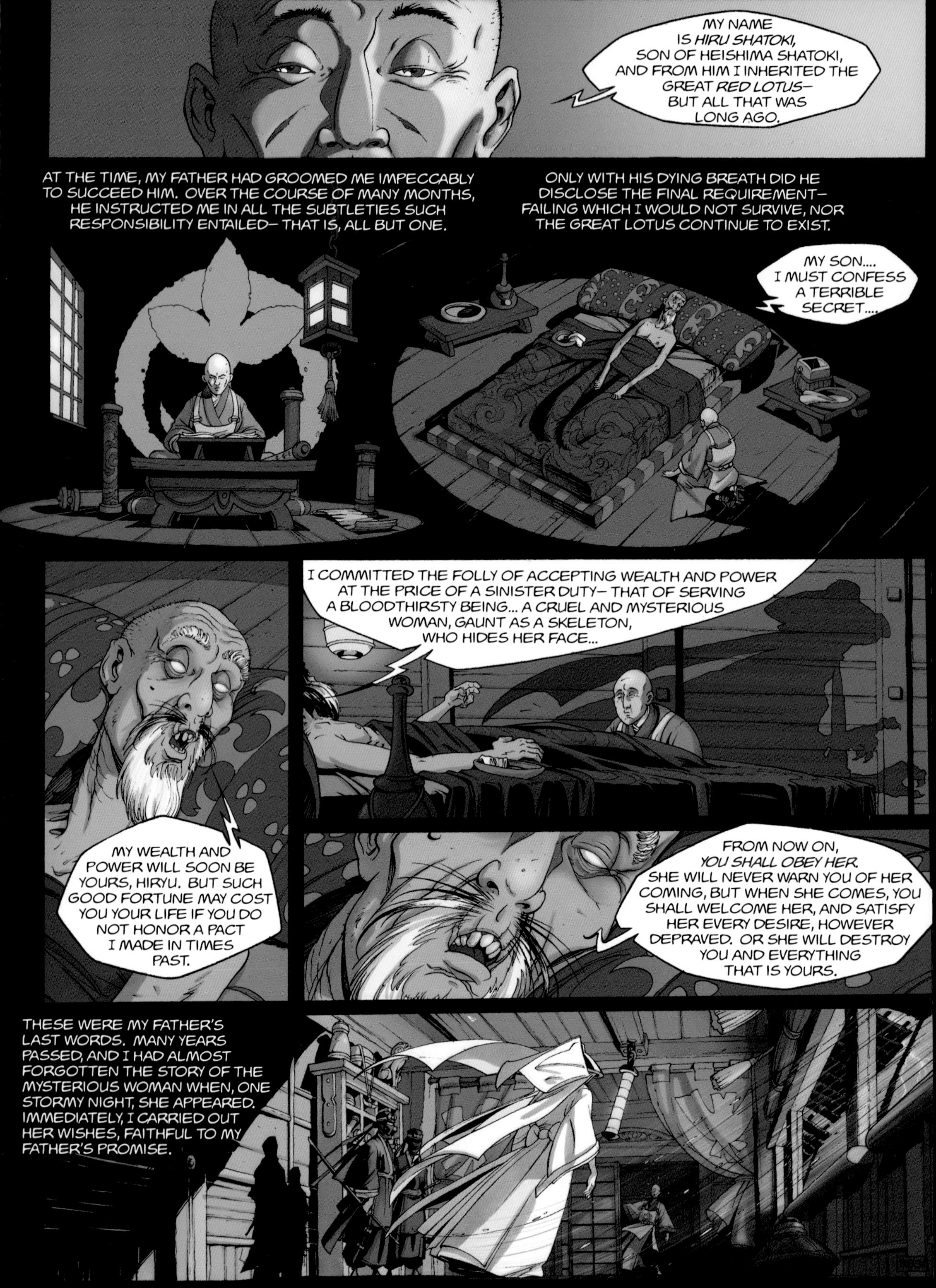
MY NAME IS *HIRU SHATOKI,* SON OF HEISHIMA SHATOKI, AND FROM HIM I INHERITED THE GREAT *RED LOTUS*— BUT ALL THAT WAS LONG AGO.
AT THE TIME, MY FATHER HAD GROOMED ME IMPECCABLY TO SUCCEED HIM. OVER THE COURSE OF MANY MONTHS, HE INSTRUCTED ME IN ALL THE SUBTLETIES SUCH RESPONSIBILITY ENTAILED— THAT IS, ALL BUT ONE.
ONLY WITH HIS DYING BREATH DID HE DISCLOSE THE FINAL REQUIREMENT— FAILING WHICH I WOULD NOT SURVIVE, NOR THE GREAT LOTUS CONTINUE TO EXIST.
MY SON.... I MUST CONFESS A TERRIBLE SECRET....
I COMMITTED THE FOLLY OF ACCEPTING WEALTH AND POWER AT THE PRICE OF A SINISTER DUTY— THAT OF SERVING A BLOODTHIRSTY BEING... A CRUEL AND MYSTERIOUS WOMAN, GAUNT AS A SKELETON, WHO HIDES HER FACE...
MY WEALTH AND POWER WILL SOON BE YOURS, HIRYU. BUT SUCH GOOD FORTUNE MAY COST YOU YOUR LIFE IF YOU DO NOT HONOR A PACT I MADE IN TIMES PAST.
FROM NOW ON, *YOU SHALL OBEY HER.* SHE WILL NEVER WARN YOU OF HER COMING, BUT WHEN SHE COMES, YOU SHALL WELCOME HER, AND SATISFY HER EVERY DESIRE, HOWEVER DEPRAVED. OR SHE WILL DESTROY YOU AND EVERYTHING THAT IS YOURS.
THESE WERE MY FATHER'S LAST WORDS. MANY YEARS PASSED, AND I HAD ALMOST FORGOTTEN THE STORY OF THE MYSTERIOUS WOMAN WHEN, ONE STORMY NIGHT, SHE APPEARED. IMMEDIATELY, I CARRIED OUT HER WISHES, FAITHFUL TO MY FATHER'S PROMISE.

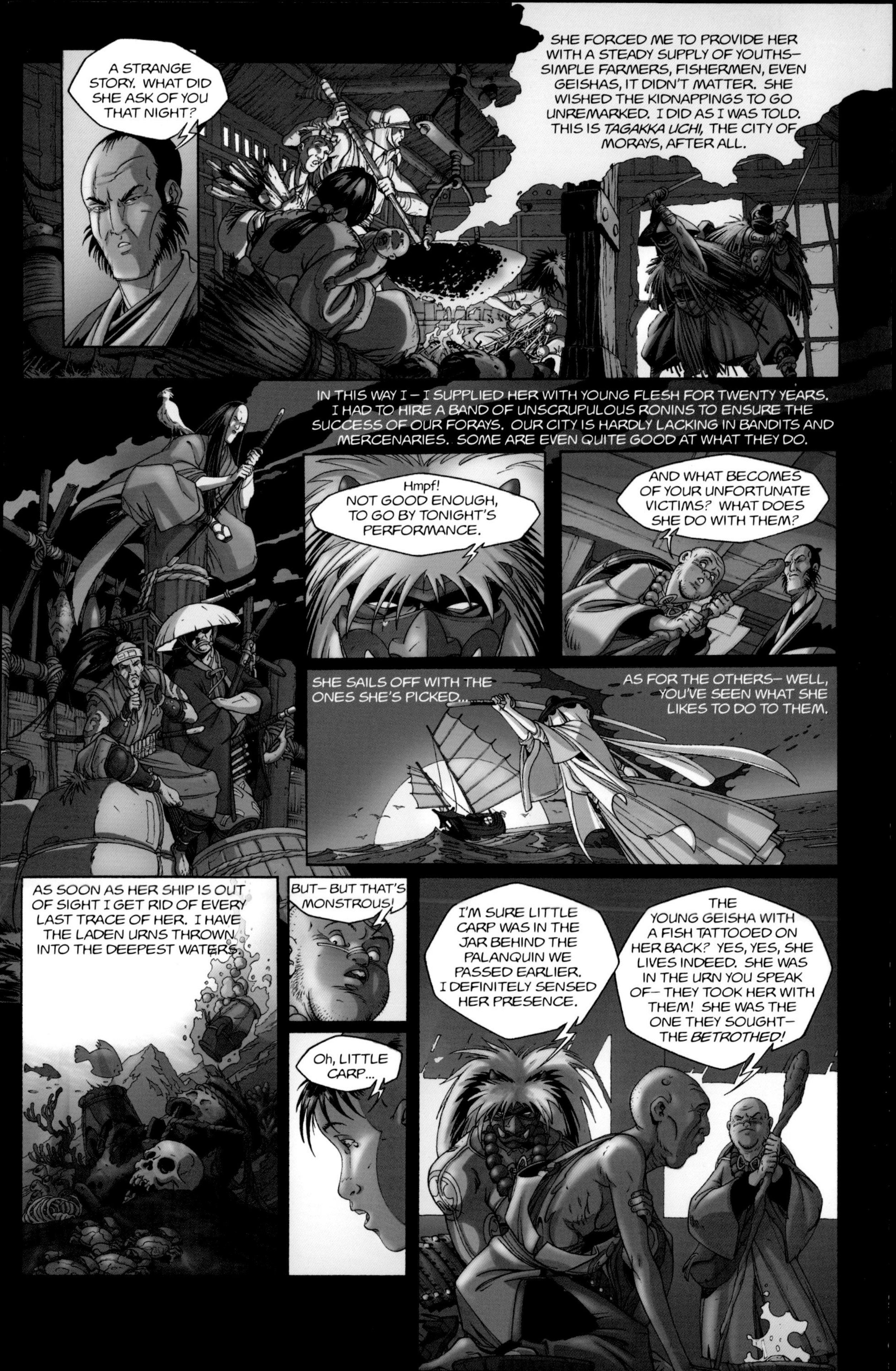
A STRANGE STORY. WHAT DID SHE ASK OF YOU THAT NIGHT?
SHE FORCED ME TO PROVIDE HER WITH A STEADY SUPPLY OF YOUTHS— SIMPLE FARMERS, FISHERMEN, EVEN GEISHAS, IT DIDN'T MATTER. SHE WISHED THE KIDNAPPINGS TO GO UNREMARKED. I DID AS I WAS TOLD. THIS IS *TAGAKKA UCHI*, THE CITY OF MORAYS, AFTER ALL.
IN THIS WAY I — I SUPPLIED HER WITH YOUNG FLESH FOR TWENTY YEARS. I HAD TO HIRE A BAND OF UNSCRUPULOUS RONINS TO ENSURE THE SUCCESS OF OUR FORAYS. OUR CITY IS HARDLY LACKING IN BANDITS AND MERCENARIES. SOME ARE EVEN QUITE GOOD AT WHAT THEY DO.
Hmpf! NOT GOOD ENOUGH, TO GO BY TONIGHT'S PERFORMANCE.
AND WHAT BECOMES OF YOUR UNFORTUNATE VICTIMS? WHAT DOES SHE DO WITH THEM?
SHE SAILS OFF WITH THE ONES SHE'S PICKED...
AS FOR THE OTHERS— WELL, YOU'VE SEEN WHAT SHE LIKES TO DO TO THEM.
AS SOON AS HER SHIP IS OUT OF SIGHT I GET RID OF EVERY LAST TRACE OF HER. I HAVE THE LADEN URNS THROWN INTO THE DEEPEST WATERS.
BUT— BUT THAT'S MONSTROUS!
Oh, LITTLE CARP...
I'M SURE LITTLE CARP WAS IN THE JAR BEHIND THE PALANQUIN WE PASSED EARLIER. I DEFINITELY SENSED HER PRESENCE.
THE YOUNG GEISHA WITH A FISH TATTOOED ON HER BACK? YES, YES, SHE LIVES INDEED. SHE WAS IN THE URN YOU SPEAK OF— THEY TOOK HER WITH THEM! SHE WAS THE ONE THEY SOUGHT— THE *BETROTHED*!

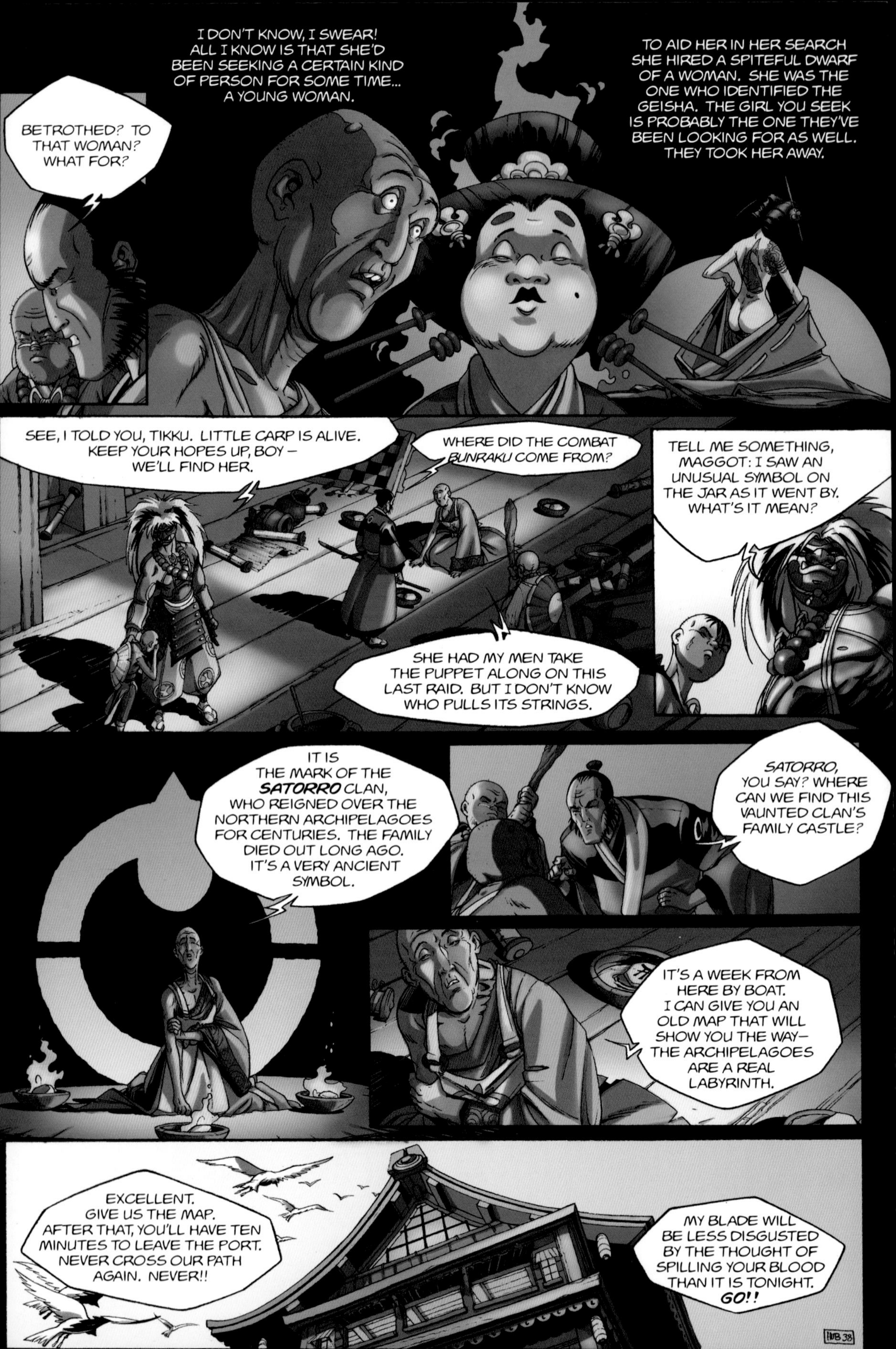
I DON'T KNOW, I SWEAR! ALL I KNOW IS THAT SHE'D BEEN SEEKING A CERTAIN KIND OF PERSON FOR SOME TIME... A YOUNG WOMAN.
BETROTHED? TO THAT WOMAN? WHAT FOR?
TO AID HER IN HER SEARCH SHE HIRED A SPITEFUL DWARF OF A WOMAN. SHE WAS THE ONE WHO IDENTIFIED THE GEISHA. THE GIRL YOU SEEK IS PROBABLY THE ONE THEY'VE BEEN LOOKING FOR AS WELL. THEY TOOK HER AWAY.
SEE, I TOLD YOU, TIKKU. LITTLE CARP IS ALIVE. KEEP YOUR HOPES UP, BOY — WE'LL FIND HER.
WHERE DID THE COMBAT *BUNRAKU* COME FROM?
SHE HAD MY MEN TAKE THE PUPPET ALONG ON THIS LAST RAID. BUT I DON'T KNOW WHO PULLS ITS STRINGS.
TELL ME SOMETHING, MAGGOT: I SAW AN UNUSUAL SYMBOL ON THE JAR AS IT WENT BY. WHAT'S IT MEAN?
IT IS THE MARK OF THE **SATORRO** CLAN, WHO REIGNED OVER THE NORTHERN ARCHIPELAGOES FOR CENTURIES. THE FAMILY DIED OUT LONG AGO. IT'S A VERY ANCIENT SYMBOL.
SATORRO, YOU SAY? WHERE CAN WE FIND THIS VAUNTED CLAN'S FAMILY CASTLE?
IT'S A WEEK FROM HERE BY BOAT. I CAN GIVE YOU AN OLD MAP THAT WILL SHOW YOU THE WAY— THE ARCHIPELAGOES ARE A REAL LABYRINTH.
EXCELLENT. GIVE US THE MAP. AFTER THAT, YOU'LL HAVE TEN MINUTES TO LEAVE THE PORT. NEVER CROSS OUR PATH AGAIN. NEVER!!
MY BLADE WILL BE LESS DISGUSTED BY THE THOUGHT OF SPILLING YOUR BLOOD THAN IT IS TONIGHT. **GO!!**
IMB 38

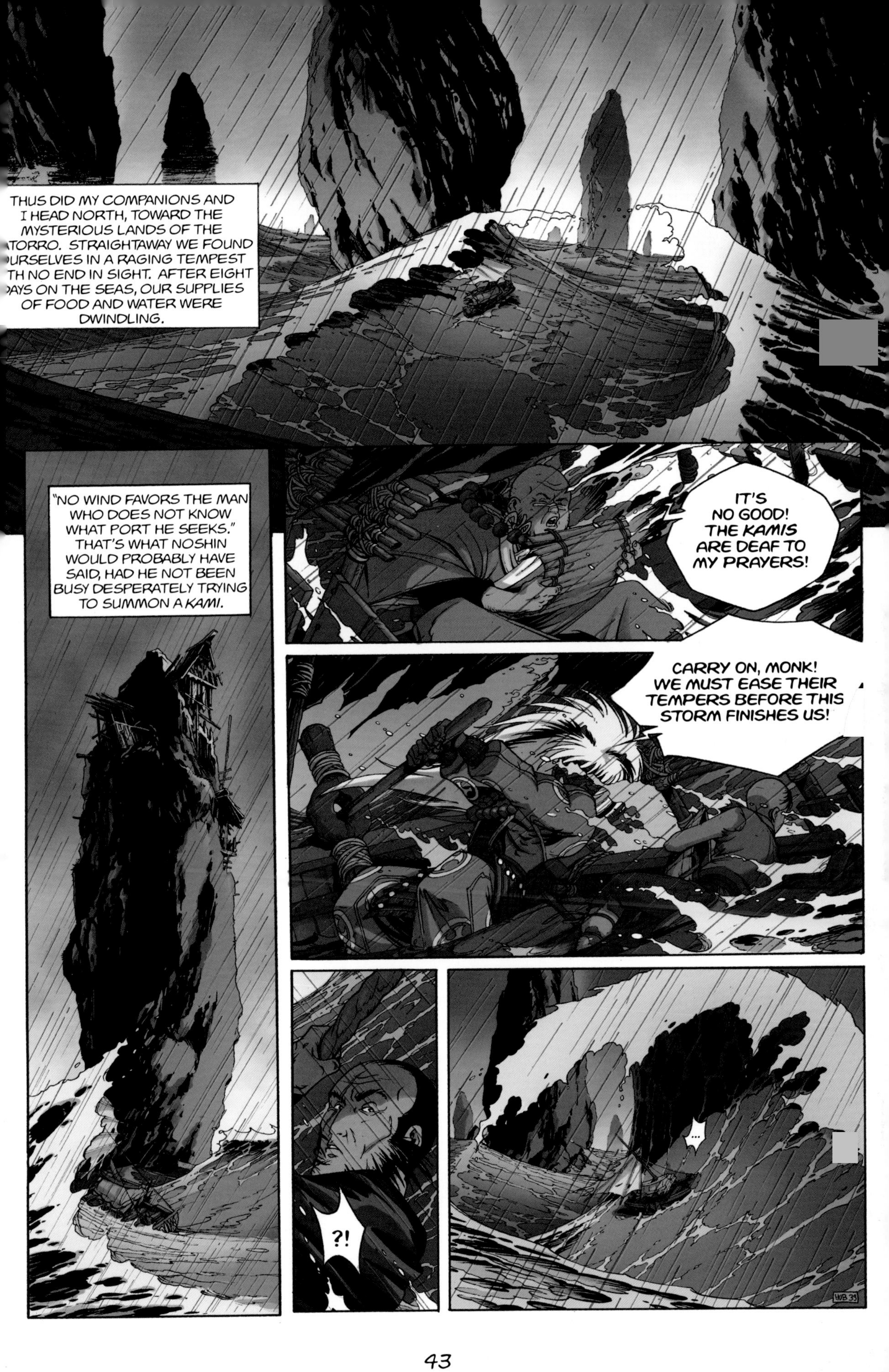
THUS DID MY COMPANIONS AND I HEAD NORTH, TOWARD THE MYSTERIOUS LANDS OF THE ATORRO. STRAIGHTAWAY WE FOUND OURSELVES IN A RAGING TEMPEST WITH NO END IN SIGHT. AFTER EIGHT DAYS ON THE SEAS, OUR SUPPLIES OF FOOD AND WATER WERE DWINDLING.
"NO WIND FAVORS THE MAN WHO DOES NOT KNOW WHAT PORT HE SEEKS." THAT'S WHAT NOSHIN WOULD PROBABLY HAVE SAID, HAD HE NOT BEEN BUSY DESPERATELY TRYING TO SUMMON A KAMI.
IT'S NO GOOD! THE KAMIS ARE DEAF TO MY PRAYERS!
CARRY ON, MONK! WE MUST EASE THEIR TEMPERS BEFORE THIS STORM FINISHES US!
?!
...
WB 39

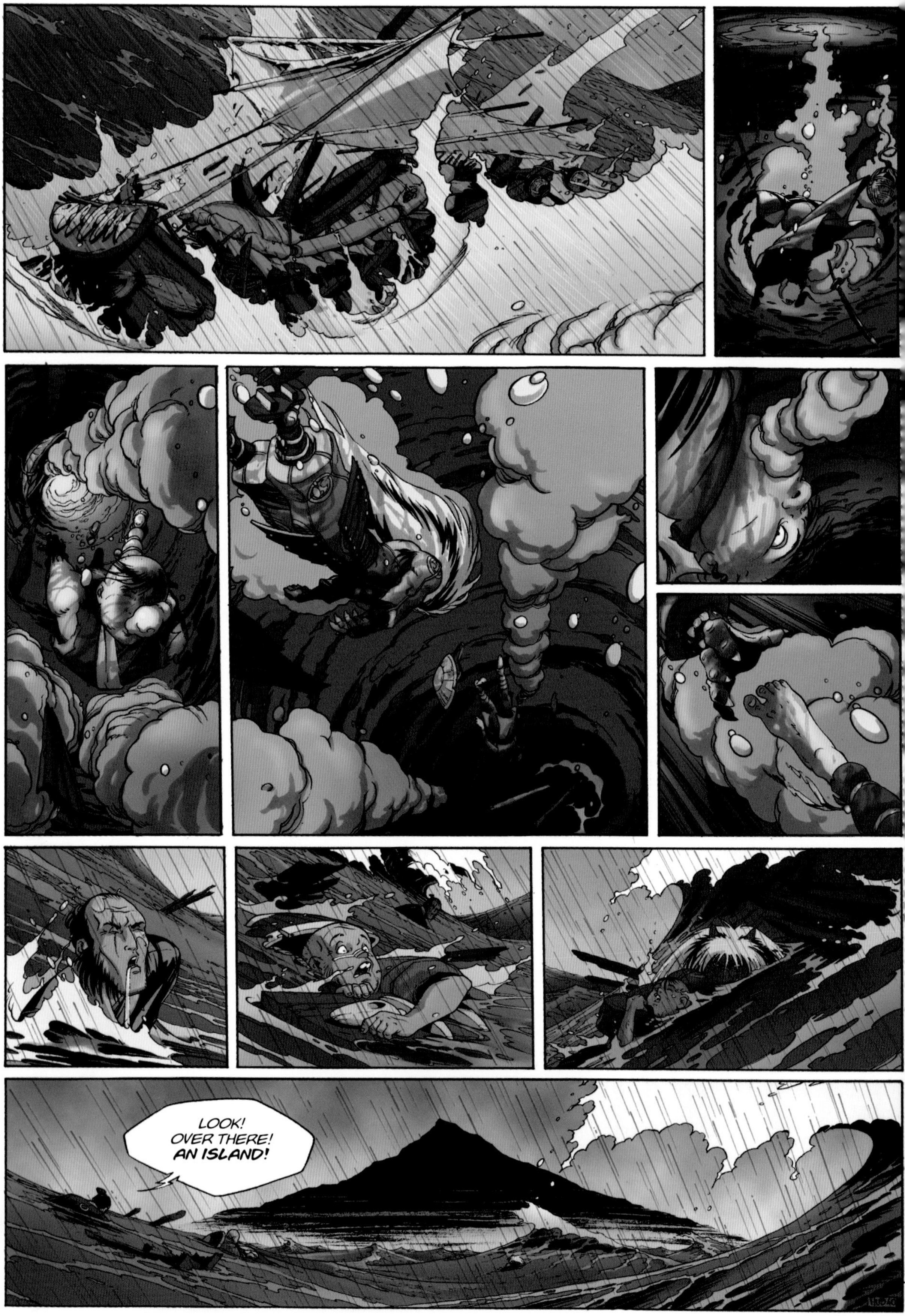
LOOK! OVER THERE! AN ISLAND!

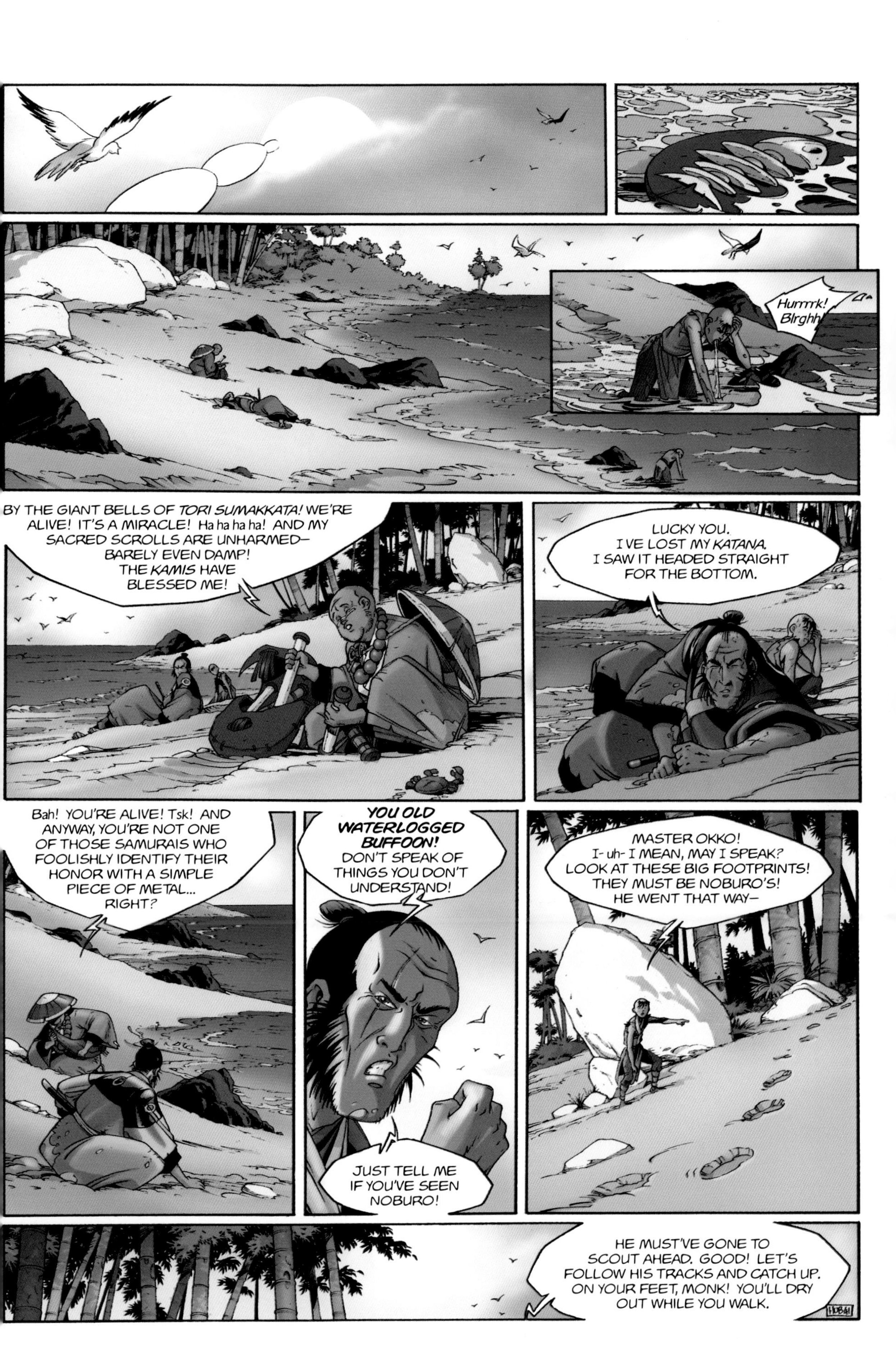
Hurrrrk! Blrghh!
BY THE GIANT BELLS OF TORI SUMAKKATA! WE'RE ALIVE! IT'S A MIRACLE! Ha ha ha ha! AND MY SACRED SCROLLS ARE UNHARMED— BARELY EVEN DAMP! THE KAMIS HAVE BLESSED ME!
LUCKY YOU. I'VE LOST MY KATANA. I SAW IT HEADED STRAIGHT FOR THE BOTTOM.
Bah! YOU'RE ALIVE! Tsk! AND ANYWAY, YOU'RE NOT ONE OF THOSE SAMURAIS WHO FOOLISHLY IDENTIFY THEIR HONOR WITH A SIMPLE PIECE OF METAL... RIGHT?
YOU OLD WATERLOGGED BUFFOON! DON'T SPEAK OF THINGS YOU DON'T UNDERSTAND!
JUST TELL ME IF YOU'VE SEEN NOBURO!
MASTER OKKO! I- uh- I MEAN, MAY I SPEAK? LOOK AT THESE BIG FOOTPRINTS! THEY MUST BE NOBURO'S! HE WENT THAT WAY—
HE MUST'VE GONE TO SCOUT AHEAD. GOOD! LET'S FOLLOW HIS TRACKS AND CATCH UP. ON YOUR FEET, MONK! YOU'LL DRY OUT WHILE YOU WALK.

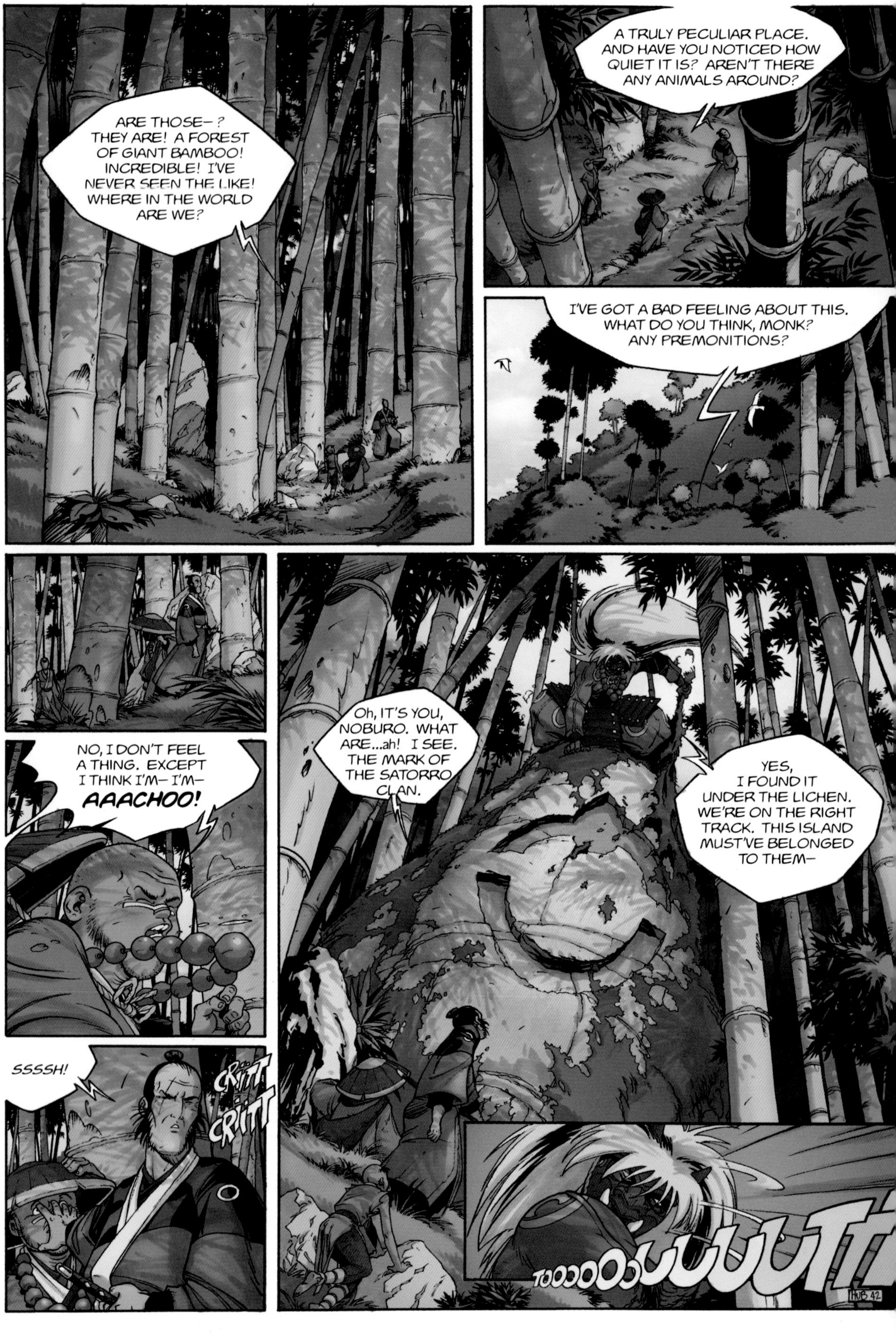
ARE THOSE—? THEY ARE! A FOREST OF GIANT BAMBOO! INCREDIBLE! I'VE NEVER SEEN THE LIKE! WHERE IN THE WORLD ARE WE?
A TRULY PECULIAR PLACE. AND HAVE YOU NOTICED HOW QUIET IT IS? AREN'T THERE ANY ANIMALS AROUND?
I'VE GOT A BAD FEELING ABOUT THIS. WHAT DO YOU THINK, MONK? ANY PREMONITIONS?
NO, I DON'T FEEL A THING. EXCEPT I THINK I'M— I'M—
AAACHOO!
SSSSH!
CRITT
CRITT
Oh, IT'S YOU, NOBURO. WHAT ARE...ah! I SEE. THE MARK OF THE SATORRO CLAN.
YES, I FOUND IT UNDER THE LICHEN. WE'RE ON THE RIGHT TRACK. THIS ISLAND MUST'VE BELONGED TO THEM—
TOOOOOOUUUUUTT
HUB 42

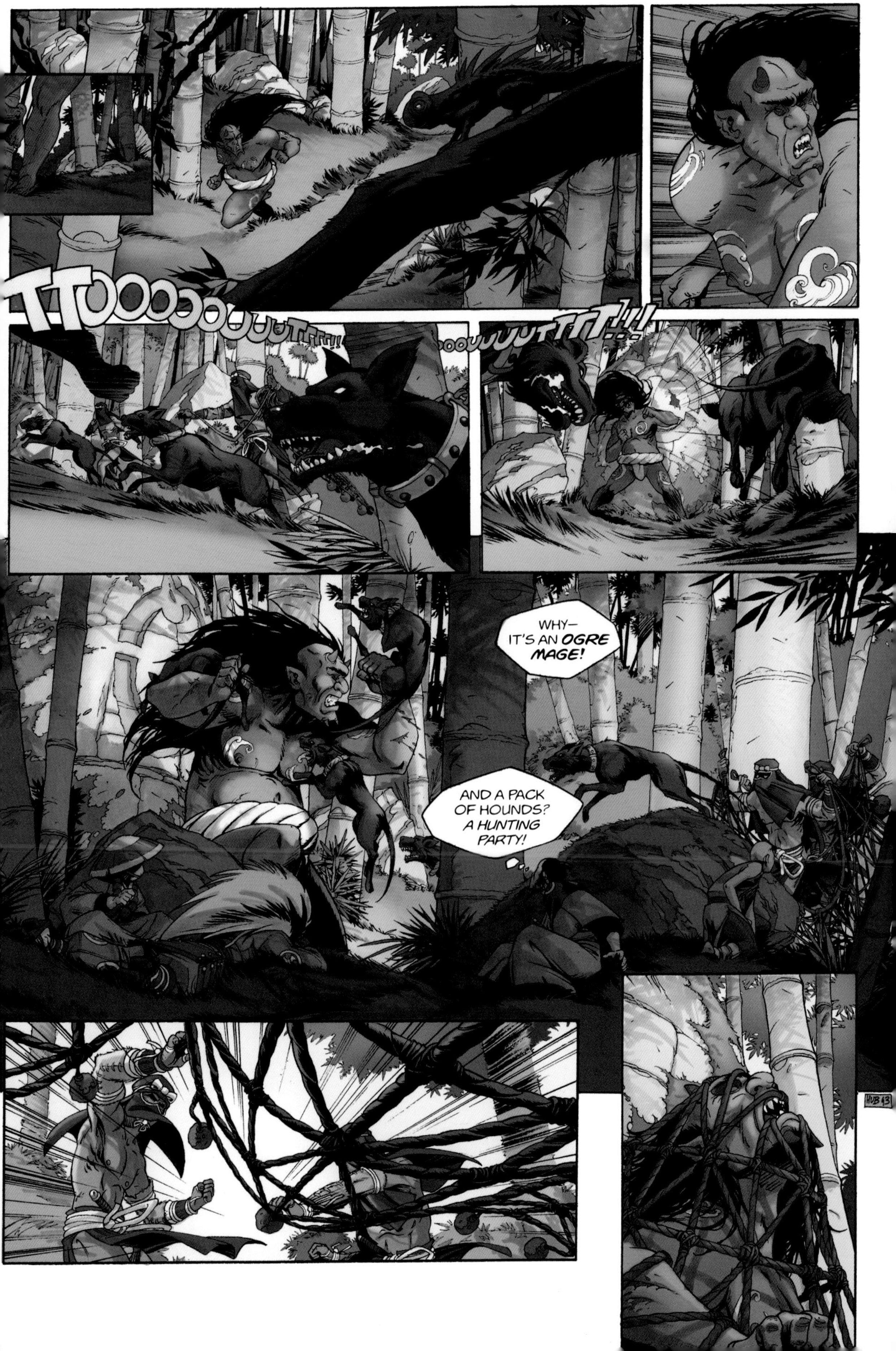
TTOOOOOOUUUUTTT!!!
WHY— IT'S AN OGRE MAGE!
AND A PACK OF HOUNDS? A HUNTING PARTY!
HUB 43

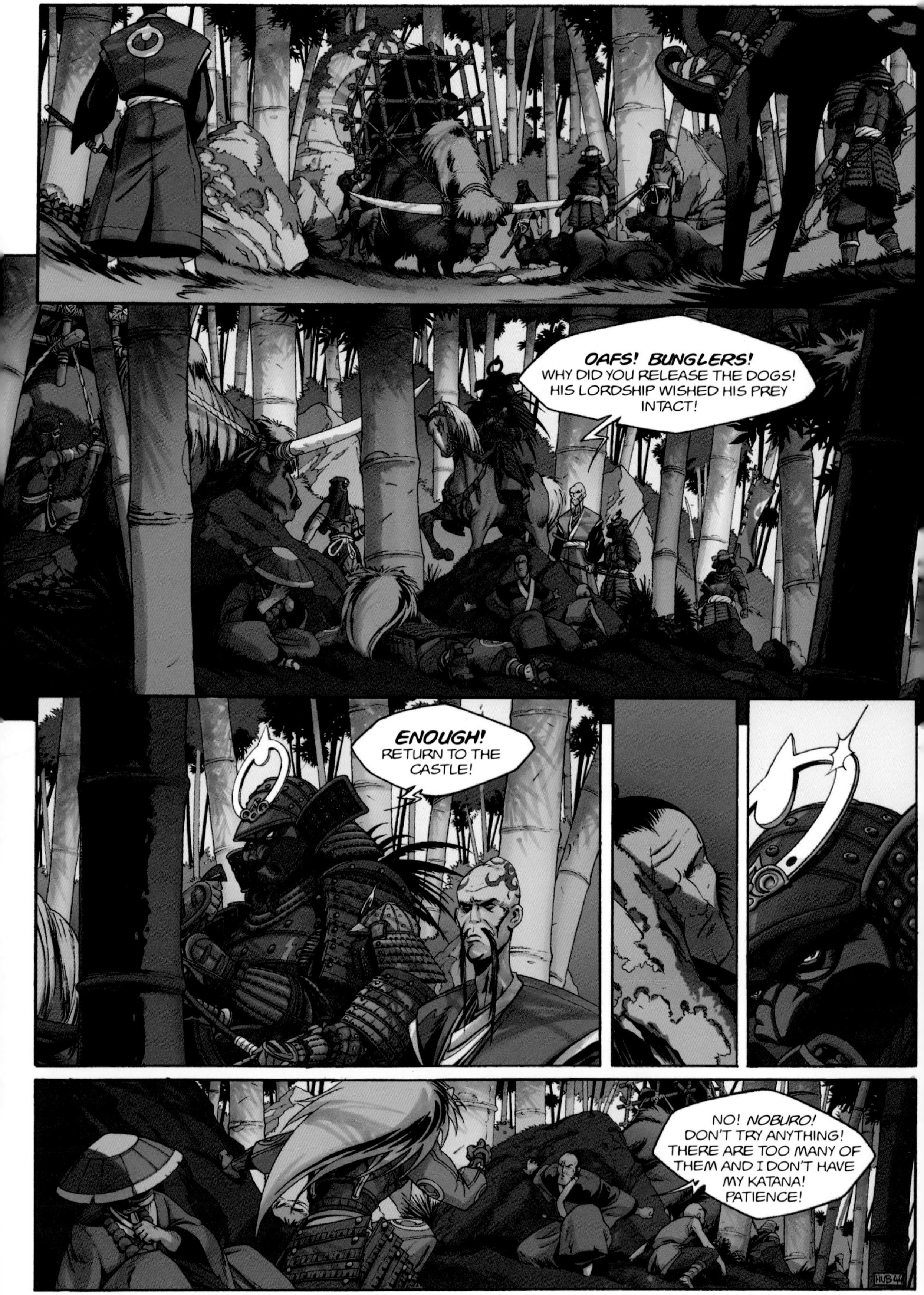
OAFS! BUNGLERS! WHY DID YOU RELEASE THE DOGS! HIS LORDSHIP WISHED HIS PREY INTACT!
ENOUGH! RETURN TO THE CASTLE!
NO! NOBURO! DON'T TRY ANYTHING! THERE ARE TOO MANY OF THEM AND I DON'T HAVE MY KATANA! PATIENCE!

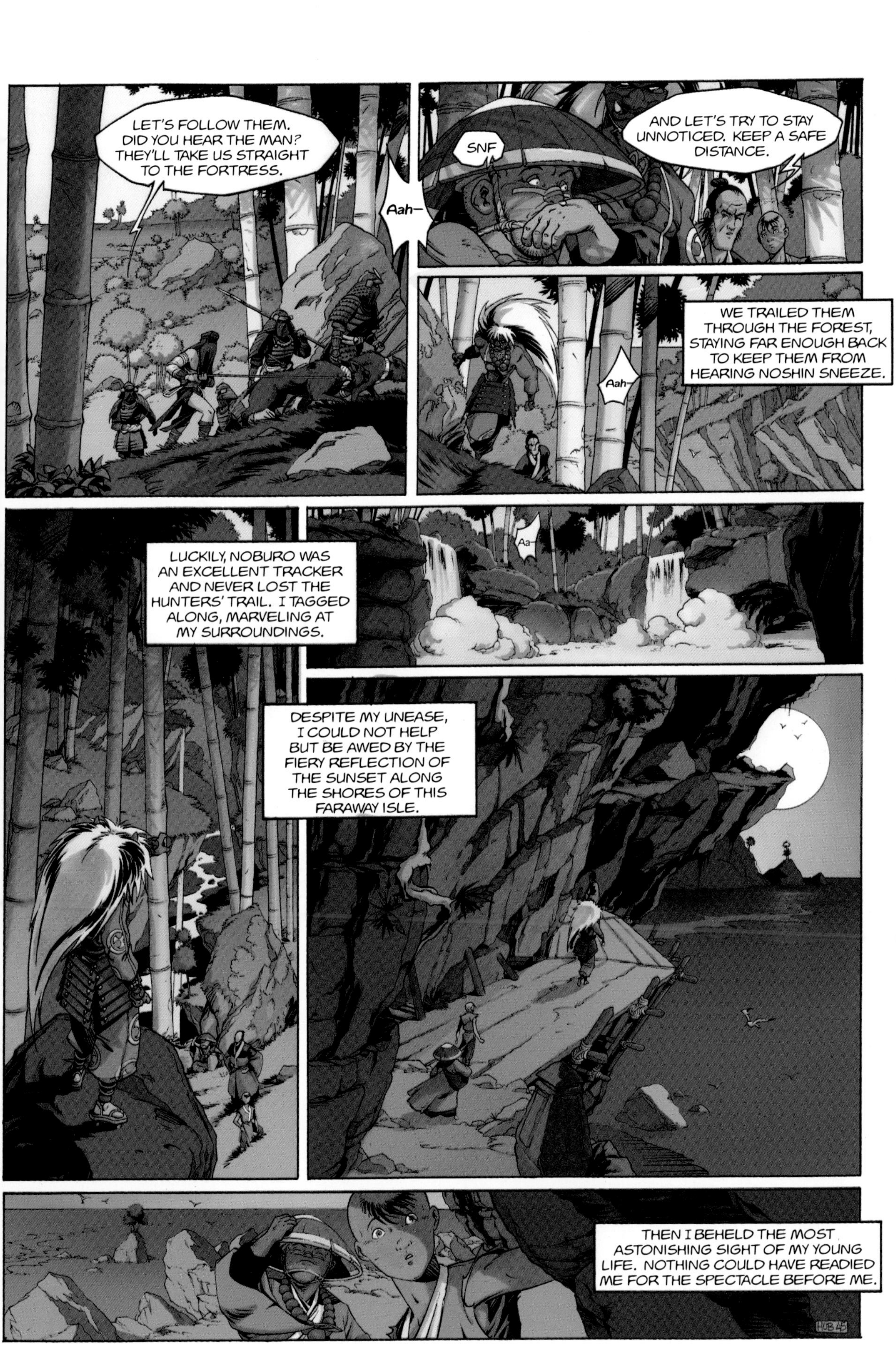
LET'S FOLLOW THEM. DID YOU HEAR THE MAN? THEY'LL TAKE US STRAIGHT TO THE FORTRESS.
Aah—
SNF
AND LET'S TRY TO STAY UNNOTICED. KEEP A SAFE DISTANCE.
Aah—
WE TRAILED THEM THROUGH THE FOREST, STAYING FAR ENOUGH BACK TO KEEP THEM FROM HEARING NOSHIN SNEEZE.
LUCKILY, NOBURO WAS AN EXCELLENT TRACKER AND NEVER LOST THE HUNTERS' TRAIL. I TAGGED ALONG, MARVELING AT MY SURROUNDINGS.
Aa
DESPITE MY UNEASE, I COULD NOT HELP BUT BE AWED BY THE FIERY REFLECTION OF THE SUNSET ALONG THE SHORES OF THIS FARAWAY ISLE.
THEN I BEHELD THE MOST ASTONISHING SIGHT OF MY YOUNG LIFE. NOTHING COULD HAVE READIED ME FOR THE SPECTACLE BEFORE ME.

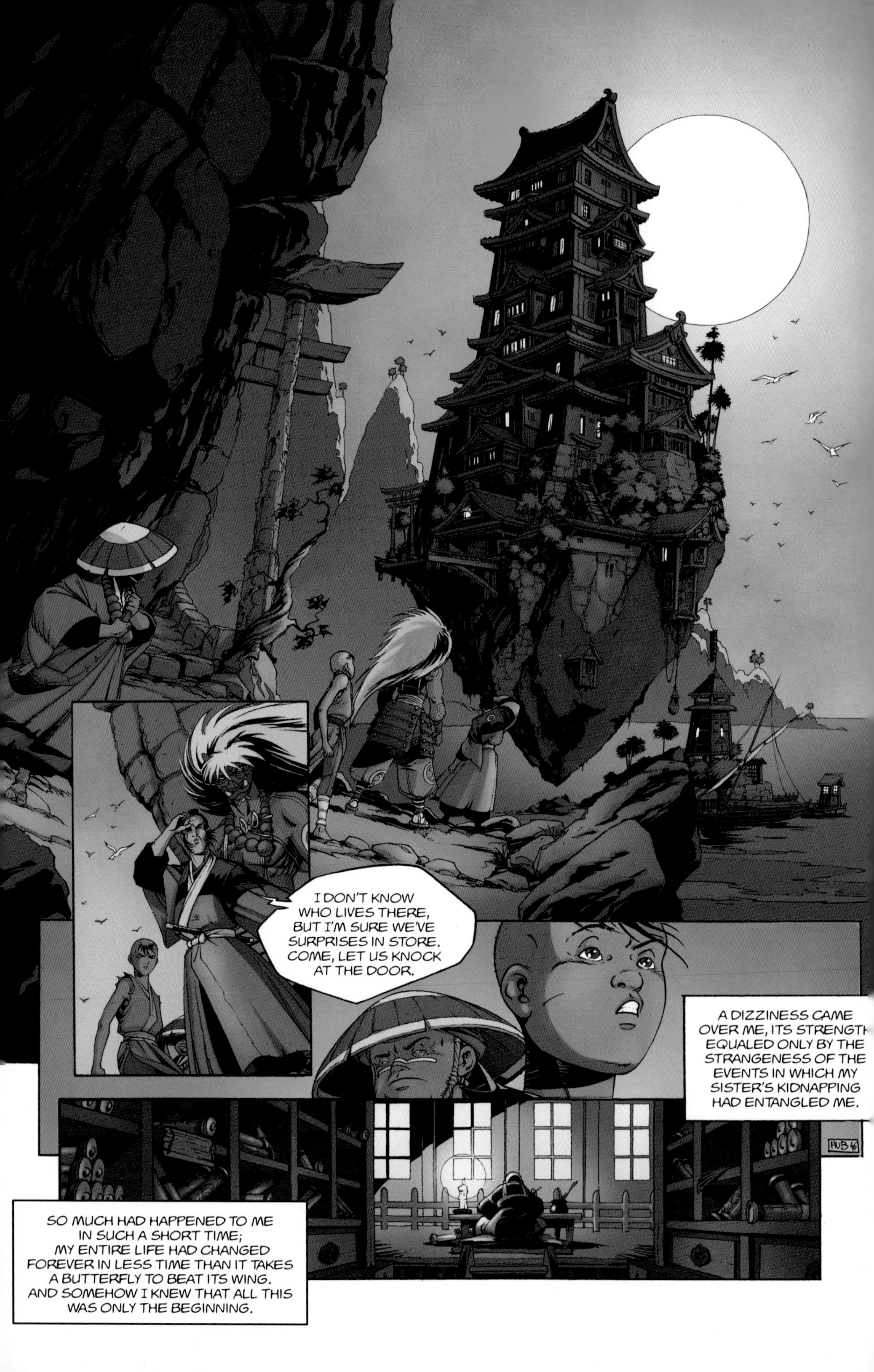
I DON'T KNOW WHO LIVES THERE, BUT I'M SURE WE'VE SURPRISES IN STORE. COME, LET US KNOCK AT THE DOOR.
A DIZZINESS CAME OVER ME, ITS STRENGTH EQUALED ONLY BY THE STRANGENESS OF THE EVENTS IN WHICH MY SISTER'S KIDNAPPING HAD ENTANGLED ME.
SO MUCH HAD HAPPENED TO ME IN SUCH A SHORT TIME; MY ENTIRE LIFE HAD CHANGED FOREVER IN LESS TIME THAN IT TAKES A BUTTERFLY TO BEAT ITS WING. AND SOMEHOW I KNEW THAT ALL THIS WAS ONLY THE BEGINNING.

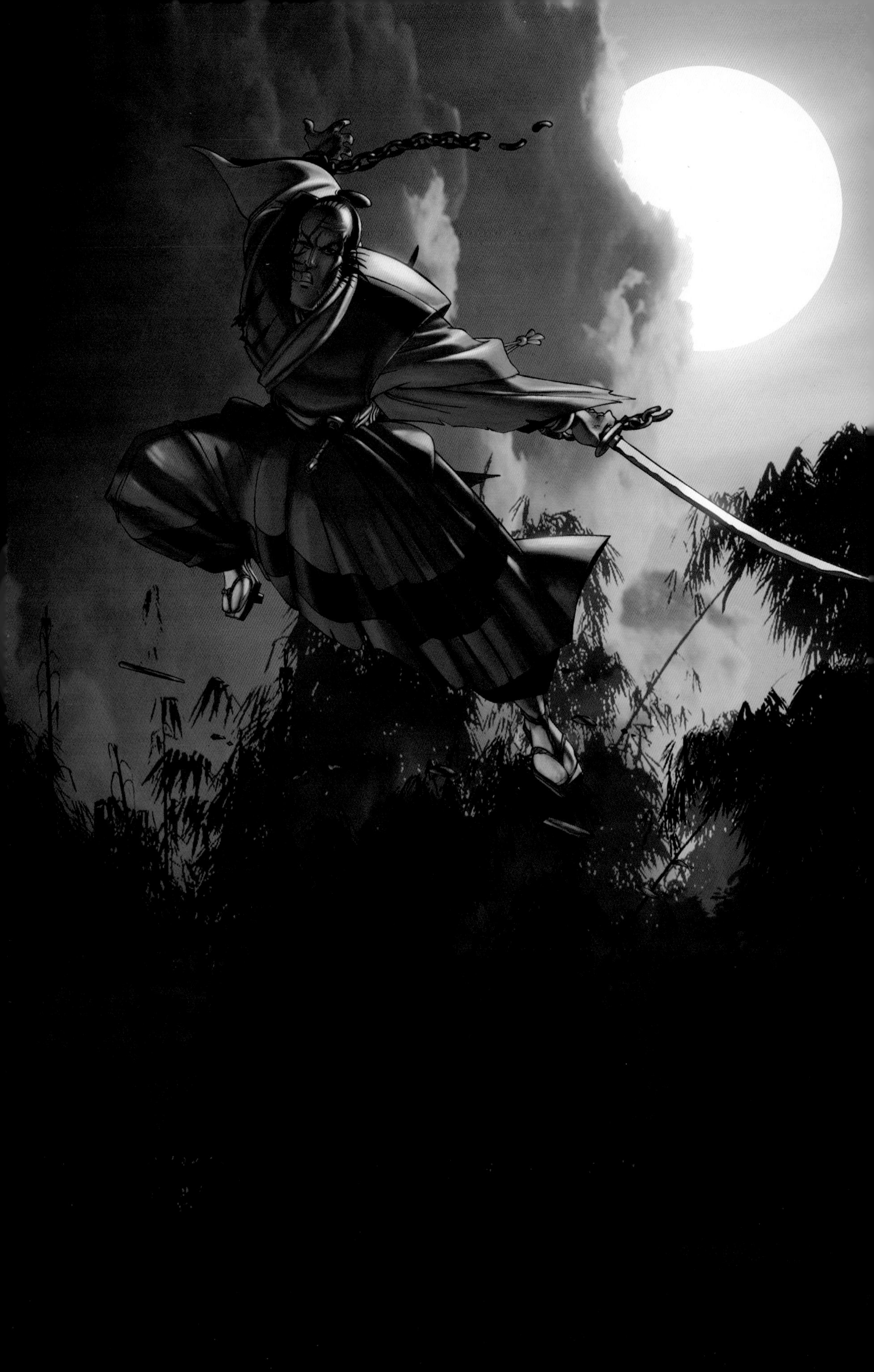

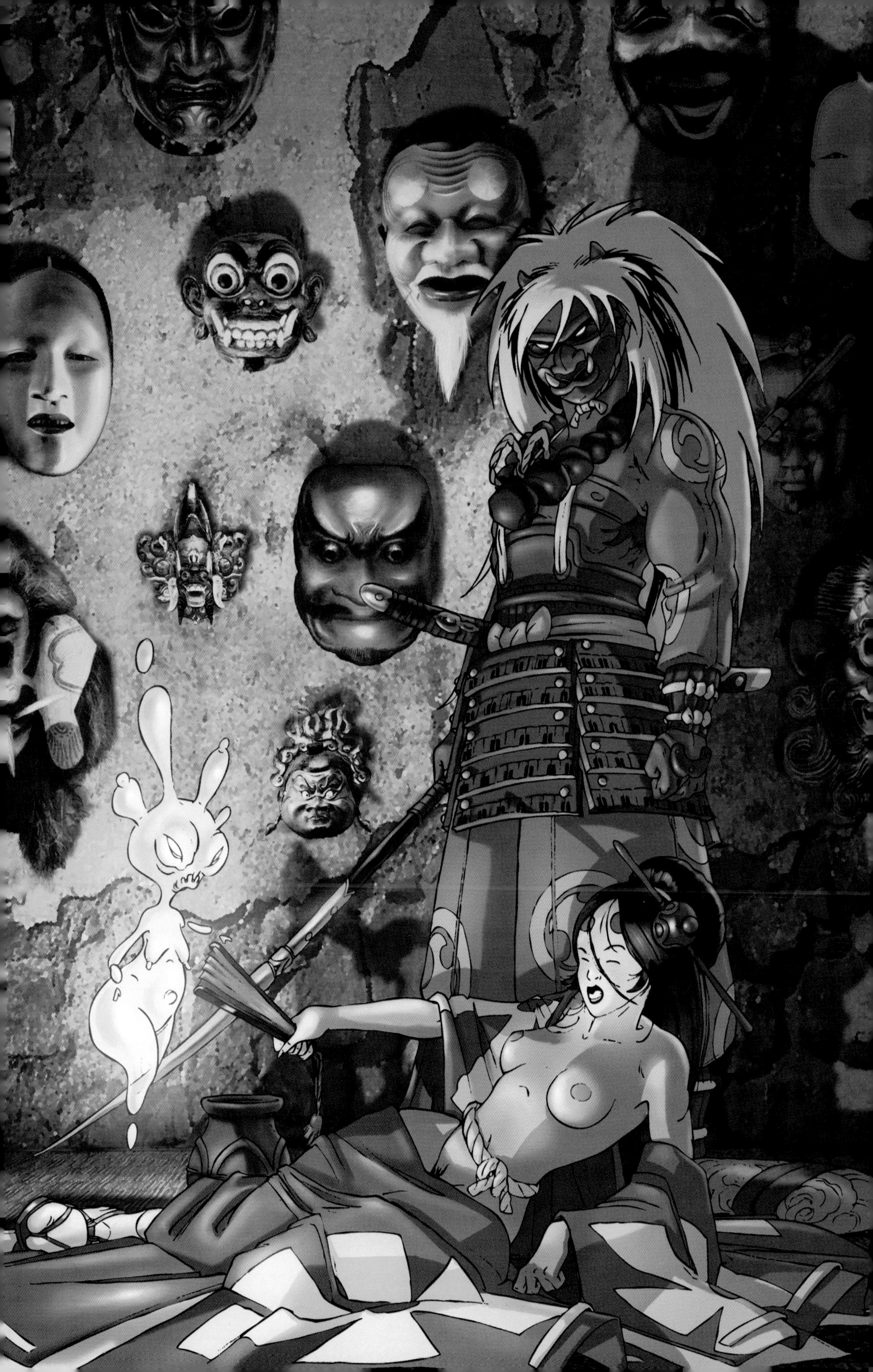

OKKO

THE CYCLE OF WATER

BOOK TWO

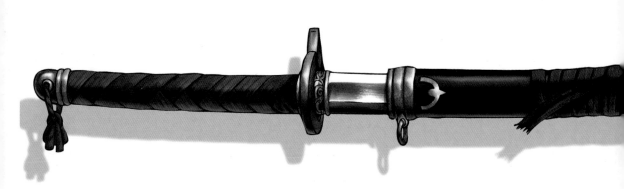

Preceding image thanks to

BRUNO GRAFF EDITIONS, BELGIUM

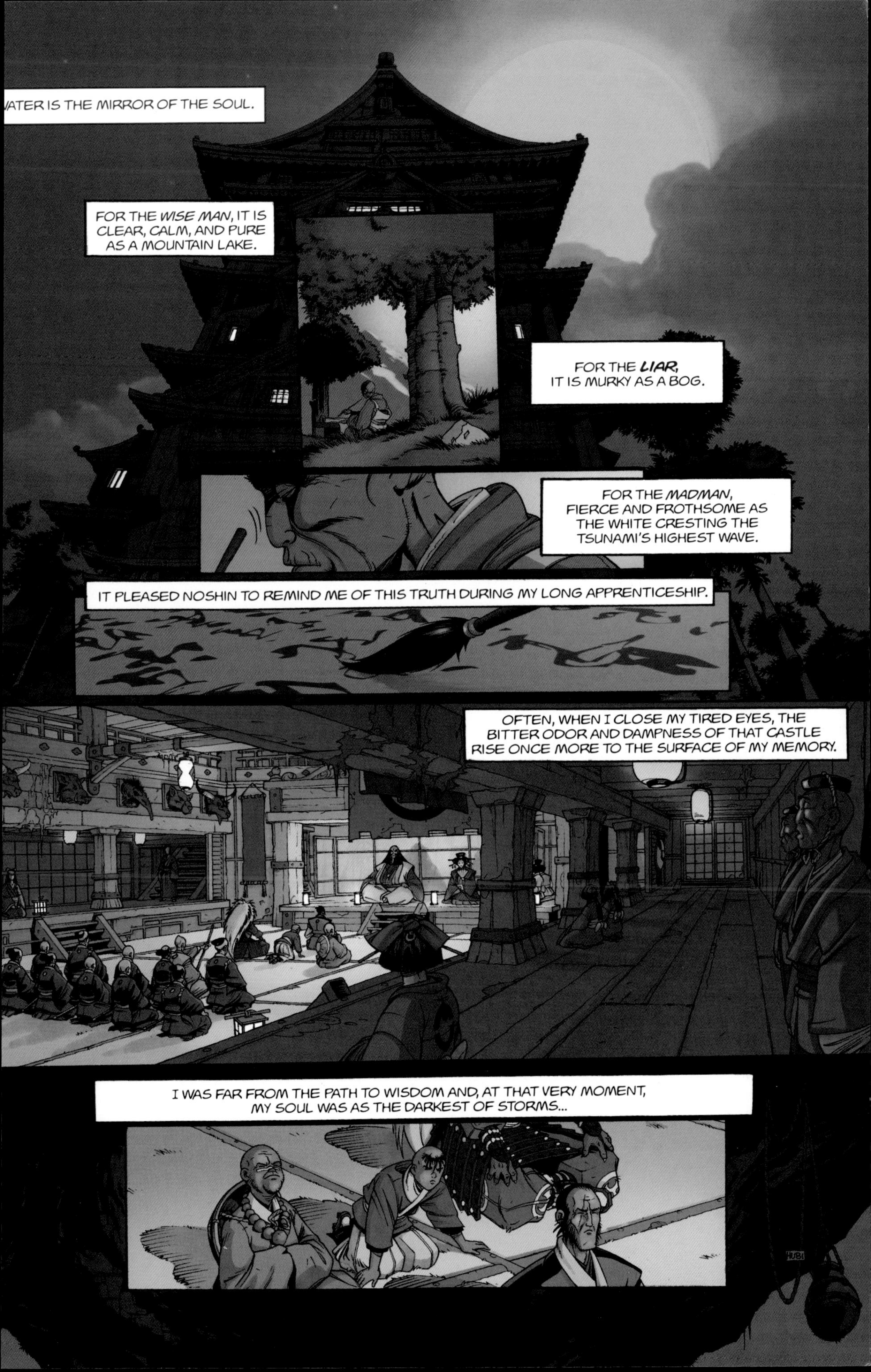

WATER IS THE MIRROR OF THE SOUL.
FOR THE *WISE MAN*, IT IS CLEAR, CALM, AND PURE AS A MOUNTAIN LAKE.
FOR THE ***LIAR***, IT IS MURKY AS A BOG.
FOR THE *MADMAN*, FIERCE AND FROTHSOME AS THE WHITE CRESTING THE TSUNAMI'S HIGHEST WAVE.
IT PLEASED NOSHIN TO REMIND ME OF THIS TRUTH DURING MY LONG APPRENTICESHIP.
OFTEN, WHEN I CLOSE MY TIRED EYES, THE BITTER ODOR AND DAMPNESS OF THAT CASTLE RISE ONCE MORE TO THE SURFACE OF MY MEMORY.
I WAS FAR FROM THE PATH TO WISDOM AND, AT THAT VERY MOMENT, MY SOUL WAS AS THE DARKEST OF STORMS...
HUBI

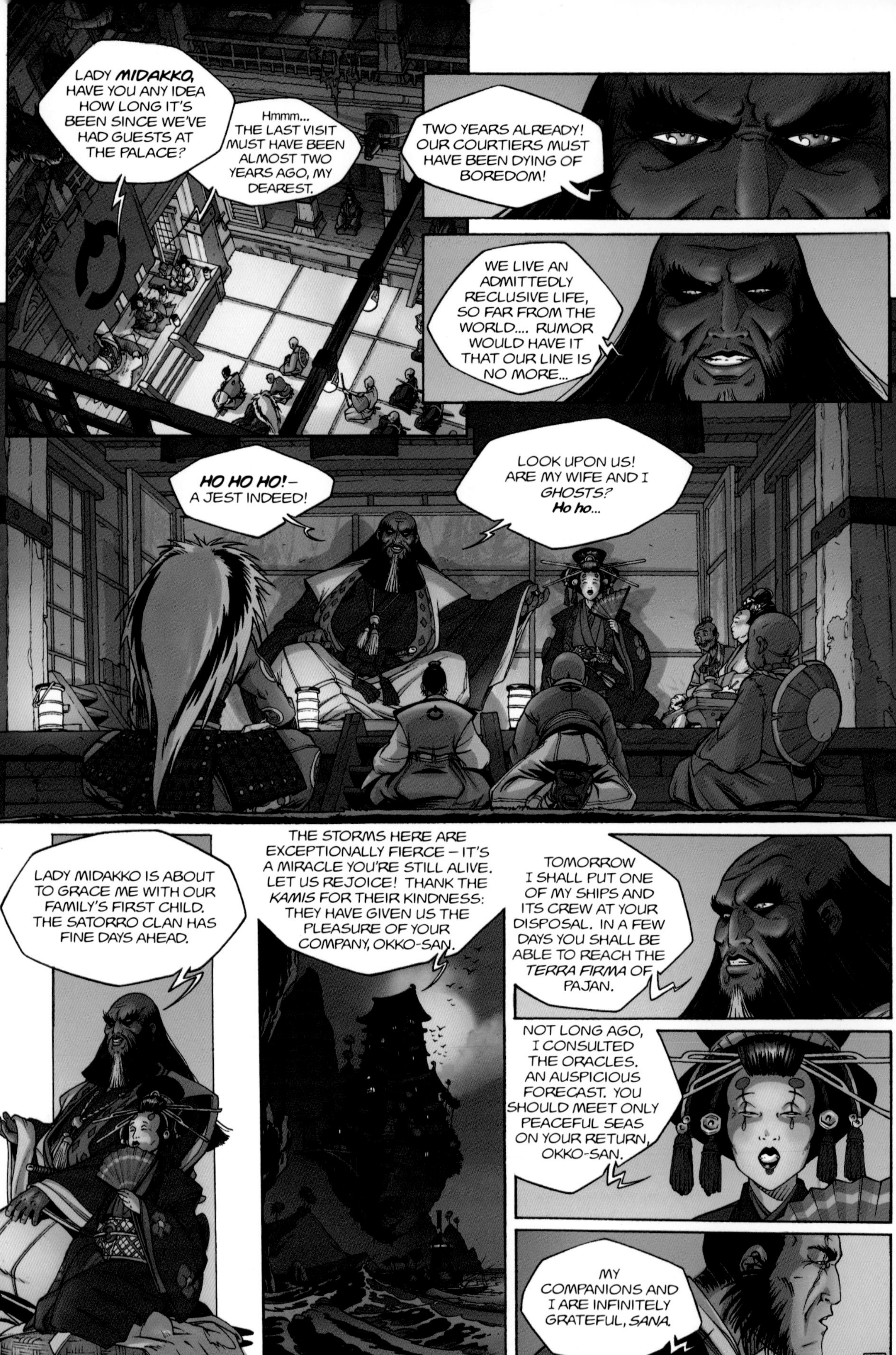
LADY **MIDAKKO,** HAVE YOU ANY IDEA HOW LONG IT'S BEEN SINCE WE'VE HAD GUESTS AT THE PALACE?
Hmmm... THE LAST VISIT MUST HAVE BEEN ALMOST TWO YEARS AGO, MY DEAREST.
TWO YEARS ALREADY! OUR COURTIERS MUST HAVE BEEN DYING OF BOREDOM!
WE LIVE AN ADMITTEDLY RECLUSIVE LIFE, SO FAR FROM THE WORLD.... RUMOR WOULD HAVE IT THAT OUR LINE IS NO MORE...
HO HO HO!– A JEST INDEED!
LOOK UPON US! ARE MY WIFE AND I *GHOSTS?* ***Ho ho...***
LADY MIDAKKO IS ABOUT TO GRACE ME WITH OUR FAMILY'S FIRST CHILD. THE SATORRO CLAN HAS FINE DAYS AHEAD.
THE STORMS HERE ARE EXCEPTIONALLY FIERCE – IT'S A MIRACLE YOU'RE STILL ALIVE. LET US REJOICE! THANK THE *KAMIS* FOR THEIR KINDNESS: THEY HAVE GIVEN US THE PLEASURE OF YOUR COMPANY, OKKO-SAN.
TOMORROW I SHALL PUT ONE OF MY SHIPS AND ITS CREW AT YOUR DISPOSAL. IN A FEW DAYS YOU SHALL BE ABLE TO REACH THE *TERRA FIRMA* OF PAJAN.
NOT LONG AGO, I CONSULTED THE ORACLES. AN AUSPICIOUS FORECAST. YOU SHOULD MEET ONLY PEACEFUL SEAS ON YOUR RETURN, OKKO-SAN.
MY COMPANIONS AND I ARE INFINITELY GRATEFUL, *SANA.*
HUB

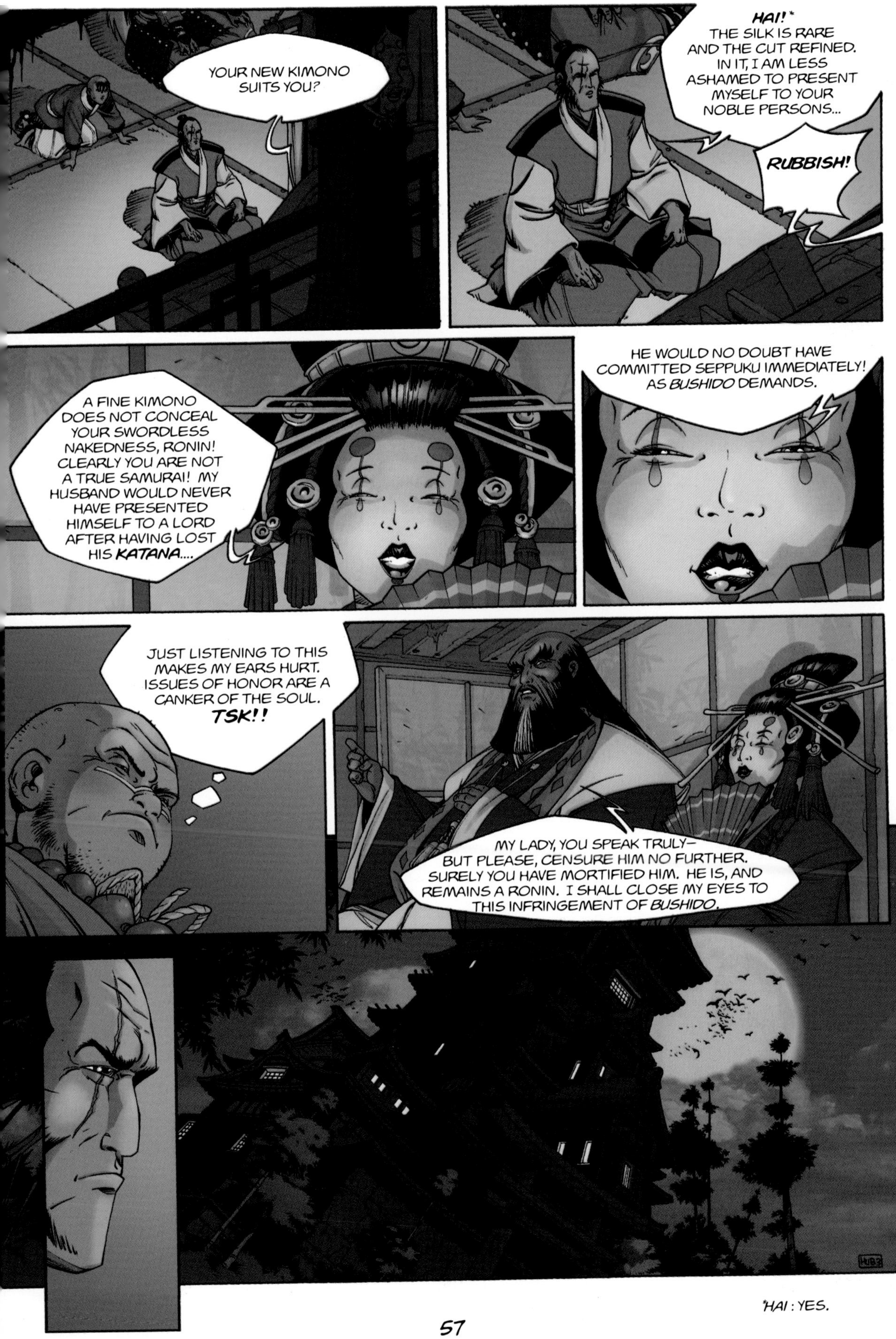
YOUR NEW KIMONO SUITS YOU?
HAI!* THE SILK IS RARE AND THE CUT REFINED. IN IT, I AM LESS ASHAMED TO PRESENT MYSELF TO YOUR NOBLE PERSONS...
RUBBISH!
A FINE KIMONO DOES NOT CONCEAL YOUR SWORDLESS NAKEDNESS, RONIN! CLEARLY YOU ARE NOT A TRUE SAMURAI! MY HUSBAND WOULD NEVER HAVE PRESENTED HIMSELF TO A LORD AFTER HAVING LOST HIS KATANA....
HE WOULD NO DOUBT HAVE COMMITTED SEPPUKU IMMEDIATELY! AS BUSHIDO DEMANDS.
JUST LISTENING TO THIS MAKES MY EARS HURT. ISSUES OF HONOR ARE A CANKER OF THE SOUL. TSK!!
MY LADY, YOU SPEAK TRULY— BUT PLEASE, CENSURE HIM NO FURTHER. SURELY YOU HAVE MORTIFIED HIM. HE IS, AND REMAINS A RONIN. I SHALL CLOSE MY EYES TO THIS INFRINGEMENT OF BUSHIDO.
HUB3

*HAI : YES.

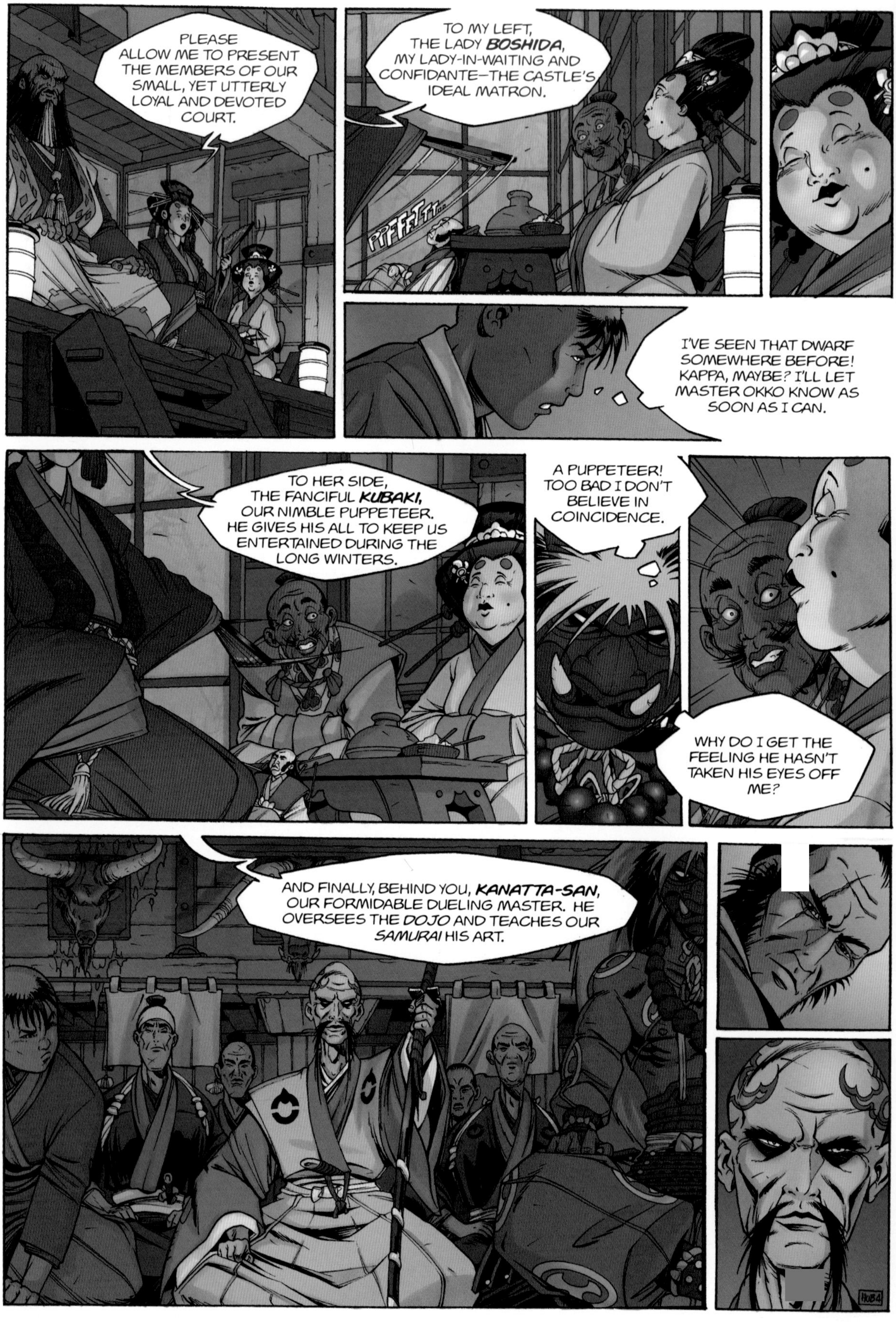
PLEASE ALLOW ME TO PRESENT THE MEMBERS OF OUR SMALL, YET UTTERLY LOYAL AND DEVOTED COURT.
TO MY LEFT, THE LADY **BOSHIDA**, MY LADY-IN-WAITING AND CONFIDANTE—THE CASTLE'S IDEAL MATRON.
PPFFFTTT...
I'VE SEEN THAT DWARF SOMEWHERE BEFORE! KAPPA, MAYBE? I'LL LET MASTER OKKO KNOW AS SOON AS I CAN.
TO HER SIDE, THE FANCIFUL **KUBAKI**, OUR NIMBLE PUPPETEER. HE GIVES HIS ALL TO KEEP US ENTERTAINED DURING THE LONG WINTERS.
A PUPPETEER! TOO BAD I DON'T BELIEVE IN COINCIDENCE.
WHY DO I GET THE FEELING HE HASN'T TAKEN HIS EYES OFF ME?
AND FINALLY, BEHIND YOU, **KANATTA-SAN**, OUR FORMIDABLE DUELING MASTER. HE OVERSEES THE *DOJO* AND TEACHES OUR *SAMURAI* HIS ART.
HUB

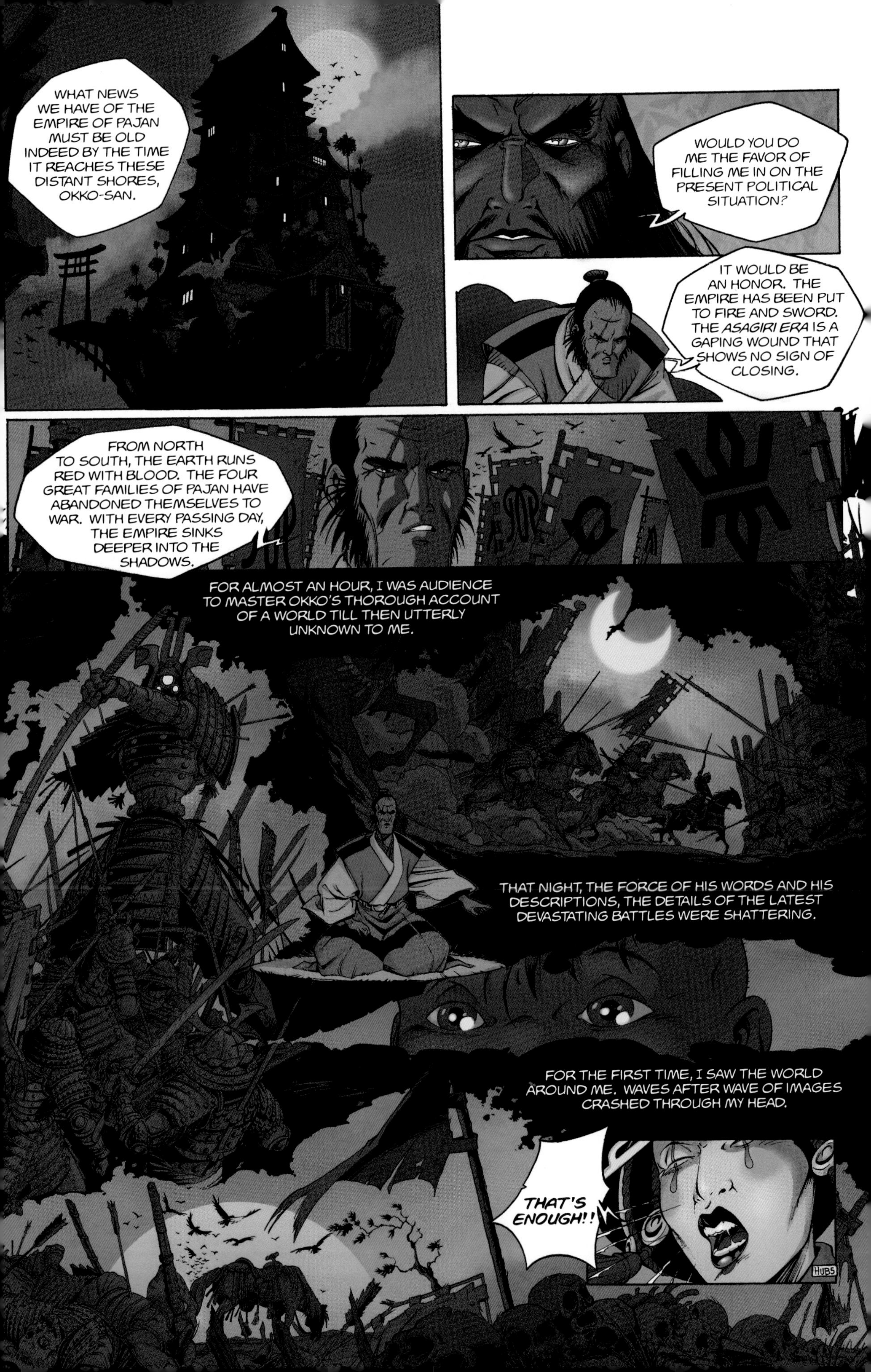
WHAT NEWS WE HAVE OF THE EMPIRE OF PAJAN MUST BE OLD INDEED BY THE TIME IT REACHES THESE DISTANT SHORES, OKKO-SAN.
WOULD YOU DO ME THE FAVOR OF FILLING ME IN ON THE PRESENT POLITICAL SITUATION?
IT WOULD BE AN HONOR. THE EMPIRE HAS BEEN PUT TO FIRE AND SWORD. THE *ASAGIRI ERA* IS A GAPING WOUND THAT SHOWS NO SIGN OF CLOSING.
FROM NORTH TO SOUTH, THE EARTH RUNS RED WITH BLOOD. THE FOUR GREAT FAMILIES OF PAJAN HAVE ABANDONED THEMSELVES TO WAR. WITH EVERY PASSING DAY, THE EMPIRE SINKS DEEPER INTO THE SHADOWS.
FOR ALMOST AN HOUR, I WAS AUDIENCE TO MASTER OKKO'S THOROUGH ACCOUNT OF A WORLD TILL THEN UTTERLY UNKNOWN TO ME.
THAT NIGHT, THE FORCE OF HIS WORDS AND HIS DESCRIPTIONS, THE DETAILS OF THE LATEST DEVASTATING BATTLES WERE SHATTERING.
FOR THE FIRST TIME, I SAW THE WORLD AROUND ME. WAVES AFTER WAVE OF IMAGES CRASHED THROUGH MY HEAD.
THAT'S ENOUGH!!
HUBS

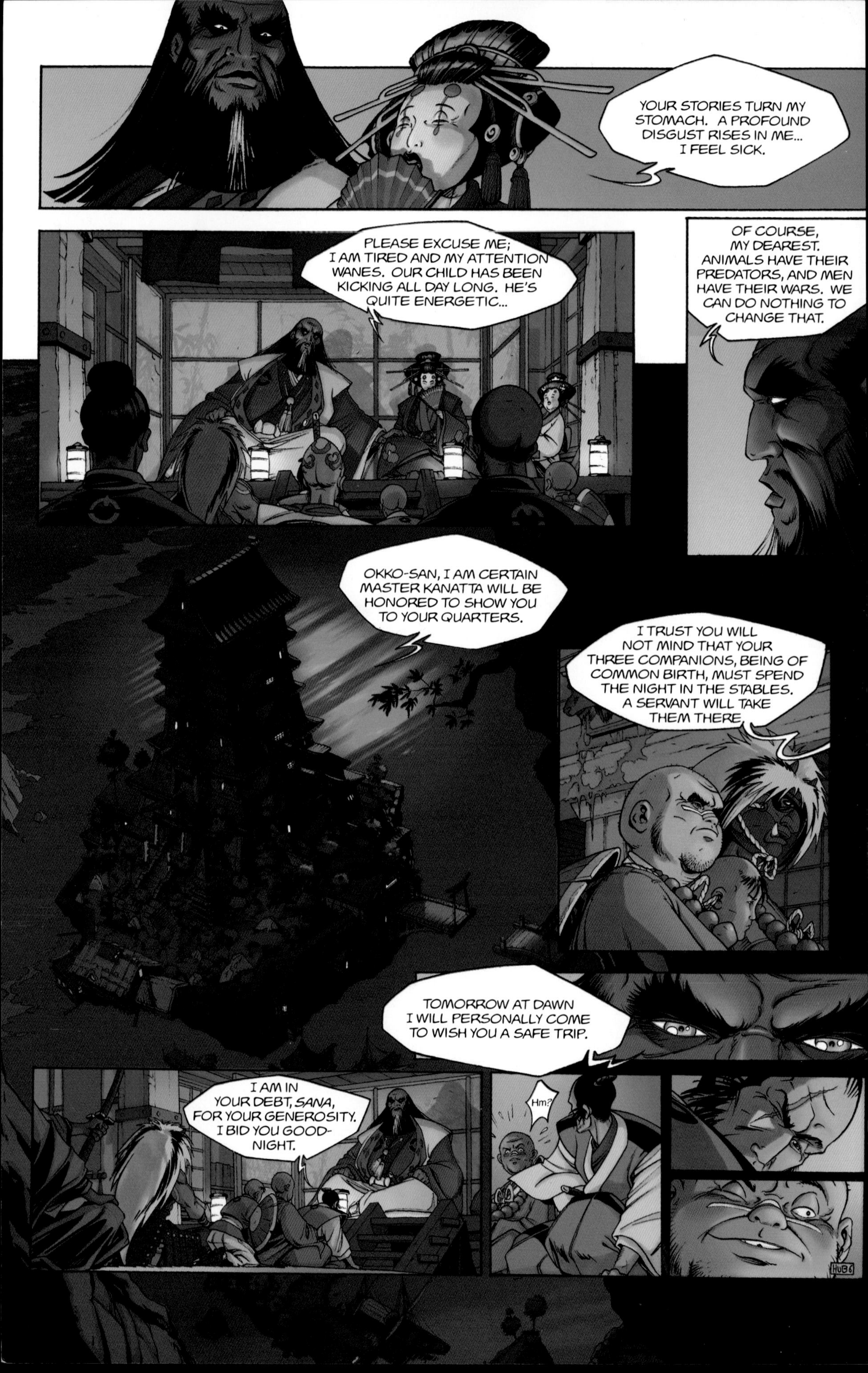
YOUR STORIES TURN MY STOMACH. A PROFOUND DISGUST RISES IN ME... I FEEL SICK.
PLEASE EXCUSE ME; I AM TIRED AND MY ATTENTION WANES. OUR CHILD HAS BEEN KICKING ALL DAY LONG. HE'S QUITE ENERGETIC...
OF COURSE, MY DEAREST. ANIMALS HAVE THEIR PREDATORS, AND MEN HAVE THEIR WARS. WE CAN DO NOTHING TO CHANGE THAT.
OKKO-SAN, I AM CERTAIN MASTER KANATTA WILL BE HONORED TO SHOW YOU TO YOUR QUARTERS.
I TRUST YOU WILL NOT MIND THAT YOUR THREE COMPANIONS, BEING OF COMMON BIRTH, MUST SPEND THE NIGHT IN THE STABLES. A SERVANT WILL TAKE THEM THERE.
TOMORROW AT DAWN I WILL PERSONALLY COME TO WISH YOU A SAFE TRIP.
I AM IN YOUR DEBT, *SANA*, FOR YOUR GENEROSITY. I BID YOU GOOD-NIGHT.
Hm?
HUB

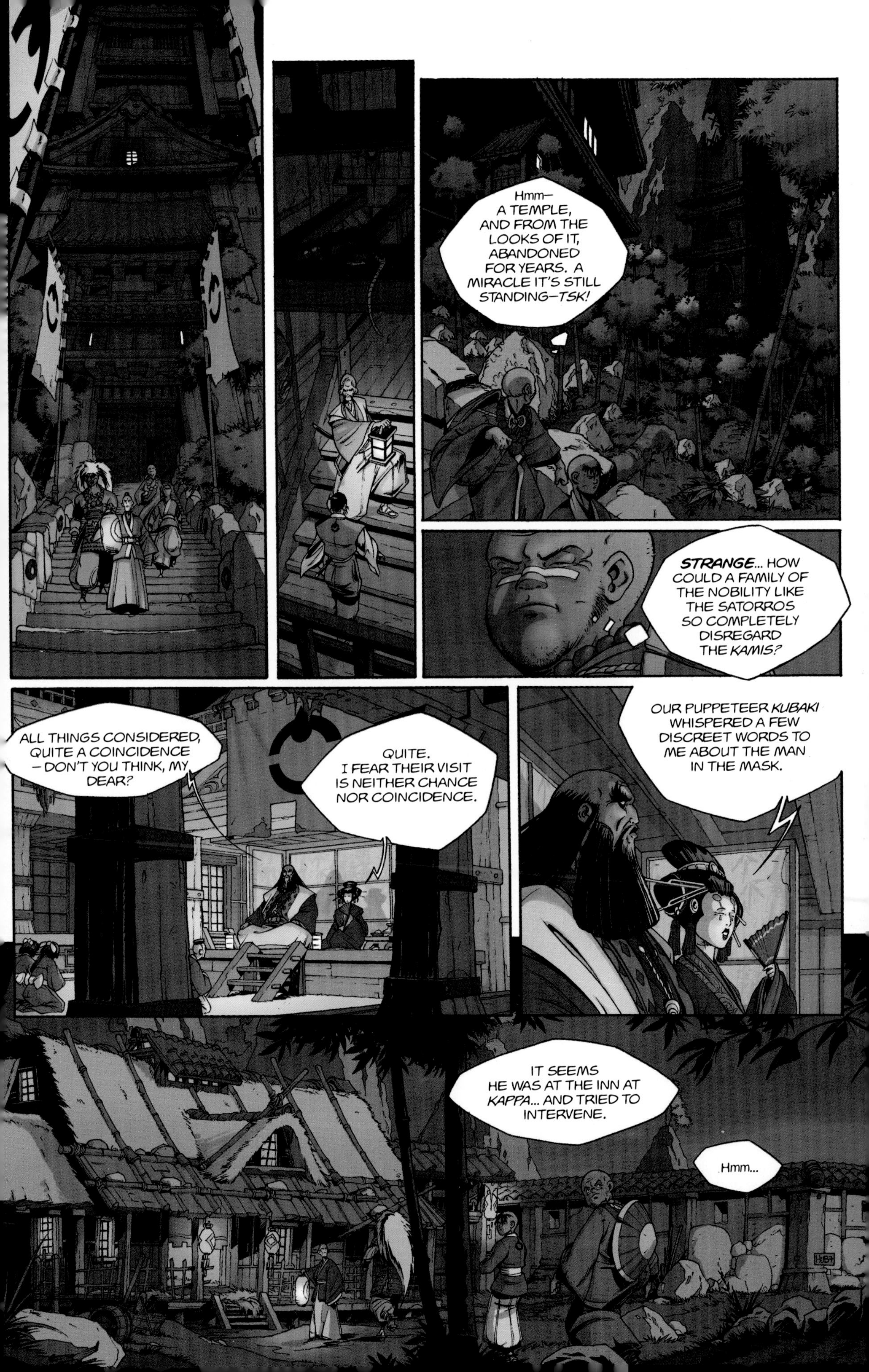
Hmm—
A TEMPLE, AND FROM THE LOOKS OF IT, ABANDONED FOR YEARS. A MIRACLE IT'S STILL STANDING—*TSK!*
STRANGE... HOW COULD A FAMILY OF THE NOBILITY LIKE THE SATORROS SO COMPLETELY DISREGARD THE *KAMIS?*
ALL THINGS CONSIDERED, QUITE A COINCIDENCE – DON'T YOU THINK, MY DEAR?
QUITE. I FEAR THEIR VISIT IS NEITHER CHANCE NOR COINCIDENCE.
OUR PUPPETEER *KUBAKI* WHISPERED A FEW DISCREET WORDS TO ME ABOUT THE MAN IN THE MASK.
IT SEEMS HE WAS AT THE INN AT *KAPPA*... AND TRIED TO INTERVENE.
Hmm...

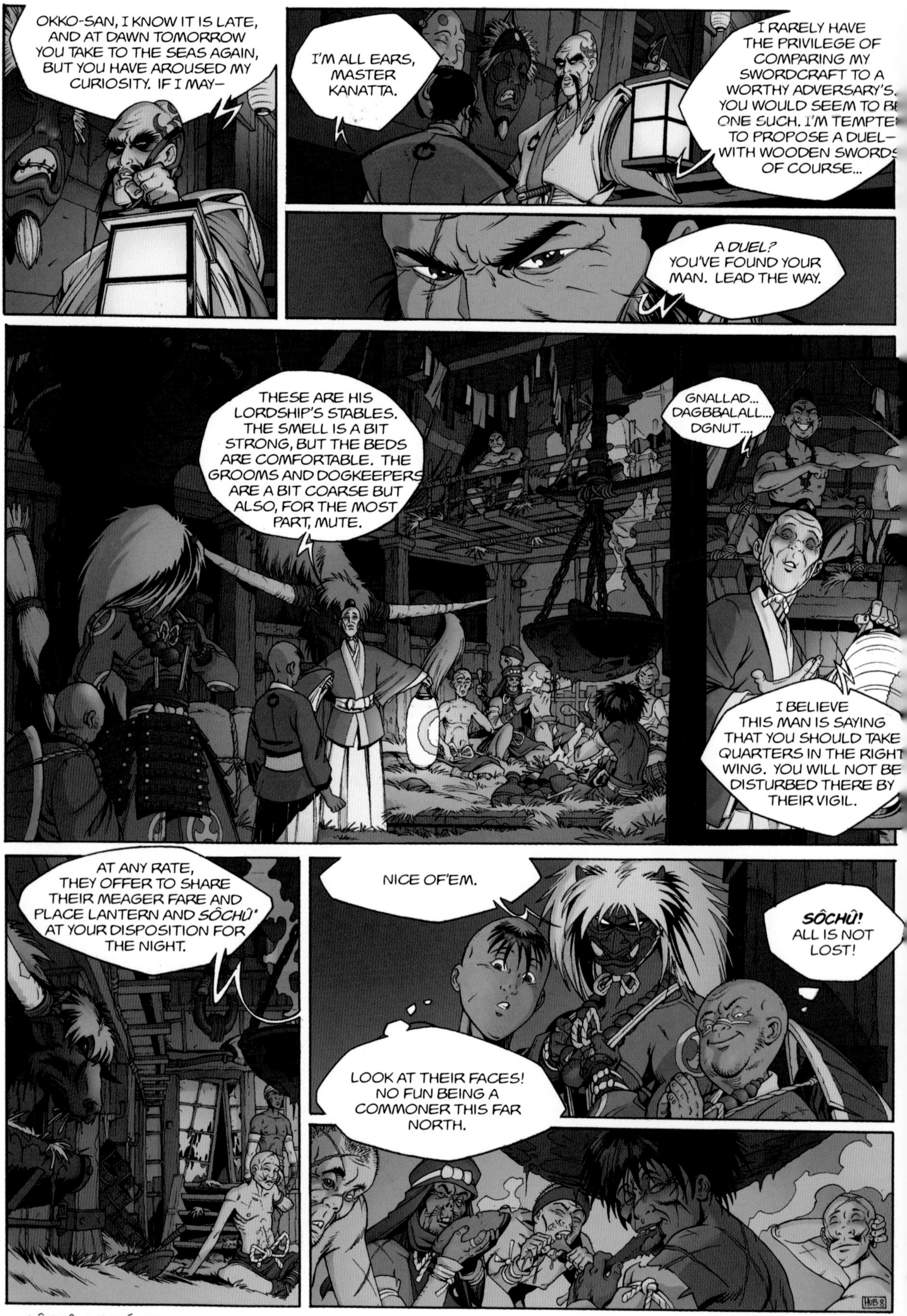
OKKO-SAN, I KNOW IT IS LATE, AND AT DAWN TOMORROW YOU TAKE TO THE SEAS AGAIN, BUT YOU HAVE AROUSED MY CURIOSITY. IF I MAY—
I'M ALL EARS, MASTER KANATTA.
I RARELY HAVE THE PRIVILEGE OF COMPARING MY SWORDCRAFT TO A WORTHY ADVERSARY'S. YOU WOULD SEEM TO BE ONE SUCH. I'M TEMPTED TO PROPOSE A DUEL—WITH WOODEN SWORDS OF COURSE...
A *DUEL?* YOU'VE FOUND YOUR MAN. LEAD THE WAY.
THESE ARE HIS LORDSHIP'S STABLES. THE SMELL IS A BIT STRONG, BUT THE BEDS ARE COMFORTABLE. THE GROOMS AND DOGKEEPERS ARE A BIT COARSE BUT ALSO, FOR THE MOST PART, MUTE.
GNALLAD... DAGBBALALL... DGNUT....
I BELIEVE THIS MAN IS SAYING THAT YOU SHOULD TAKE QUARTERS IN THE RIGHT WING. YOU WILL NOT BE DISTURBED THERE BY THEIR VIGIL.
AT ANY RATE, THEY OFFER TO SHARE THEIR MEAGER FARE AND PLACE LANTERN AND *SÔCHÛ** AT YOUR DISPOSITION FOR THE NIGHT.
NICE OF'EM.
SÔCHÛ! ALL IS NOT LOST!
LOOK AT THEIR FACES! NO FUN BEING A COMMONER THIS FAR NORTH.
HUB 8

SÔCHÛ: A SAKÉ OF POOR QUALITY.

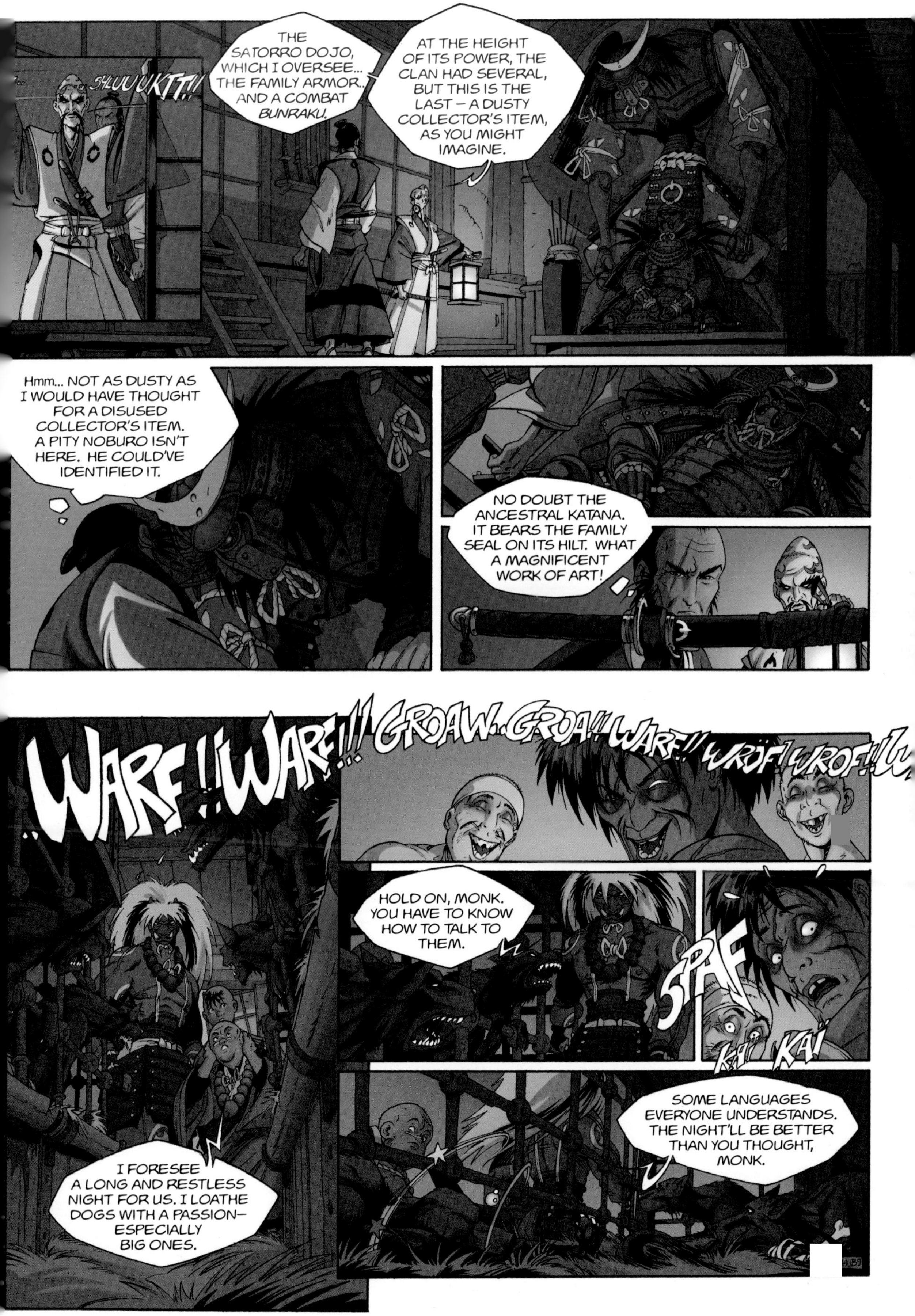
SHLUUUKTT!!
THE SATORRO DOJO, WHICH I OVERSEE... THE FAMILY ARMOR... AND A COMBAT BUNRAKU.
AT THE HEIGHT OF ITS POWER, THE CLAN HAD SEVERAL, BUT THIS IS THE LAST – A DUSTY COLLECTOR'S ITEM, AS YOU MIGHT IMAGINE.
Hmm... NOT AS DUSTY AS I WOULD HAVE THOUGHT FOR A DISUSED COLLECTOR'S ITEM. A PITY NOBURO ISN'T HERE. HE COULD'VE IDENTIFIED IT.
NO DOUBT THE ANCESTRAL KATANA. IT BEARS THE FAMILY SEAL ON ITS HILT. WHAT A MAGNIFICENT WORK OF ART!
WARF!! WARF!!! GROAW.. GROA!! WARF!! WROF! WROF!!
HOLD ON, MONK. YOU HAVE TO KNOW HOW TO TALK TO THEM.
SPAF
KAI KAI
SOME LANGUAGES EVERYONE UNDERSTANDS. THE NIGHT'LL BE BETTER THAN YOU THOUGHT, MONK.
I FORESEE A LONG AND RESTLESS NIGHT FOR US. I LOATHE DOGS WITH A PASSION– ESPECIALLY BIG ONES.

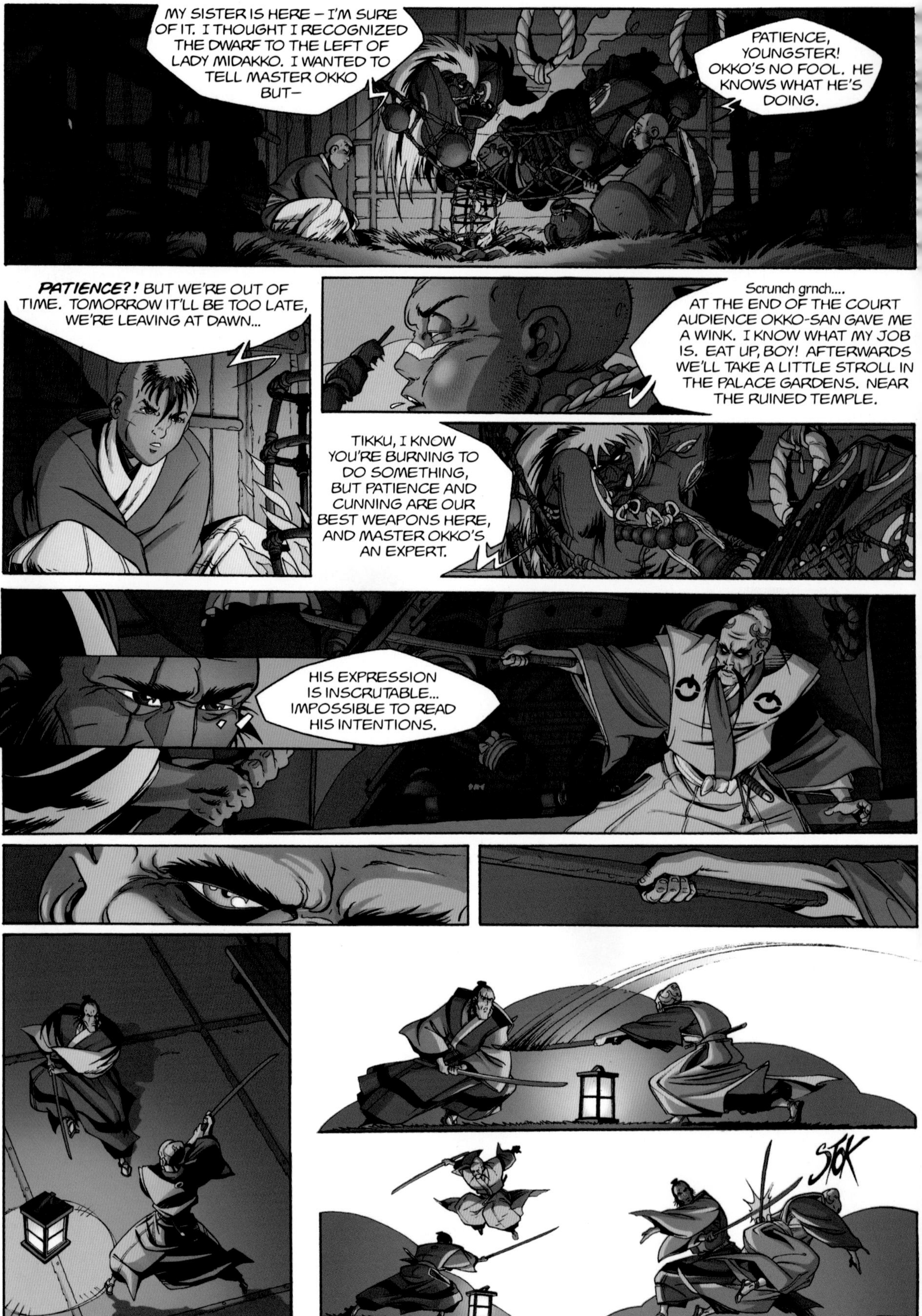
MY SISTER IS HERE – I'M SURE OF IT. I THOUGHT I RECOGNIZED THE DWARF TO THE LEFT OF LADY MIDAKKO. I WANTED TO TELL MASTER OKKO BUT–
PATIENCE, YOUNGSTER! OKKO'S NO FOOL. HE KNOWS WHAT HE'S DOING.
PATIENCE?! BUT WE'RE OUT OF TIME. TOMORROW IT'LL BE TOO LATE, WE'RE LEAVING AT DAWN...
Scrunch grnch.... AT THE END OF THE COURT AUDIENCE OKKO-SAN GAVE ME A WINK. I KNOW WHAT MY JOB IS. EAT UP, BOY! AFTERWARDS WE'LL TAKE A LITTLE STROLL IN THE PALACE GARDENS. NEAR THE RUINED TEMPLE.
TIKKU, I KNOW YOU'RE BURNING TO DO SOMETHING, BUT PATIENCE AND CUNNING ARE OUR BEST WEAPONS HERE, AND MASTER OKKO'S AN EXPERT.
HIS EXPRESSION IS INSCRUTABLE... IMPOSSIBLE TO READ HIS INTENTIONS.
STOK
HUB 10

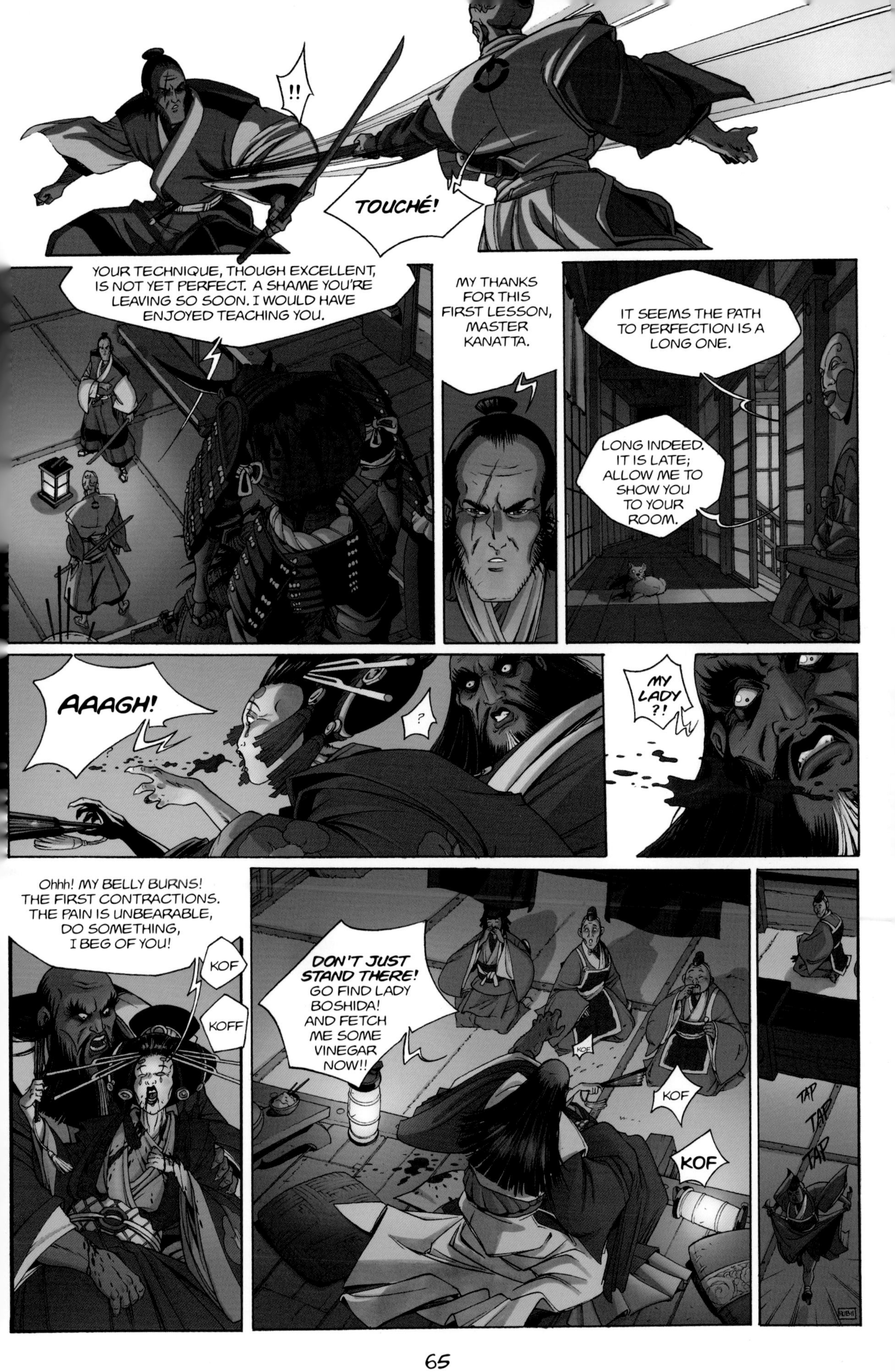
!!
TOUCHÉ!
YOUR TECHNIQUE, THOUGH EXCELLENT, IS NOT YET PERFECT. A SHAME YOU'RE LEAVING SO SOON. I WOULD HAVE ENJOYED TEACHING YOU.
MY THANKS FOR THIS FIRST LESSON, MASTER KANATTA.
IT SEEMS THE PATH TO PERFECTION IS A LONG ONE.
LONG INDEED. IT IS LATE; ALLOW ME TO SHOW YOU TO YOUR ROOM.
AAAGH!
?
MY LADY ?!
Ohhh! MY BELLY BURNS! THE FIRST CONTRACTIONS. THE PAIN IS UNBEARABLE, DO SOMETHING, I BEG OF YOU!
KOF
KOFF
DON'T JUST STAND THERE! GO FIND LADY BOSHIDA! AND FETCH ME SOME VINEGAR NOW!!
KOF
KOF
KOF
TAP
TAP
TAP

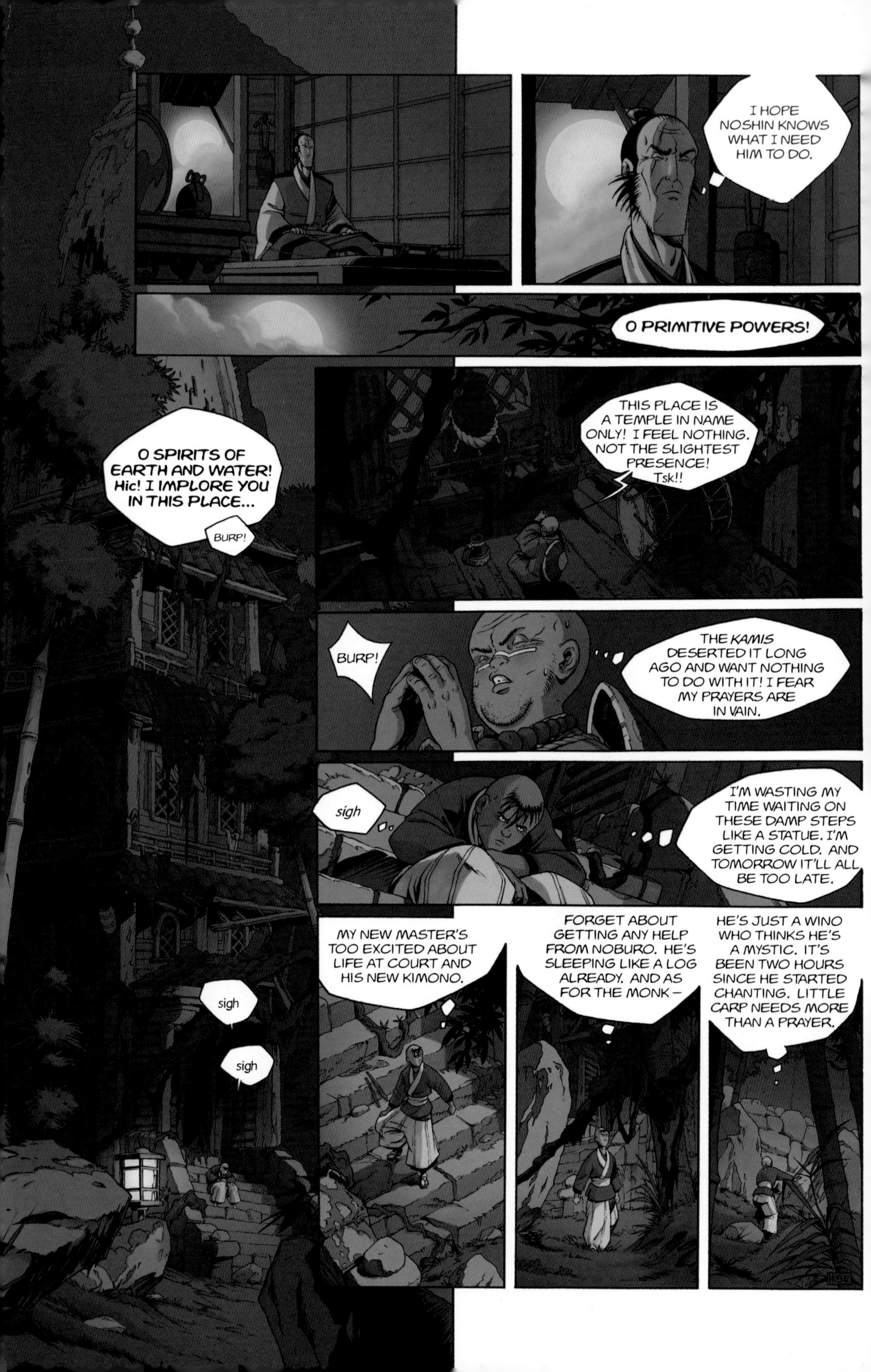
I HOPE NOSHIN KNOWS WHAT I NEED HIM TO DO.
O PRIMITIVE POWERS!
O SPIRITS OF EARTH AND WATER! Hic! I IMPLORE YOU IN THIS PLACE...
BURP!
THIS PLACE IS A TEMPLE IN NAME ONLY! I FEEL NOTHING. NOT THE SLIGHTEST PRESENCE! Tsk!!
BURP!
THE KAMIS DESERTED IT LONG AGO AND WANT NOTHING TO DO WITH IT! I FEAR MY PRAYERS ARE IN VAIN.
sigh
I'M WASTING MY TIME WAITING ON THESE DAMP STEPS LIKE A STATUE. I'M GETTING COLD. AND TOMORROW IT'LL ALL BE TOO LATE.
sigh
sigh
MY NEW MASTER'S TOO EXCITED ABOUT LIFE AT COURT AND HIS NEW KIMONO.
FORGET ABOUT GETTING ANY HELP FROM NOBURO. HE'S SLEEPING LIKE A LOG ALREADY. AND AS FOR THE MONK –
HE'S JUST A WINO WHO THINKS HE'S A MYSTIC. IT'S BEEN TWO HOURS SINCE HE STARTED CHANTING. LITTLE CARP NEEDS MORE THAN A PRAYER.

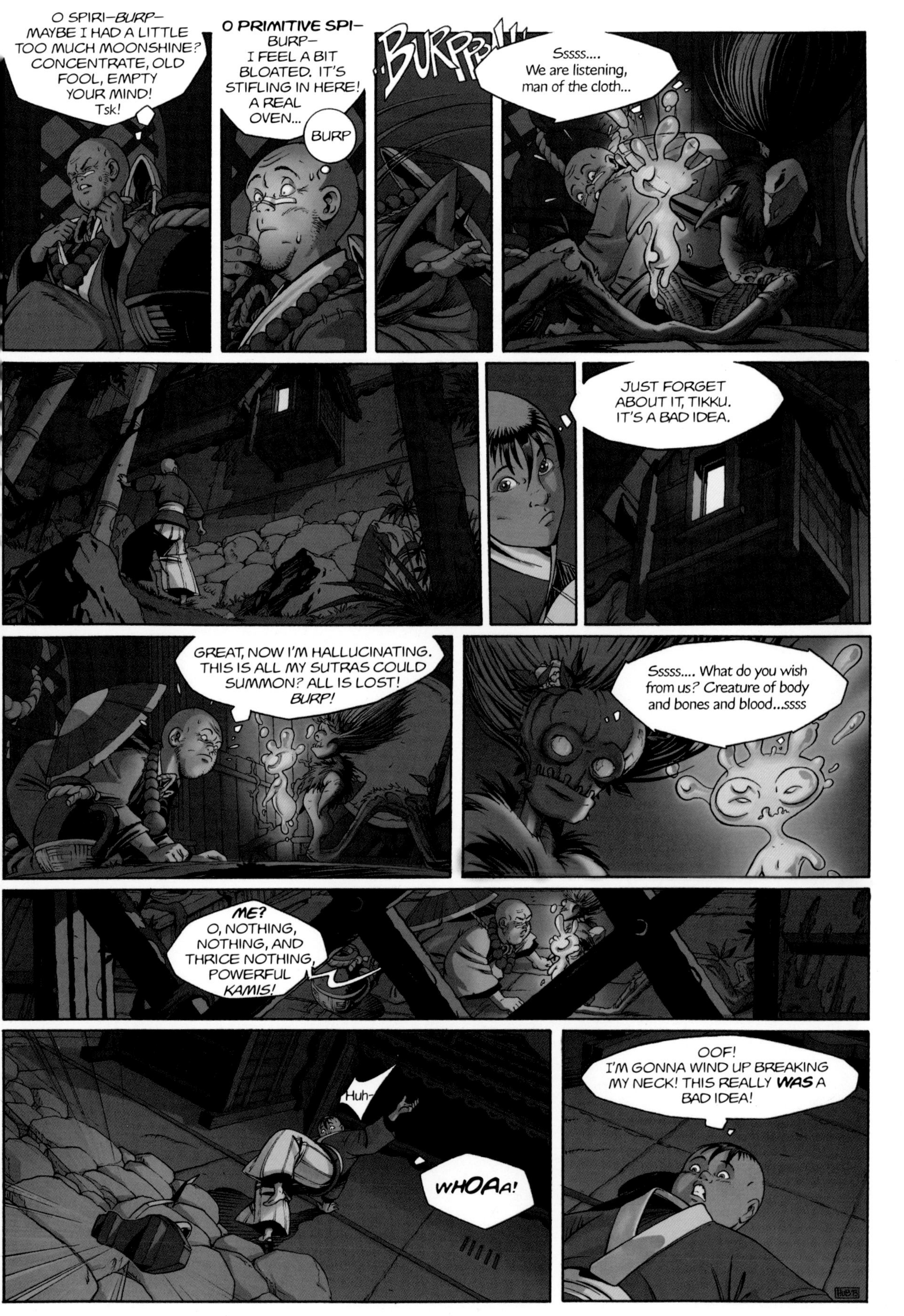
O SPIRI–BURP– MAYBE I HAD A LITTLE TOO MUCH MOONSHINE? CONCENTRATE, OLD FOOL, EMPTY YOUR MIND! Tsk!
O PRIMITIVE SPI– BURP– I FEEL A BIT BLOATED. IT'S STIFLING IN HERE! A REAL OVEN...
BURP
BURPPP
Sssss.... We are listening, man of the cloth...
JUST FORGET ABOUT IT, TIKKU. IT'S A BAD IDEA.
GREAT, NOW I'M HALLUCINATING. THIS IS ALL MY SUTRAS COULD SUMMON? ALL IS LOST! BURP!
Sssss.... What do you wish from us? Creature of body and bones and blood...ssss
ME? O, NOTHING, NOTHING, AND THRICE NOTHING, POWERFUL KAMIS!
Huh–
WHOAA!
OOF! I'M GONNA WIND UP BREAKING MY NECK! THIS REALLY WAS A BAD IDEA!

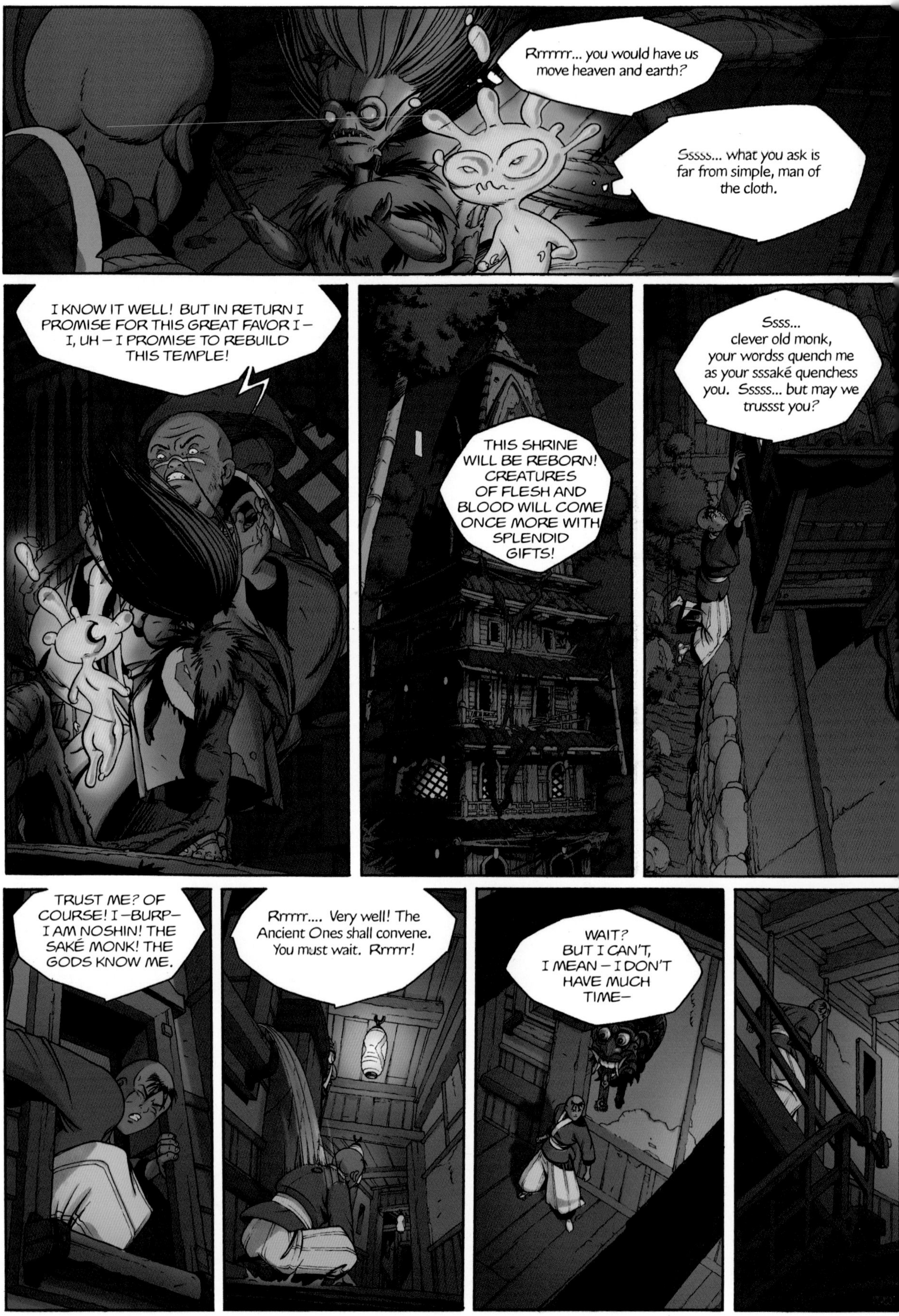

Rrrrrr... you would have us move heaven and earth?
Sssss... what you ask is far from simple, man of the cloth.
I KNOW IT WELL! BUT IN RETURN I PROMISE FOR THIS GREAT FAVOR I– I, UH – I PROMISE TO REBUILD THIS TEMPLE!
THIS SHRINE WILL BE REBORN! CREATURES OF FLESH AND BLOOD WILL COME ONCE MORE WITH SPLENDID GIFTS!
Ssss... clever old monk, your wordss quench me as your sssaké quenchess you. Sssss... but may we trussst you?
TRUST ME? OF COURSE! I –BURP– I AM NOSHIN! THE SAKÉ MONK! THE GODS KNOW ME.
Rrrrr.... Very well! The Ancient Ones shall convene. You must wait. Rrrrr!
WAIT? BUT I CAN'T, I MEAN – I DON'T HAVE MUCH TIME–

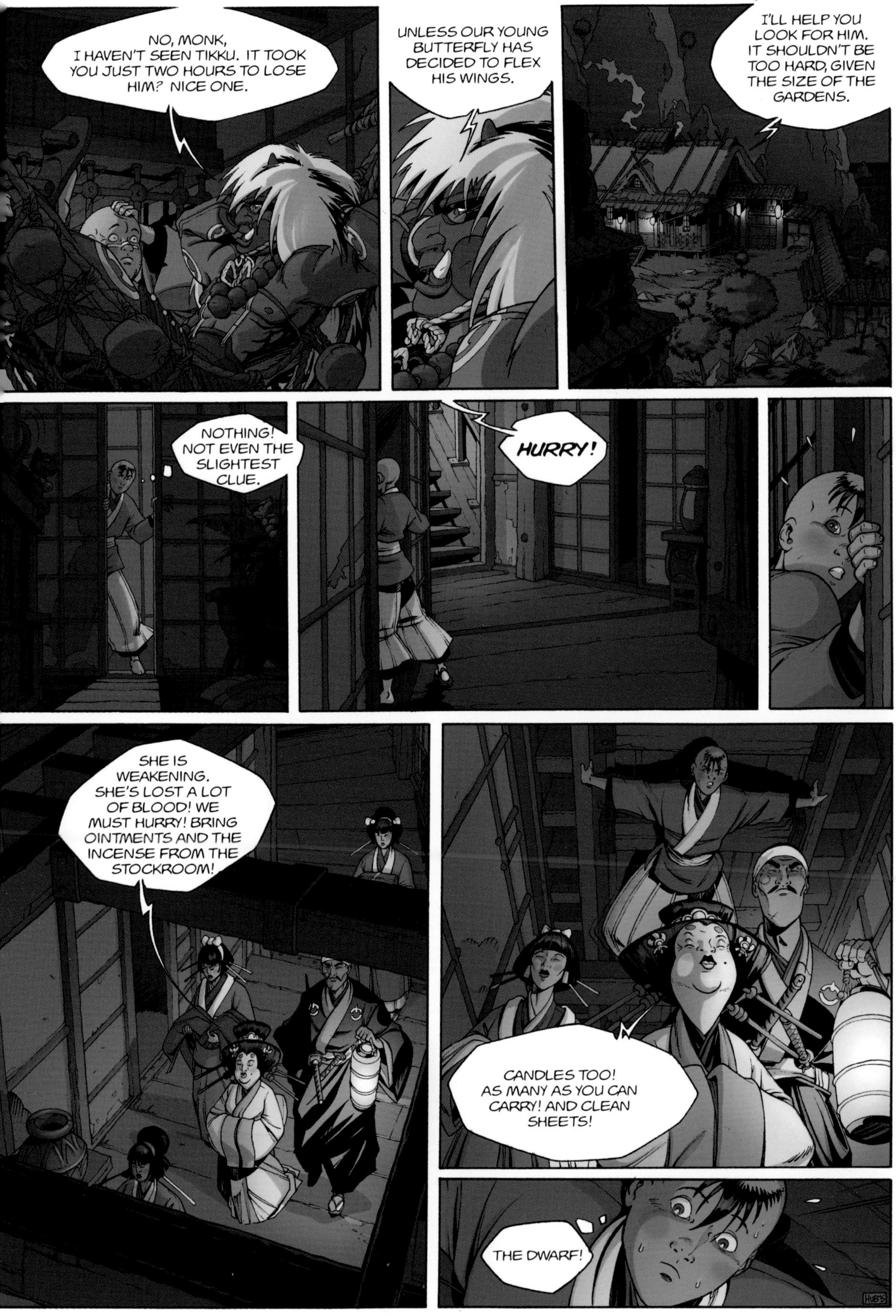
NO, MONK, I HAVEN'T SEEN TIKKU. IT TOOK YOU JUST TWO HOURS TO LOSE HIM? NICE ONE.
UNLESS OUR YOUNG BUTTERFLY HAS DECIDED TO FLEX HIS WINGS.
I'LL HELP YOU LOOK FOR HIM. IT SHOULDN'T BE TOO HARD, GIVEN THE SIZE OF THE GARDENS.
NOTHING! NOT EVEN THE SLIGHTEST CLUE.
HURRY!
SHE IS WEAKENING. SHE'S LOST A LOT OF BLOOD! WE MUST HURRY! BRING OINTMENTS AND THE INCENSE FROM THE STOCKROOM!
CANDLES TOO! AS MANY AS YOU CAN CARRY! AND CLEAN SHEETS!
THE DWARF!
HUB'S

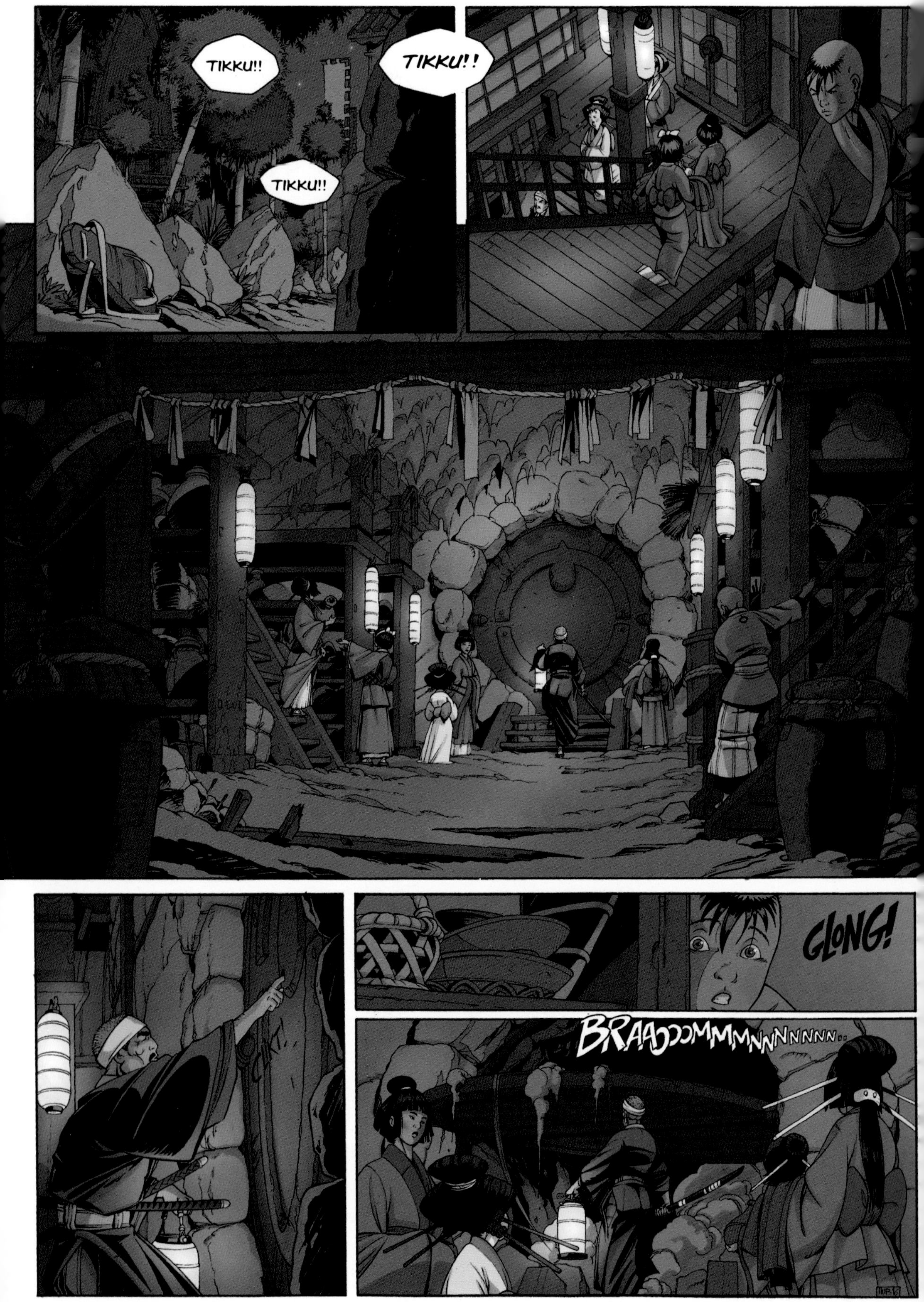
TIKKU!!
TIKKU!!
TIKKU!!
GLONG!
BRAAOOMMMNNNNNNN..

HELLO? TIKKU?!

Sshhh! STOP CRYING LIKE A STUCK PIG!

HE'S NOT GOING TO ANSWER. I FOUND HIS *GETA** AT THE BASE OF THE WALL. SEEMS OUR YOUNG PEASANT HAS UNFORTUNATELY TAKEN THE INITIATIVE...

O MY KAMIS!

TIKKU!!

BROoAAAAMMPPppp!!

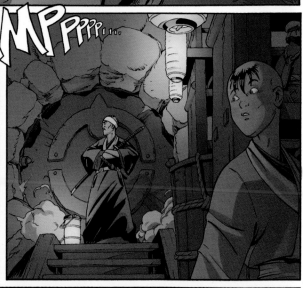

*GETA: WOODEN SANDAL WITH AN ELEVATED BASE.

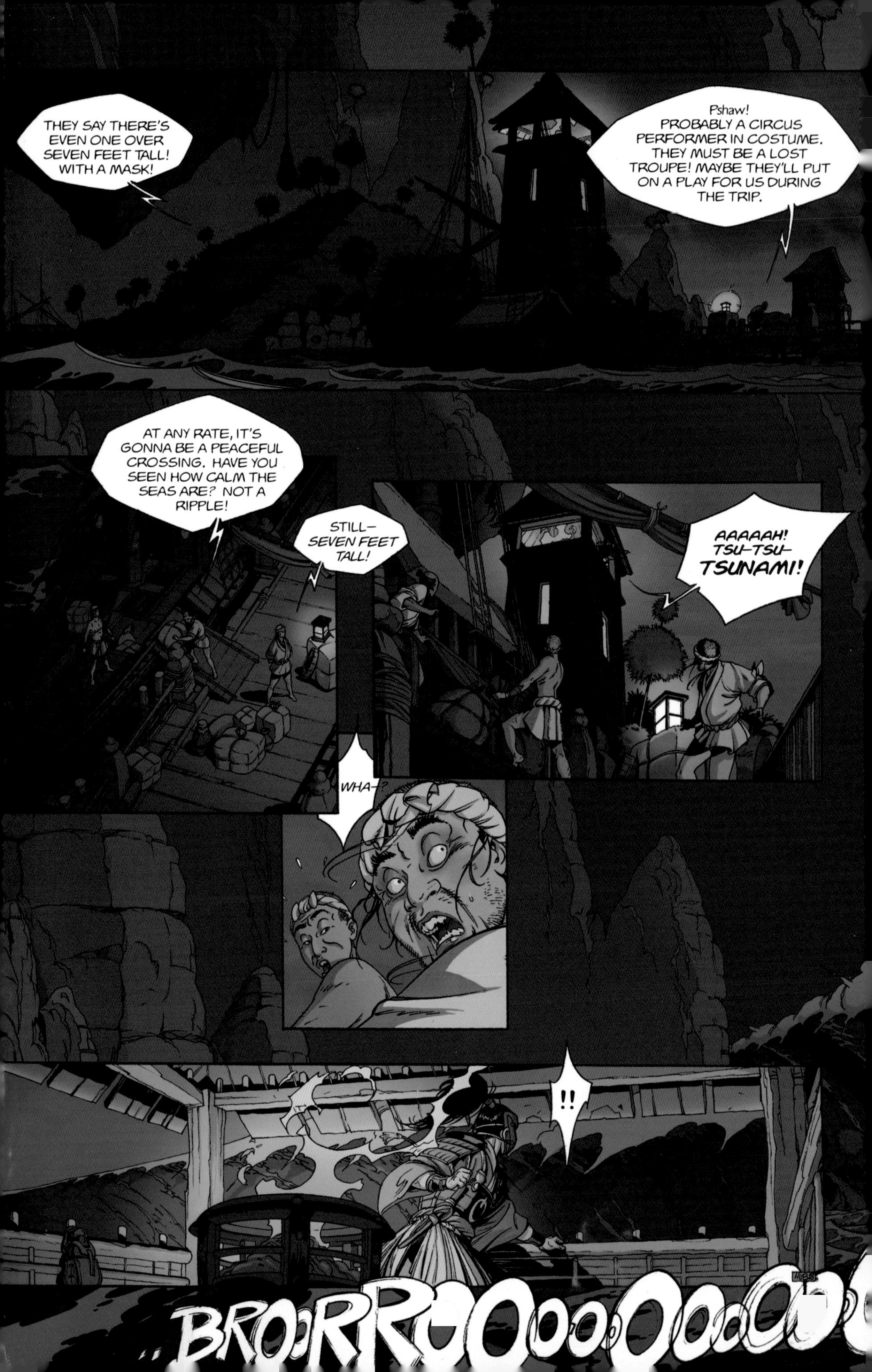
THEY SAY THERE'S EVEN ONE OVER SEVEN FEET TALL! WITH A MASK!
Pshaw! PROBABLY A CIRCUS PERFORMER IN COSTUME. THEY MUST BE A LOST TROUPE! MAYBE THEY'LL PUT ON A PLAY FOR US DURING THE TRIP.
AT ANY RATE, IT'S GONNA BE A PEACEFUL CROSSING. HAVE YOU SEEN HOW CALM THE SEAS ARE? NOT A RIPPLE!
STILL— SEVEN FEET TALL!
AAAAAH! TSU-TSU-TSUNAMI!
WHA—?
!!
..BROORRROOOOOOOOO
HUB38

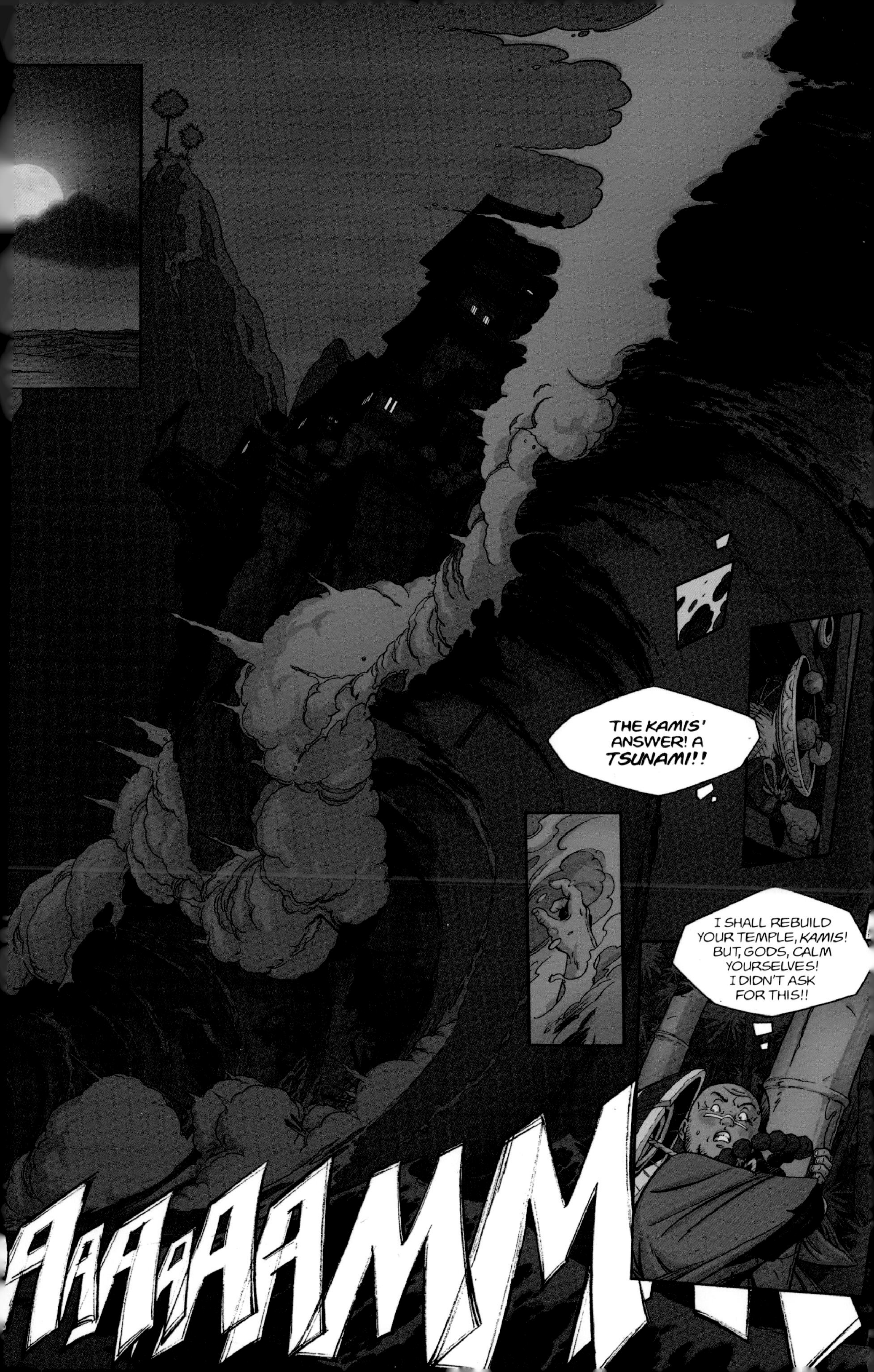
THE *KAMIS'* ANSWER! A *TSUNAMI*!!
I SHALL REBUILD YOUR TEMPLE, *KAMIS*! BUT, GODS, CALM YOURSELVES! I DIDN'T ASK FOR THIS!!

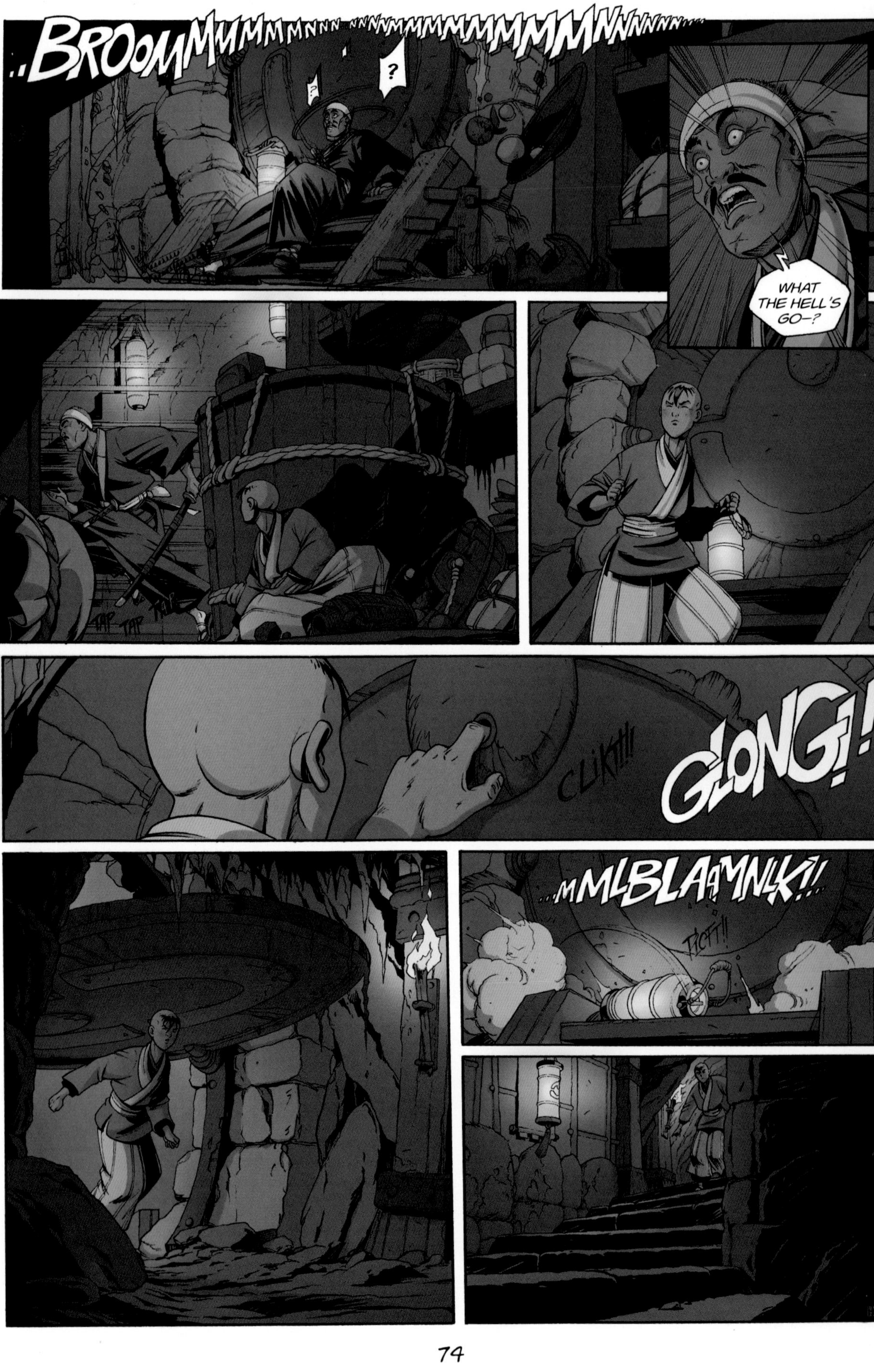
..BROOMMMMMMMNNN NNNMMMMMMMMMMNNNNNN...
?
?
WHAT THE HELL'S GO–?
TAP TAP TAP
CLIK!!!
GLONG!!
...MMLBLAAMNLK!!..
TICT!!

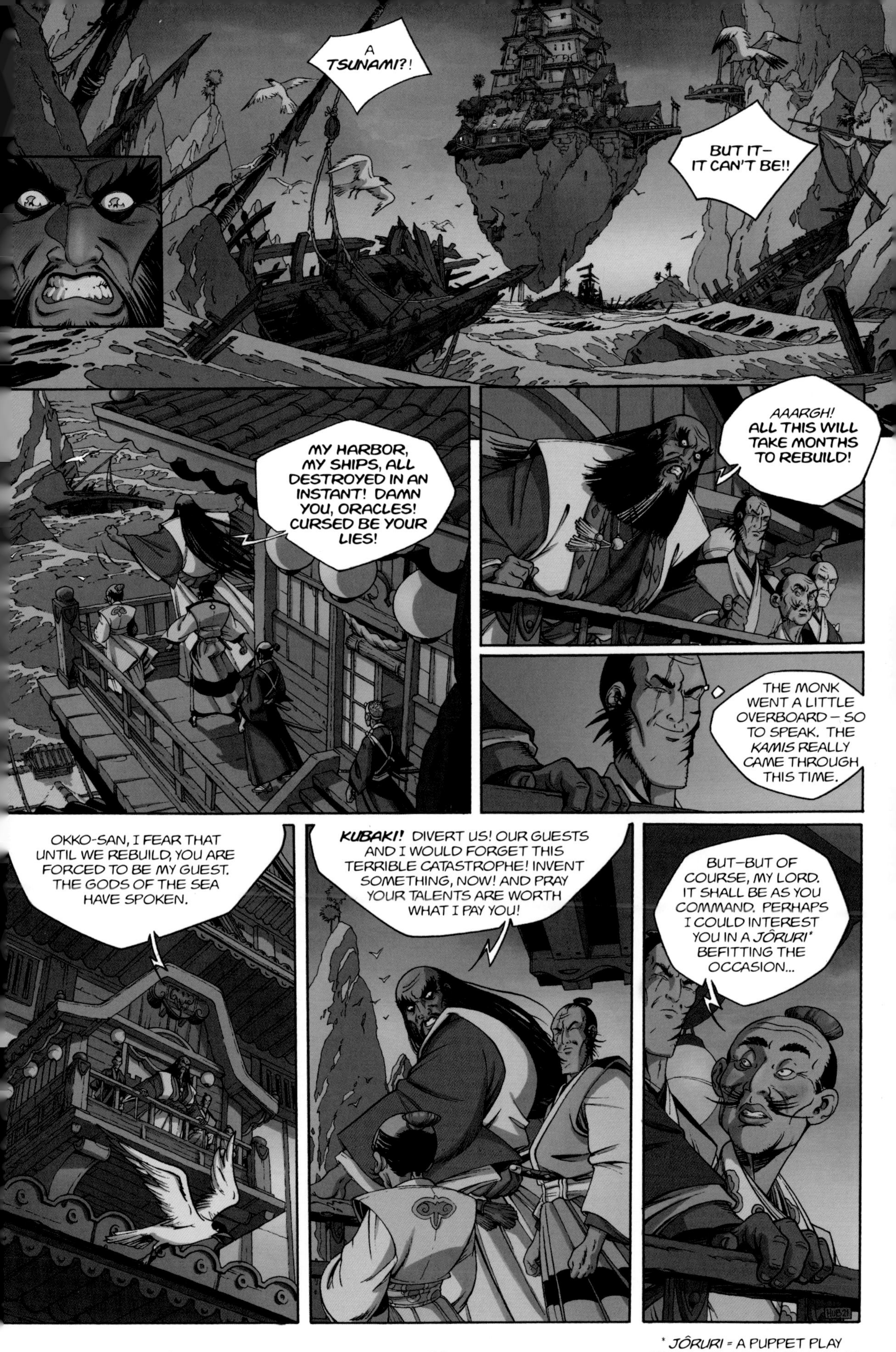
A TSUNAMI?!
BUT IT— IT CAN'T BE!!
MY HARBOR, MY SHIPS, ALL DESTROYED IN AN INSTANT! DAMN YOU, ORACLES! CURSED BE YOUR LIES!
AAARGH! ALL THIS WILL TAKE MONTHS TO REBUILD!
THE MONK WENT A LITTLE OVERBOARD – SO TO SPEAK. THE KAMIS REALLY CAME THROUGH THIS TIME.
OKKO-SAN, I FEAR THAT UNTIL WE REBUILD, YOU ARE FORCED TO BE MY GUEST. THE GODS OF THE SEA HAVE SPOKEN.
KUBAKI! DIVERT US! OUR GUESTS AND I WOULD FORGET THIS TERRIBLE CATASTROPHE! INVENT SOMETHING, NOW! AND PRAY YOUR TALENTS ARE WORTH WHAT I PAY YOU!
BUT—BUT OF COURSE, MY LORD. IT SHALL BE AS YOU COMMAND. PERHAPS I COULD INTEREST YOU IN A JÔRURI* BEFITTING THE OCCASION...
HUB 21

* *JÔRURI* = A PUPPET PLAY WITH SUNG ACCOMPANIMENT.

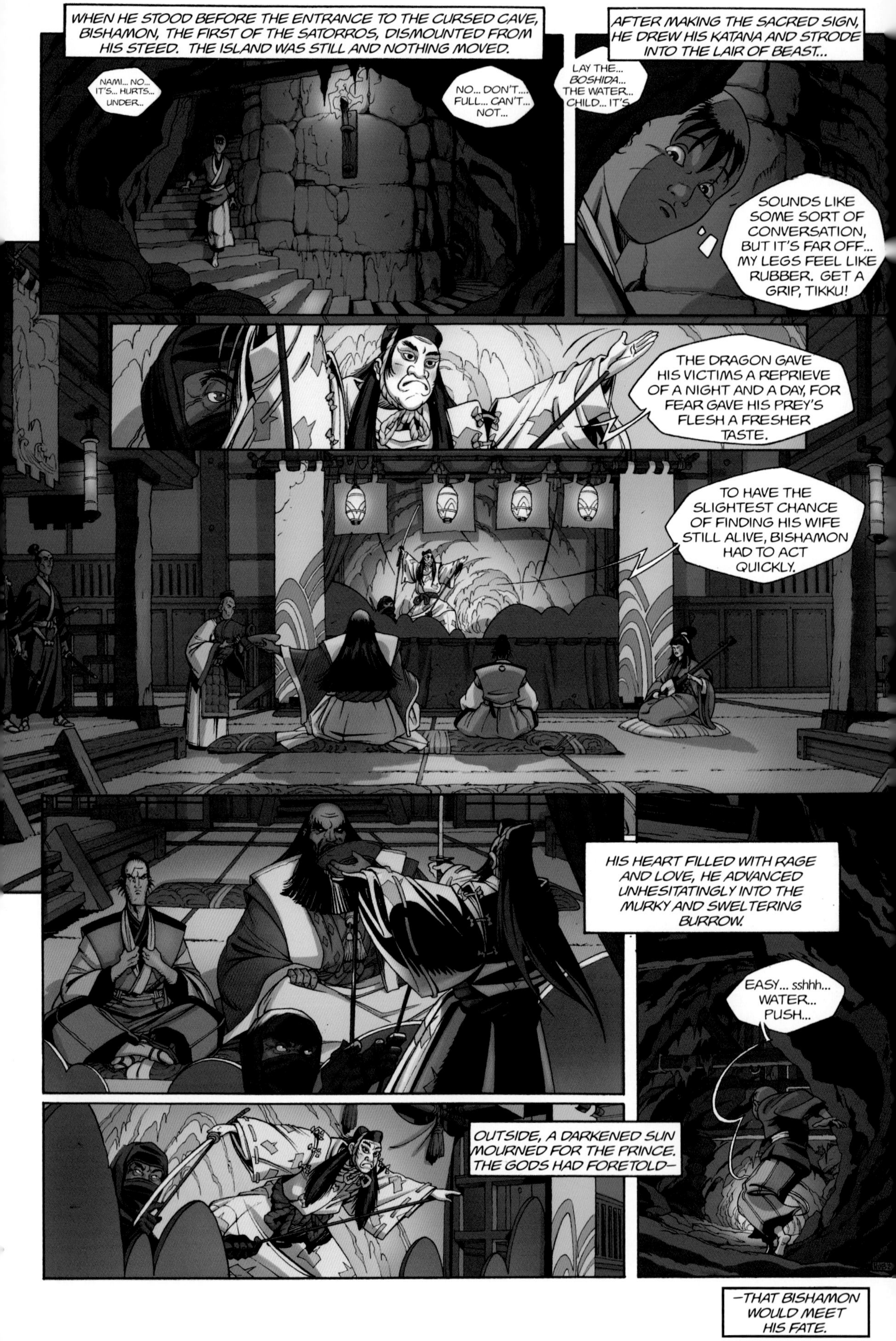
WHEN HE STOOD BEFORE THE ENTRANCE TO THE CURSED CAVE, BISHAMON, THE FIRST OF THE SATORROS, DISMOUNTED FROM HIS STEED. THE ISLAND WAS STILL AND NOTHING MOVED.
NAMI... NO... IT'S... HURTS... UNDER...
NO... DON'T... FULL... CAN'T... NOT...
AFTER MAKING THE SACRED SIGN, HE DREW HIS KATANA AND STRODE INTO THE LAIR OF BEAST...
LAY THE... BOSHIDA... THE WATER... CHILD... IT'S...
SOUNDS LIKE SOME SORT OF CONVERSATION, BUT IT'S FAR OFF... MY LEGS FEEL LIKE RUBBER. GET A GRIP, TIKKU!
THE DRAGON GAVE HIS VICTIMS A REPRIEVE OF A NIGHT AND A DAY, FOR FEAR GAVE HIS PREY'S FLESH A FRESHER TASTE.
TO HAVE THE SLIGHTEST CHANCE OF FINDING HIS WIFE STILL ALIVE, BISHAMON HAD TO ACT QUICKLY.
HIS HEART FILLED WITH RAGE AND LOVE, HE ADVANCED UNHESITATINGLY INTO THE MURKY AND SWELTERING BURROW.
EASY... sshhh... WATER... PUSH...
OUTSIDE, A DARKENED SUN MOURNED FOR THE PRINCE. THE GODS HAD FORETOLD—
—THAT BISHAMON WOULD MEET HIS FATE.

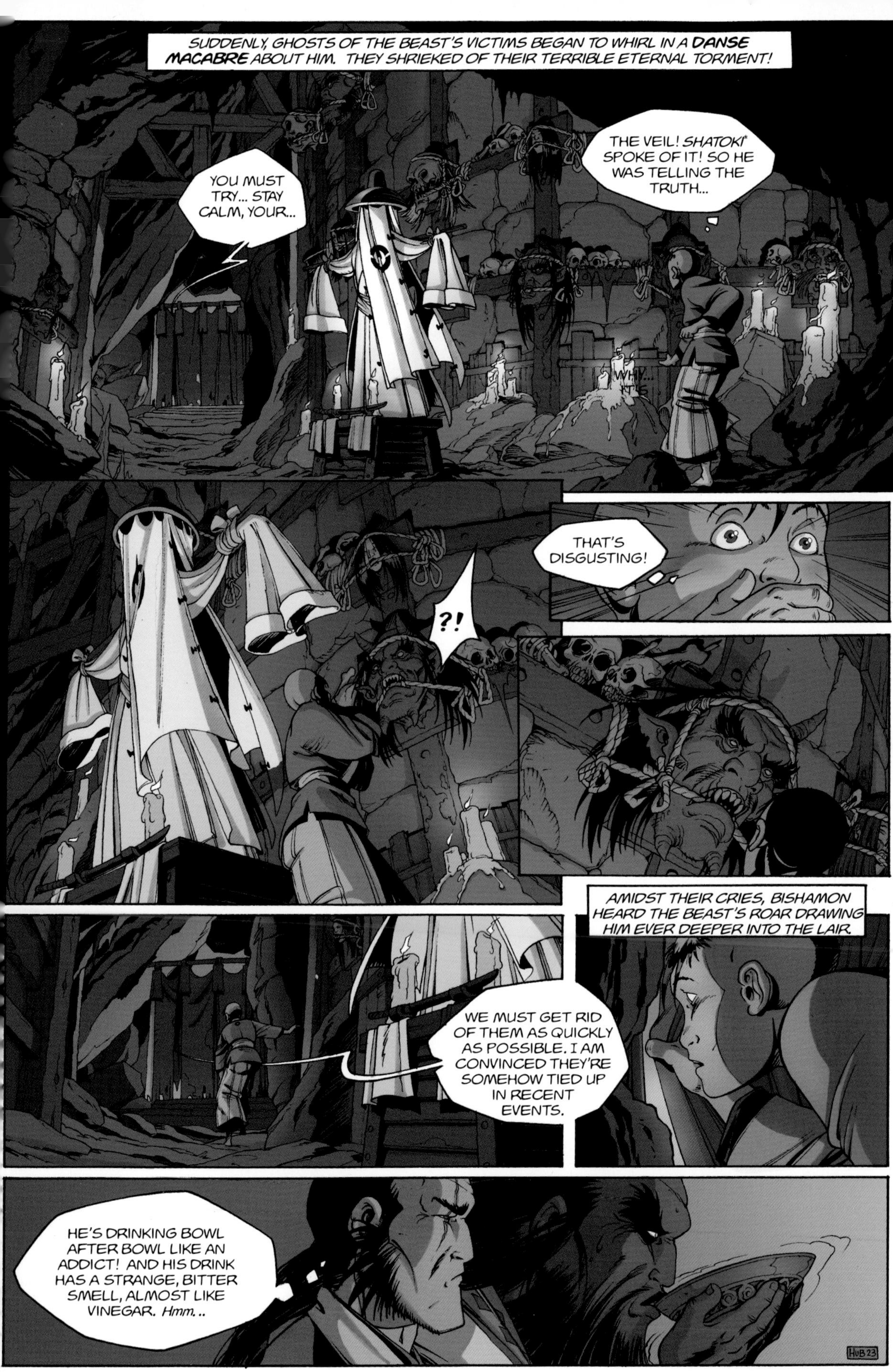
SUDDENLY, GHOSTS OF THE BEAST'S VICTIMS BEGAN TO WHIRL IN A **DANSE MACABRE** ABOUT HIM. THEY SHRIEKED OF THEIR TERRIBLE ETERNAL TORMENT!
YOU MUST TRY... STAY CALM, YOUR...
THE VEIL! *SHATOKI** SPOKE OF IT! SO HE WAS TELLING THE TRUTH...
?!
THAT'S DISGUSTING!
AMIDST THEIR CRIES, BISHAMON HEARD THE BEAST'S ROAR DRAWING HIM EVER DEEPER INTO THE LAIR.
WE MUST GET RID OF THEM AS QUICKLY AS POSSIBLE. I AM CONVINCED THEY'RE SOMEHOW TIED UP IN RECENT EVENTS.
HE'S DRINKING BOWL AFTER BOWL LIKE AN ADDICT! AND HIS DRINK HAS A STRANGE, BITTER SMELL, ALMOST LIKE VINEGAR. *Hmm...*
HUB 23

* *HIRYU SHATOKI*: SEE ISSUE #2 OF *OKKO: THE CYCLE OF WATER.*

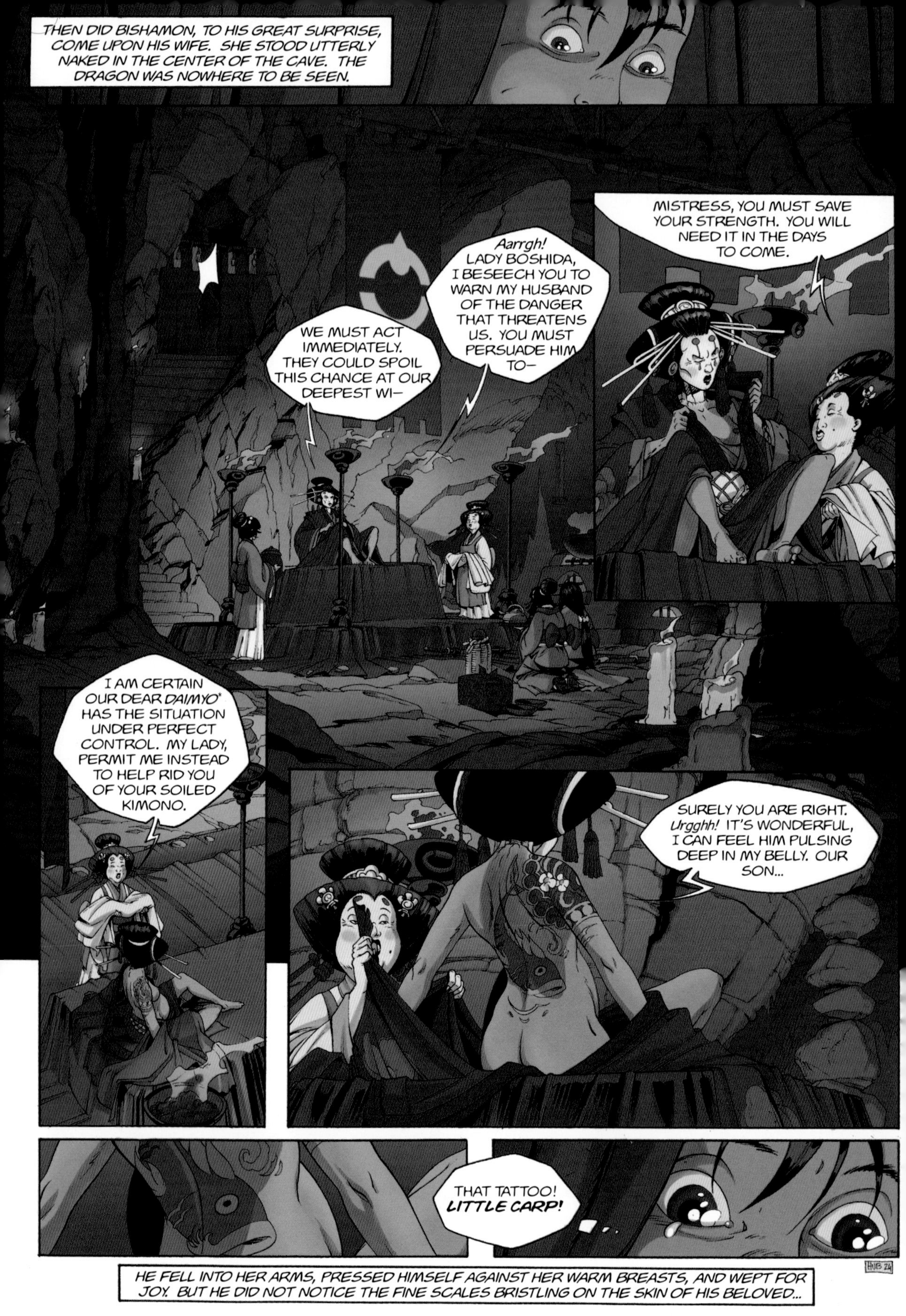
THEN DID BISHAMON, TO HIS GREAT SURPRISE, COME UPON HIS WIFE. SHE STOOD UTTERLY NAKED IN THE CENTER OF THE CAVE. THE DRAGON WAS NOWHERE TO BE SEEN.
WE MUST ACT IMMEDIATELY. THEY COULD SPOIL THIS CHANCE AT OUR DEEPEST WI—
Aarrgh! LADY BOSHIDA, I BESEECH YOU TO WARN MY HUSBAND OF THE DANGER THAT THREATENS US. YOU MUST PERSUADE HIM TO—
MISTRESS, YOU MUST SAVE YOUR STRENGTH. YOU WILL NEED IT IN THE DAYS TO COME.
I AM CERTAIN OUR DEAR *DAIMYO** HAS THE SITUATION UNDER PERFECT CONTROL. MY LADY, PERMIT ME INSTEAD TO HELP RID YOU OF YOUR SOILED KIMONO.
SURELY YOU ARE RIGHT. *Urgghh!* IT'S WONDERFUL, I CAN FEEL HIM PULSING DEEP IN MY BELLY. OUR SON...
THAT TATTOO! ***LITTLE CARP!***
HUB 24
HE FELL INTO HER ARMS, PRESSED HIMSELF AGAINST HER WARM BREASTS, AND WEPT FOR JOY. BUT HE DID NOT NOTICE THE FINE SCALES BRISTLING ON THE SKIN OF HIS BELOVED...

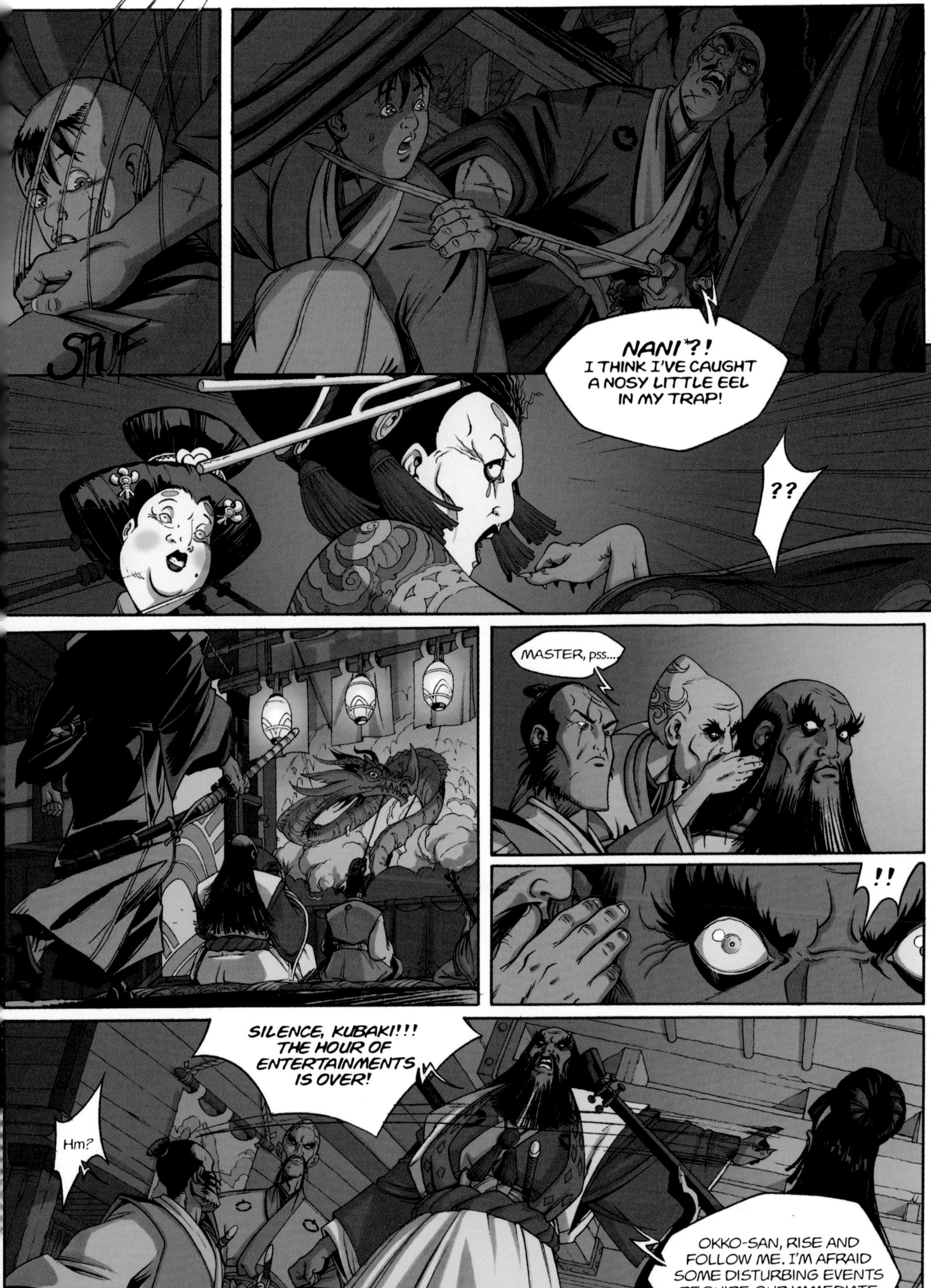

SNIF
NANI*?! I THINK I'VE CAUGHT A NOSY LITTLE EEL IN MY TRAP!
??
MASTER, pss...
!!
SILENCE, KUBAKI!!! THE HOUR OF ENTERTAINMENTS IS OVER!
Hm?
OKKO-SAN, RISE AND FOLLOW ME. I'M AFRAID SOME DISTURBING EVENTS REQUIRE OUR IMMEDIATE ATTENTION.
HUB 25

*NANI: WHAT?

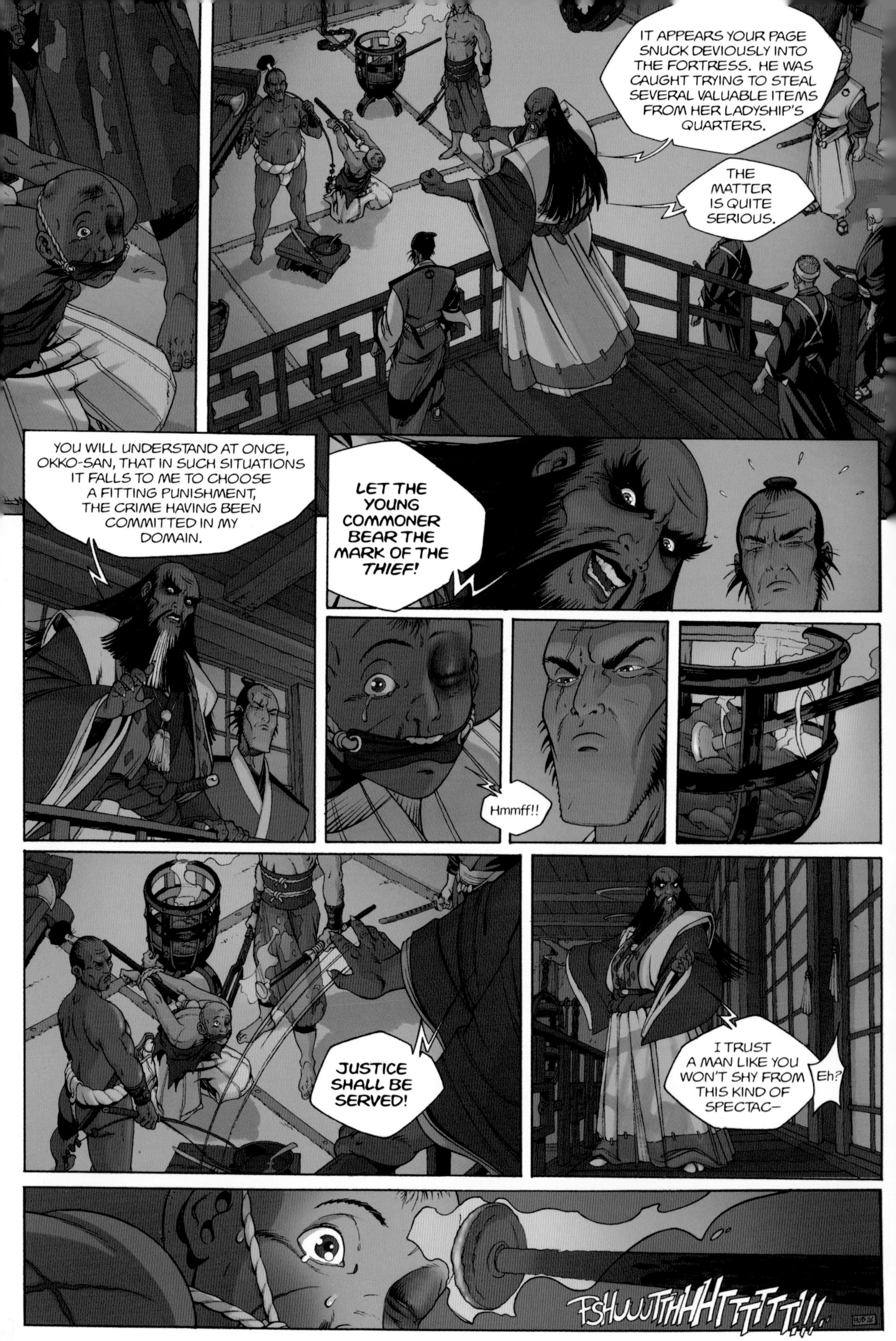
IT APPEARS YOUR PAGE SNUCK DEVIOUSLY INTO THE FORTRESS. HE WAS CAUGHT TRYING TO STEAL SEVERAL VALUABLE ITEMS FROM HER LADYSHIP'S QUARTERS.
THE MATTER IS QUITE SERIOUS.
YOU WILL UNDERSTAND AT ONCE, OKKO-SAN, THAT IN SUCH SITUATIONS IT FALLS TO ME TO CHOOSE A FITTING PUNISHMENT, THE CRIME HAVING BEEN COMMITTED IN MY DOMAIN.
LET THE YOUNG COMMONER BEAR THE MARK OF THE *THIEF!*
Hmmff!!
JUSTICE SHALL BE SERVED!
I TRUST A MAN LIKE YOU WON'T SHY FROM THIS KIND OF SPECTAC–
Eh?
FSHUUUTTHHHTTTTTT!!!

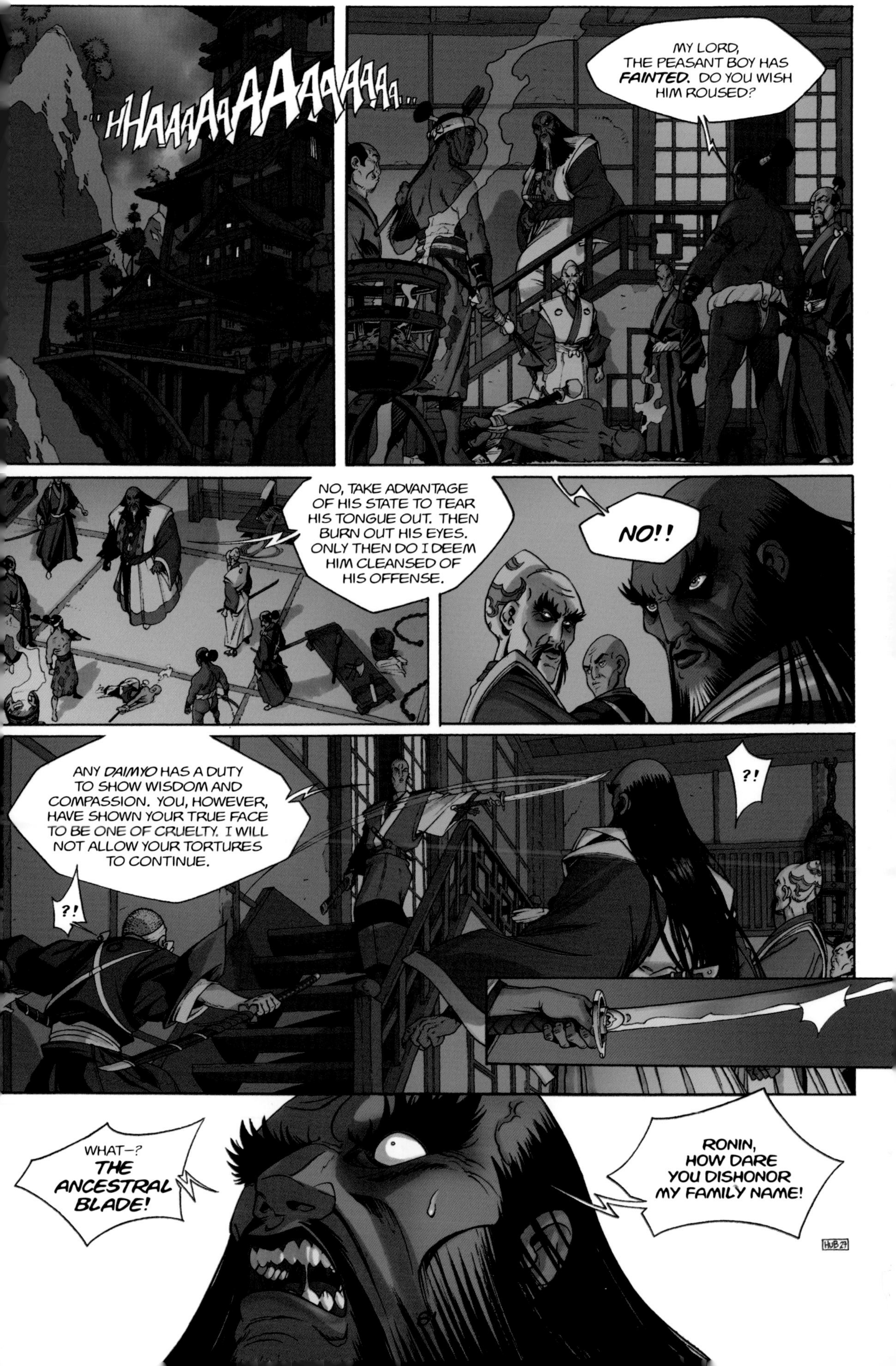
...HHAAAAAAAAAaaaaa...
MY LORD, THE PEASANT BOY HAS FAINTED. DO YOU WISH HIM ROUSED?
NO, TAKE ADVANTAGE OF HIS STATE TO TEAR HIS TONGUE OUT. THEN BURN OUT HIS EYES. ONLY THEN DO I DEEM HIM CLEANSED OF HIS OFFENSE.
NO!!
ANY DAIMYO HAS A DUTY TO SHOW WISDOM AND COMPASSION. YOU, HOWEVER, HAVE SHOWN YOUR TRUE FACE TO BE ONE OF CRUELTY. I WILL NOT ALLOW YOUR TORTURES TO CONTINUE.
?!
?!
WHAT—? THE ANCESTRAL BLADE!
RONIN, HOW DARE YOU DISHONOR MY FAMILY NAME!
HUB 2?

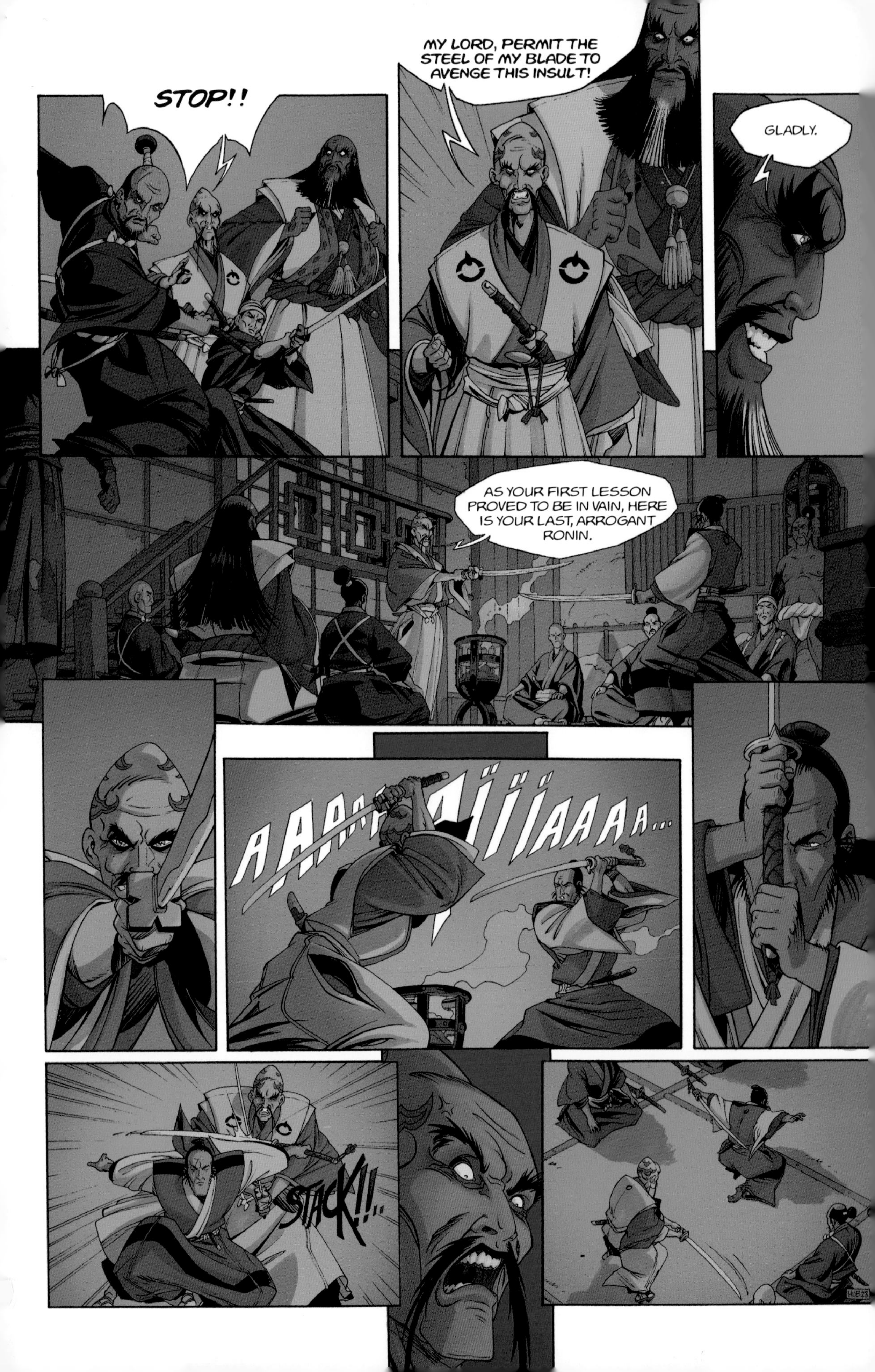
STOP!!
MY LORD, PERMIT THE STEEL OF MY BLADE TO AVENGE THIS INSULT!
GLADLY.
AS YOUR FIRST LESSON PROVED TO BE IN VAIN, HERE IS YOUR LAST, ARROGANT RONIN.
AAAAAIIIIAAAAA...
STACK!!!

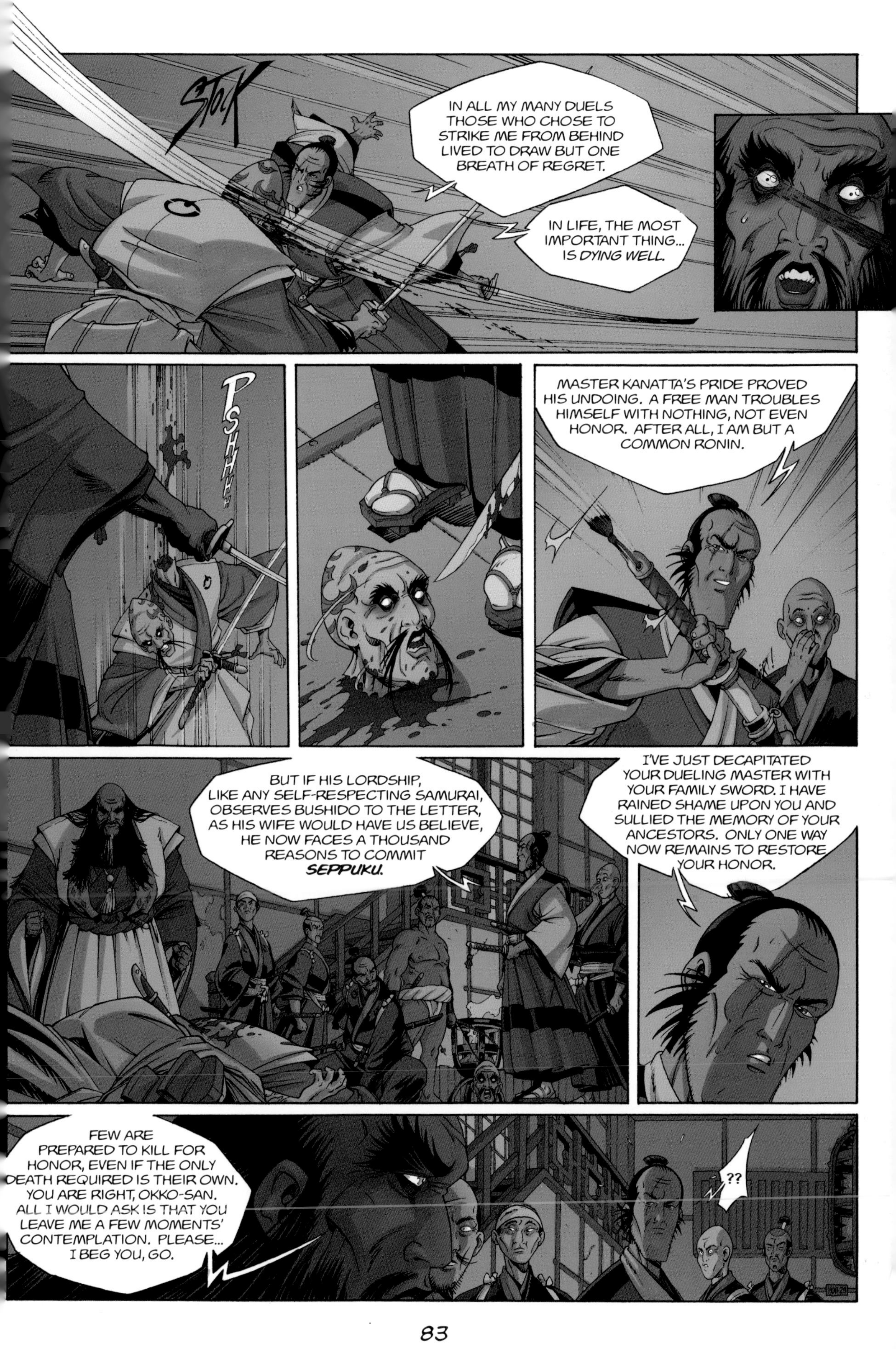
STOCK
IN ALL MY MANY DUELS THOSE WHO CHOSE TO STRIKE ME FROM BEHIND LIVED TO DRAW BUT ONE BREATH OF REGRET.
IN LIFE, THE MOST IMPORTANT THING... IS DYING WELL.
PSHHH
MASTER KANATTA'S PRIDE PROVED HIS UNDOING. A FREE MAN TROUBLES HIMSELF WITH NOTHING, NOT EVEN HONOR. AFTER ALL, I AM BUT A COMMON RONIN.
BUT IF HIS LORDSHIP, LIKE ANY SELF-RESPECTING SAMURAI, OBSERVES BUSHIDO TO THE LETTER, AS HIS WIFE WOULD HAVE US BELIEVE, HE NOW FACES A THOUSAND REASONS TO COMMIT SEPPUKU.
I'VE JUST DECAPITATED YOUR DUELING MASTER WITH YOUR FAMILY SWORD. I HAVE RAINED SHAME UPON YOU AND SULLIED THE MEMORY OF YOUR ANCESTORS. ONLY ONE WAY NOW REMAINS TO RESTORE YOUR HONOR.
FEW ARE PREPARED TO KILL FOR HONOR, EVEN IF THE ONLY DEATH REQUIRED IS THEIR OWN. YOU ARE RIGHT, OKKO-SAN. ALL I WOULD ASK IS THAT YOU LEAVE ME A FEW MOMENTS' CONTEMPLATION. PLEASE... I BEG YOU, GO.
??

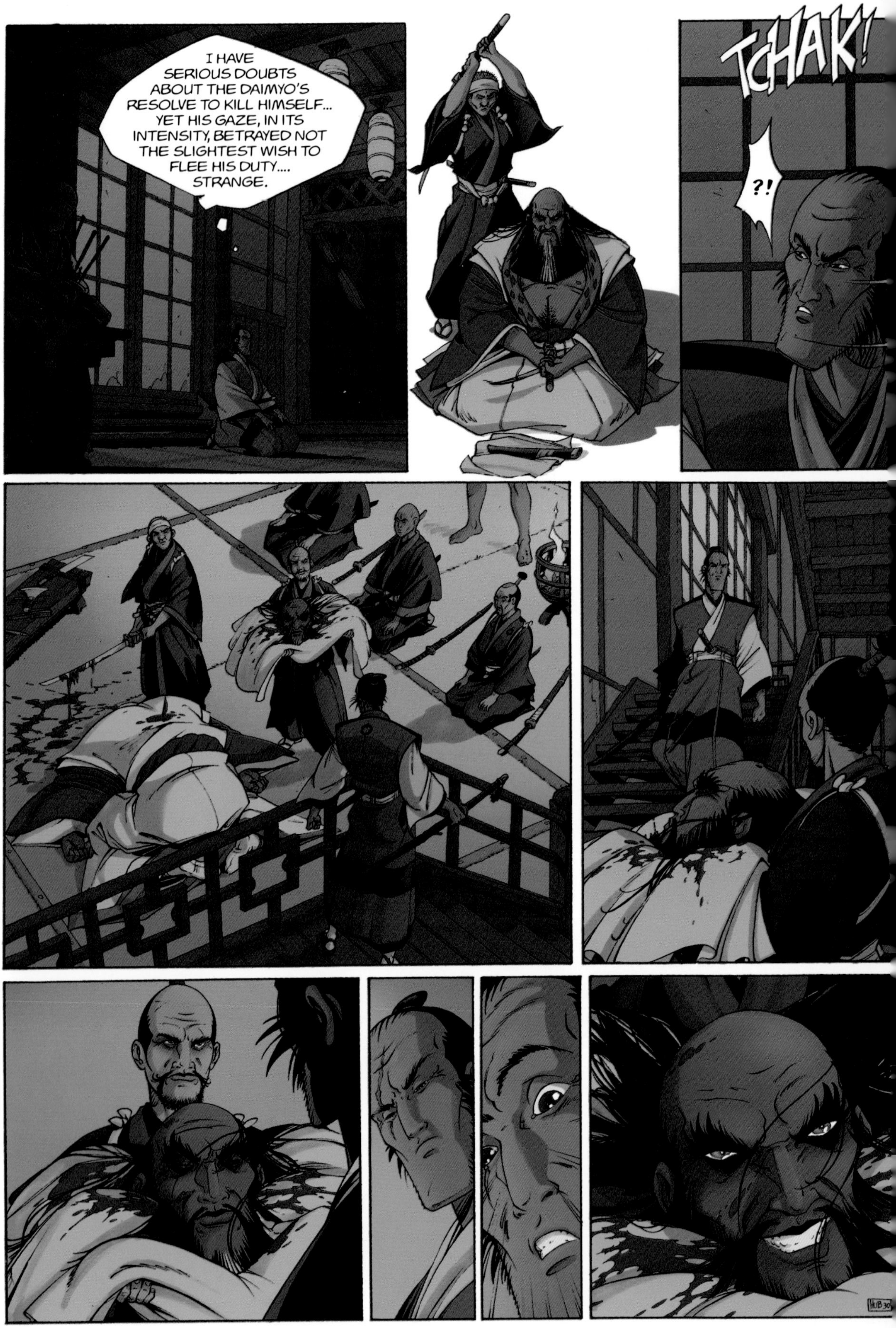
I HAVE SERIOUS DOUBTS ABOUT THE DAIMYO'S RESOLVE TO KILL HIMSELF... YET HIS GAZE, IN ITS INTENSITY, BETRAYED NOT THE SLIGHTEST WISH TO FLEE HIS DUTY.... STRANGE.
TCHAK!
?!

PAK!

WHAT NONSENSE, REHEARSING KATAS IN SUCH DRIVING RAIN AS THIS!

Unnhh! DON'T YOU KNOW ummph THE OLD SAYING whff! **WHILE YOU SLEEP, YOUR ENEMY TRAINS...** Hmmff!

SPAK!

NOBURO-SAN: IF YOU WOULD ACCOMPANY ME.... YOUR MASTER AWAITS!

ON MY WAY.

WAIT FOR ME HERE. I'LL BE BACK SOON AS I CAN.

"WAIT HERE, NOBURO," "I'LL BE BACK, NOBURO," AND WHO'S STUCK IN THE RAIN OUTSIDE THE STUPID CASTL, huh? I'M NO MAN OF ACTION, BUT ALL THE SAME I'M GETTING TIRED OF SITTING AROUND, AND THE SITUATION HARDLY SEEMS TO BE IMPROVING...

...BBRRROOOOOOAAAMMNnn!!

RRRRUUMMBLVVVGGNNN....

HE – HE AWAITS YOU HERE... INSIDE THE DOJO.

OKKO? ... Hm?!

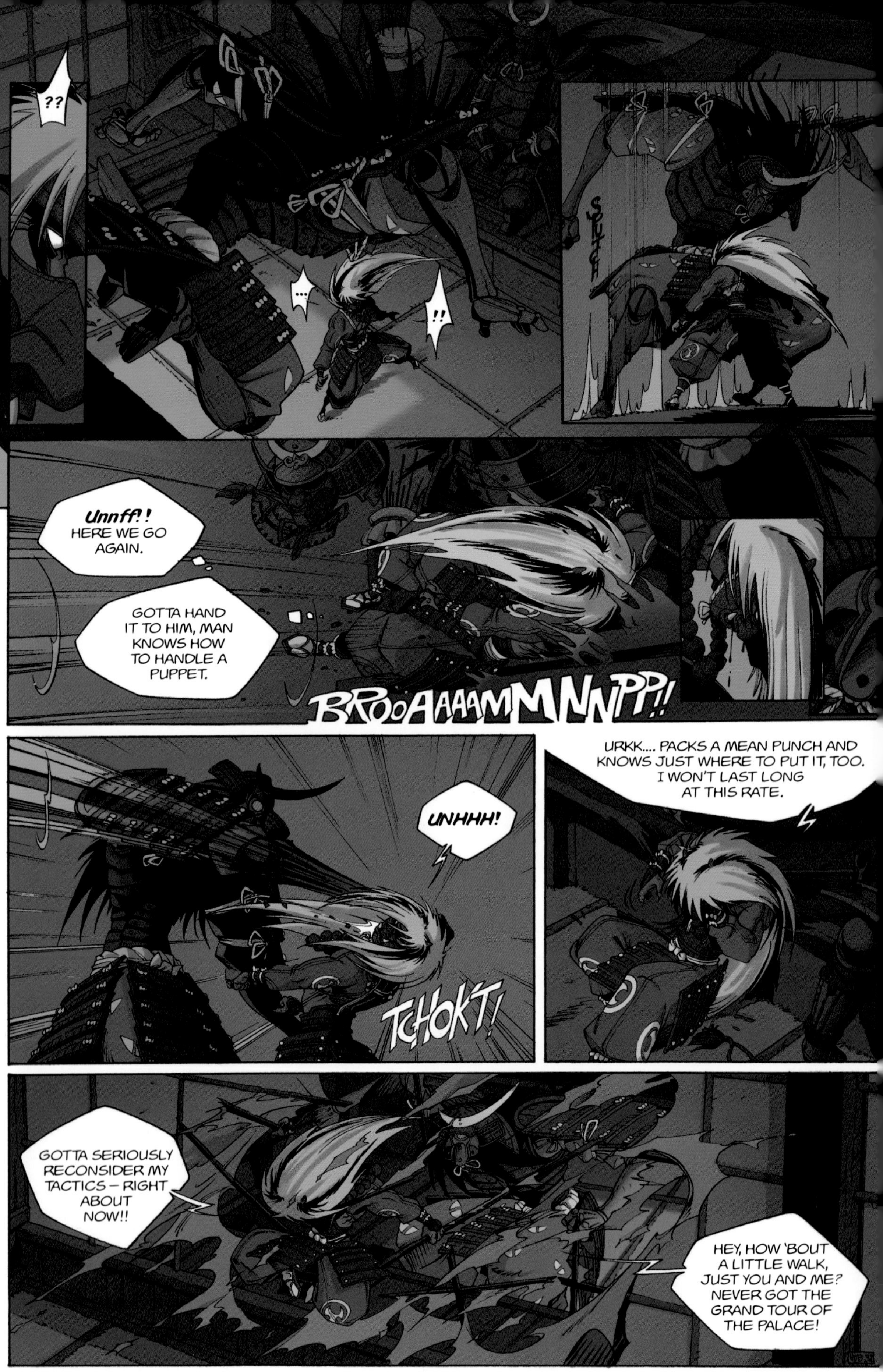
??
...
!!
SPLUTCH
Unnff!! HERE WE GO AGAIN.
GOTTA HAND IT TO HIM, MAN KNOWS HOW TO HANDLE A PUPPET.
BROOAAAAMMNNPP!!
UNHHH!
TCHOK'T!
URKK.... PACKS A MEAN PUNCH AND KNOWS JUST WHERE TO PUT IT, TOO. I WON'T LAST LONG AT THIS RATE.
GOTTA SERIOUSLY RECONSIDER MY TACTICS – RIGHT ABOUT NOW!!
HEY, HOW 'BOUT A LITTLE WALK, JUST YOU AND ME? NEVER GOT THE GRAND TOUR OF THE PALACE!

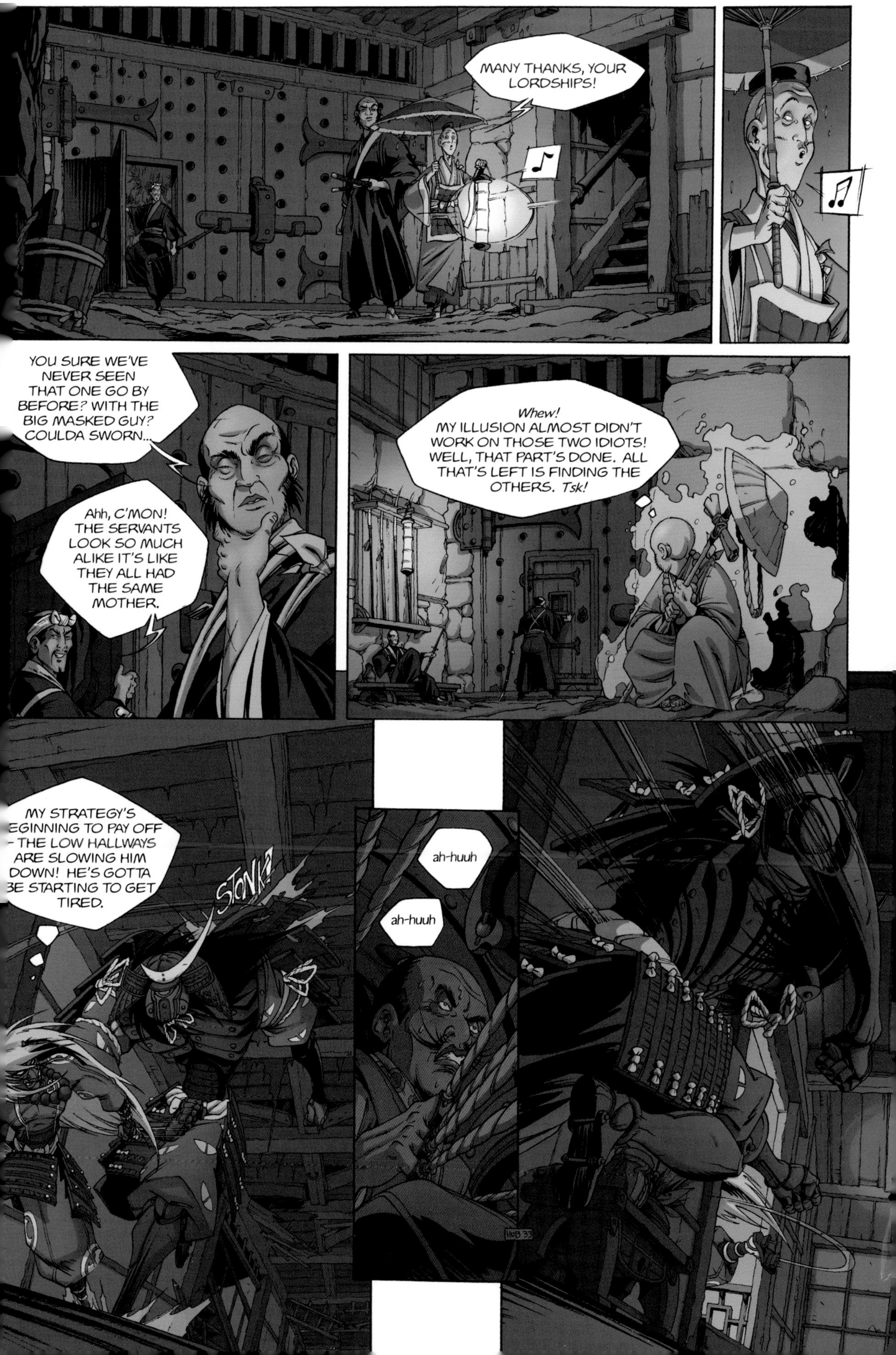

MANY THANKS, YOUR LORDSHIPS!
YOU SURE WE'VE NEVER SEEN THAT ONE GO BY BEFORE? WITH THE BIG MASKED GUY? COULDA SWORN...
Ahh, C'MON! THE SERVANTS LOOK SO MUCH ALIKE IT'S LIKE THEY ALL HAD THE SAME MOTHER.
Whew! MY ILLUSION ALMOST DIDN'T WORK ON THOSE TWO IDIOTS! WELL, THAT PART'S DONE. ALL THAT'S LEFT IS FINDING THE OTHERS. *Tsk!*
MY STRATEGY'S BEGINNING TO PAY OFF - THE LOW HALLWAYS ARE SLOWING HIM DOWN! HE'S GOTTA BE STARTING TO GET TIRED.
STONK?
ah-huuh
ah-huuh

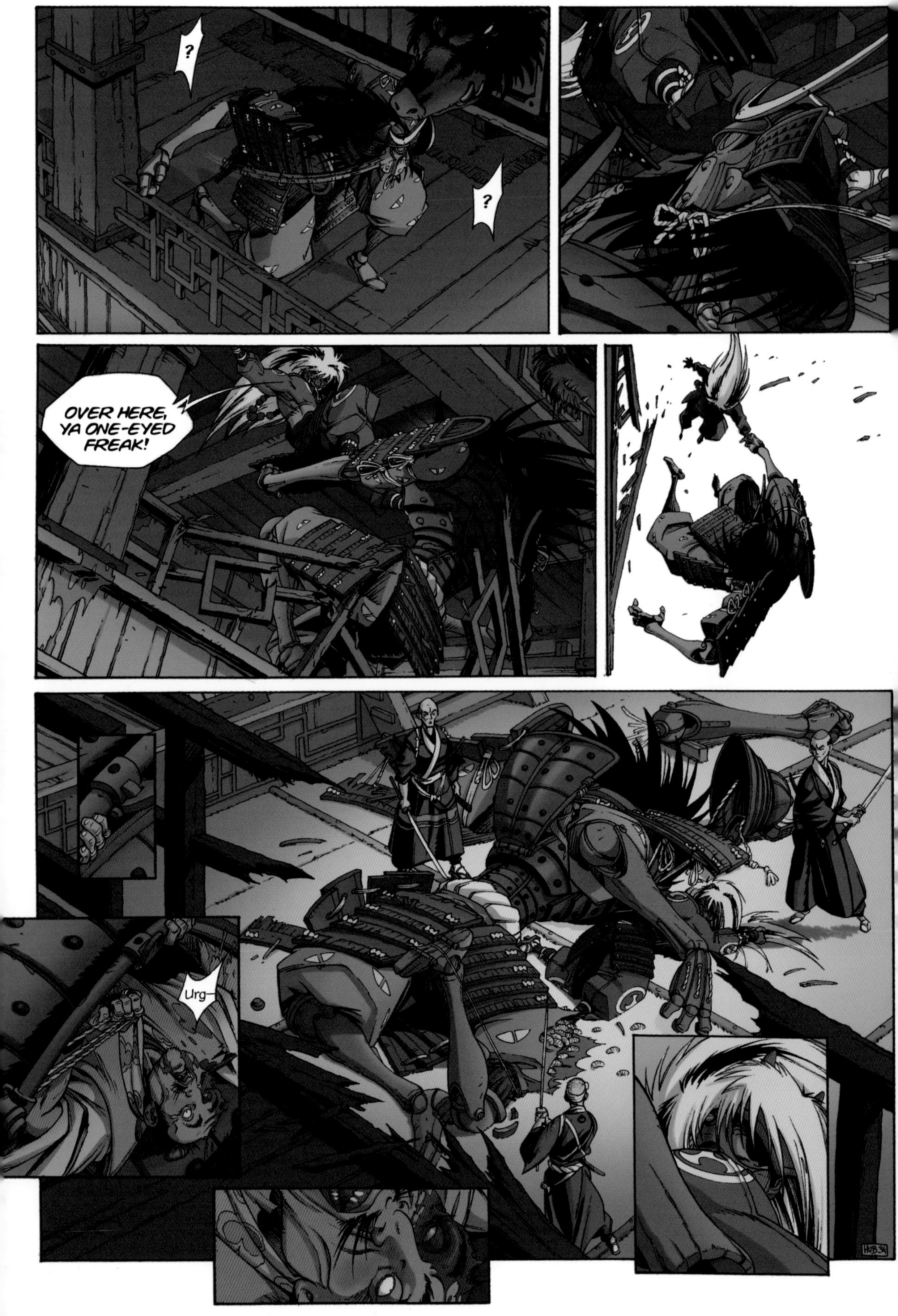
?
?
OVER HERE, YA ONE-EYED FREAK!
Urg—
HUB.34

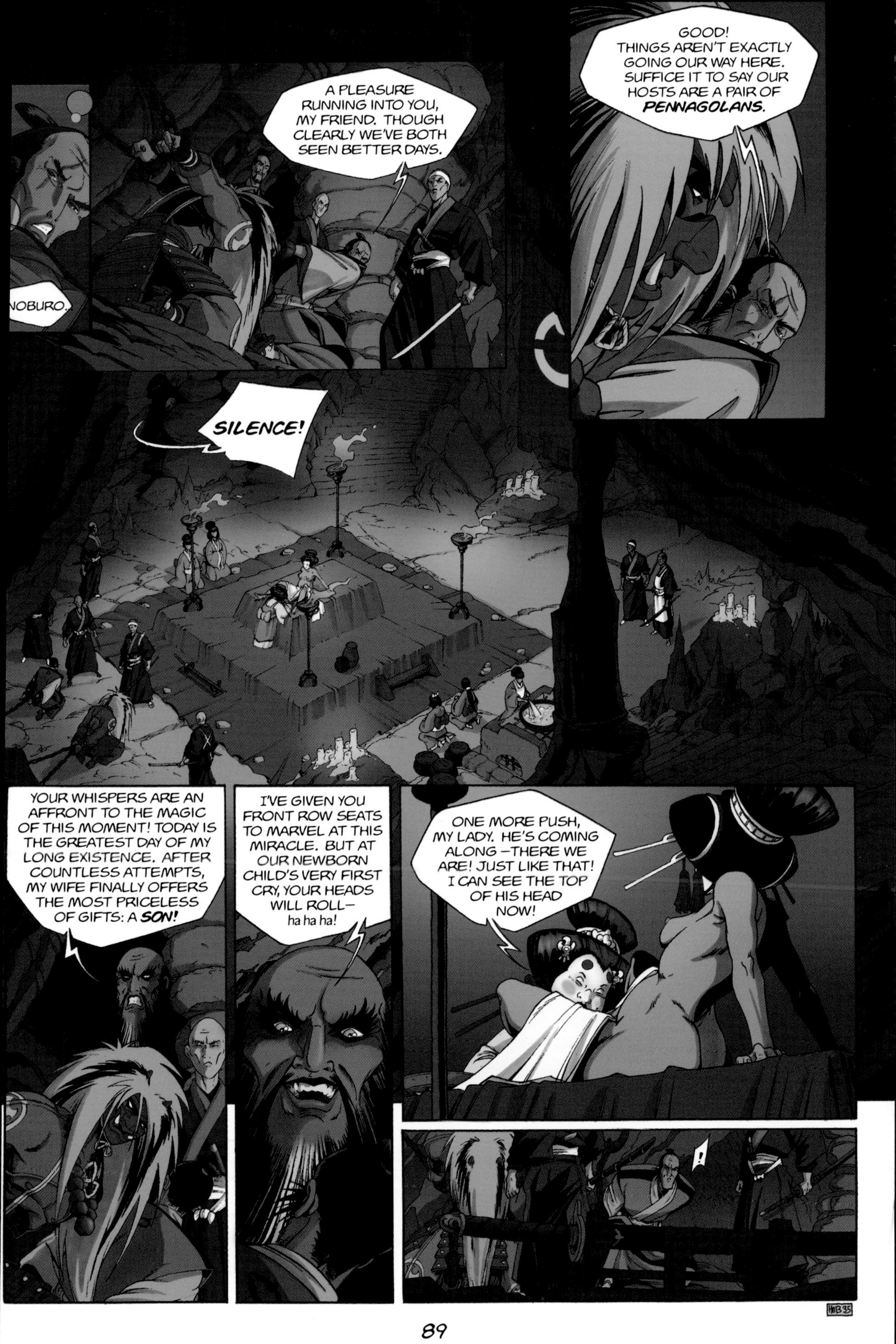
NOBURO...
A PLEASURE RUNNING INTO YOU, MY FRIEND. THOUGH CLEARLY WE'VE BOTH SEEN BETTER DAYS.
GOOD! THINGS AREN'T EXACTLY GOING OUR WAY HERE. SUFFICE IT TO SAY OUR HOSTS ARE A PAIR OF PENNAGOLANS.
SILENCE!
YOUR WHISPERS ARE AN AFFRONT TO THE MAGIC OF THIS MOMENT! TODAY IS THE GREATEST DAY OF MY LONG EXISTENCE. AFTER COUNTLESS ATTEMPTS, MY WIFE FINALLY OFFERS THE MOST PRICELESS OF GIFTS: A SON!
I'VE GIVEN YOU FRONT ROW SEATS TO MARVEL AT THIS MIRACLE. BUT AT OUR NEWBORN CHILD'S VERY FIRST CRY, YOUR HEADS WILL ROLL— ha ha ha!
ONE MORE PUSH, MY LADY. HE'S COMING ALONG —THERE WE ARE! JUST LIKE THAT! I CAN SEE THE TOP OF HIS HEAD NOW!
!

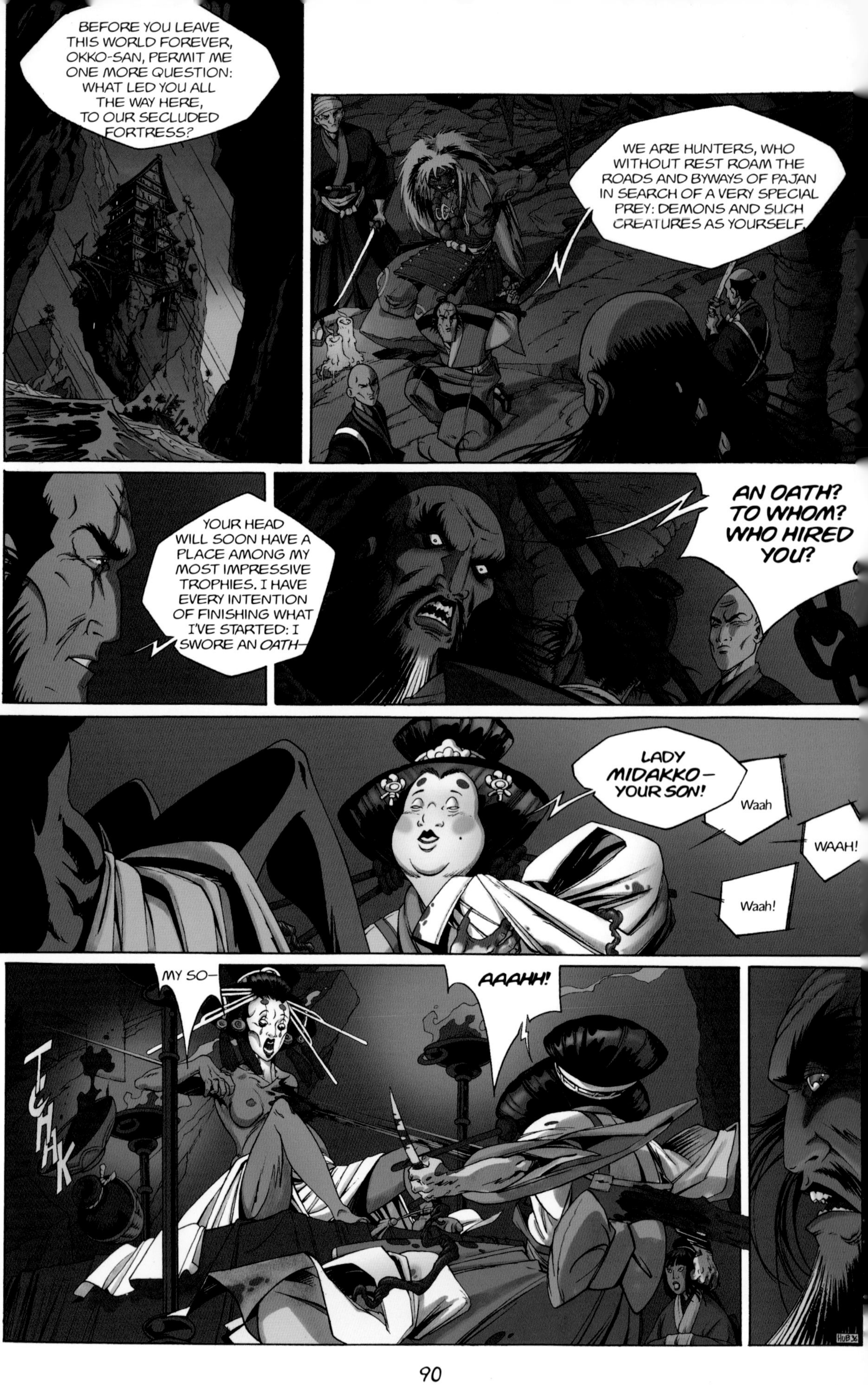
BEFORE YOU LEAVE THIS WORLD FOREVER, OKKO-SAN, PERMIT ME ONE MORE QUESTION: WHAT LED YOU ALL THE WAY HERE, TO OUR SECLUDED FORTRESS?
WE ARE HUNTERS, WHO WITHOUT REST ROAM THE ROADS AND BYWAYS OF PAJAN IN SEARCH OF A VERY SPECIAL PREY: DEMONS AND SUCH CREATURES AS YOURSELF.
YOUR HEAD WILL SOON HAVE A PLACE AMONG MY MOST IMPRESSIVE TROPHIES. I HAVE EVERY INTENTION OF FINISHING WHAT I'VE STARTED: I SWORE AN *OATH*—
AN OATH? TO WHOM? WHO HIRED YOU?
LADY MIDAKKO— YOUR SON!
Waah
WAAH!
Waah!
MY SO—
AAAHH!
TCHAK

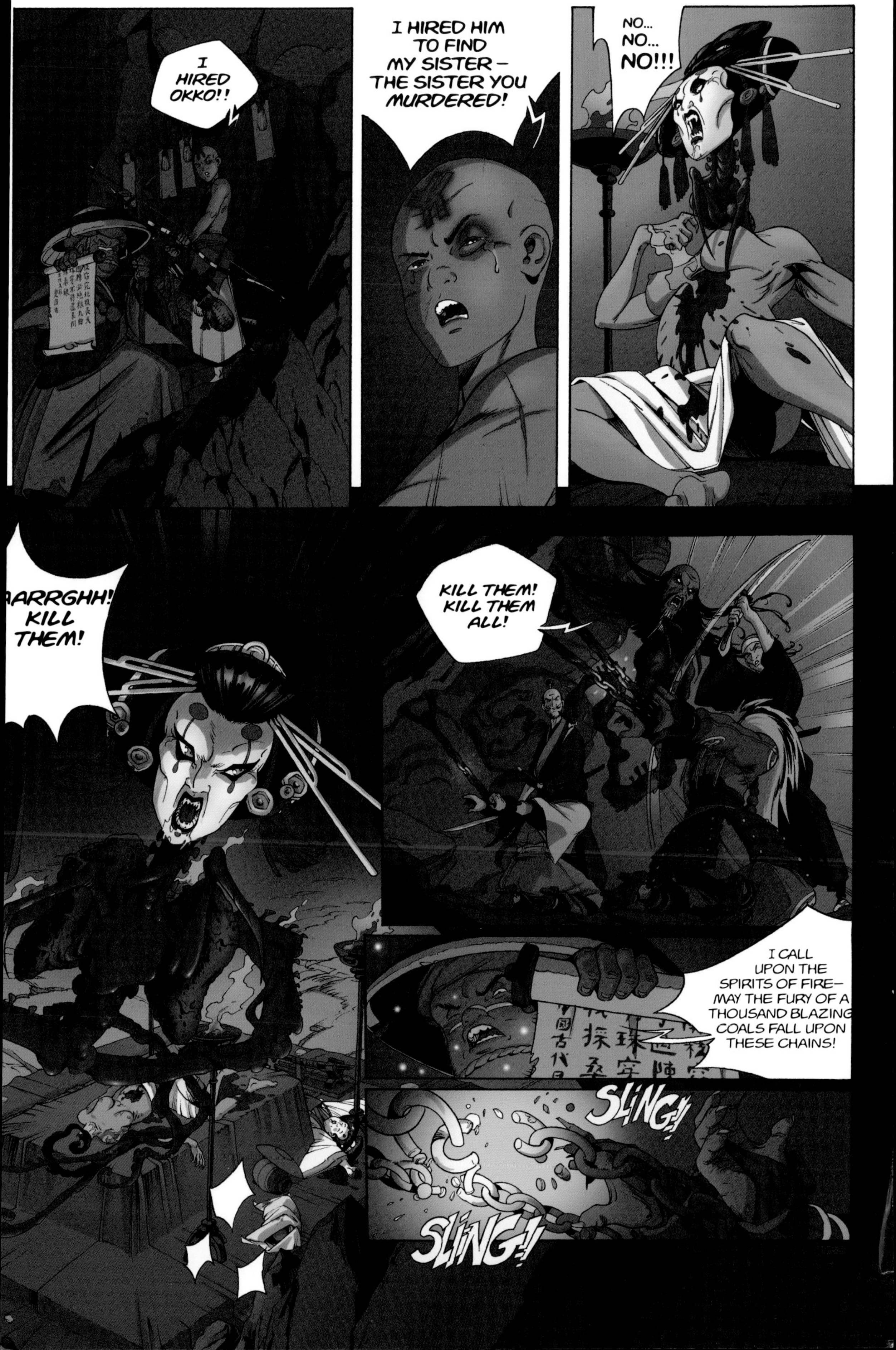
I HIRED OKKO!!
I HIRED HIM TO FIND MY SISTER – THE SISTER YOU MURDERED!
NO... NO... NO!!!
ARRGHH! KILL THEM!
KILL THEM! KILL THEM ALL!
I CALL UPON THE SPIRITS OF FIRE– MAY THE FURY OF A THOUSAND BLAZING COALS FALL UPON THESE CHAINS!
SLING!!
SLING!!

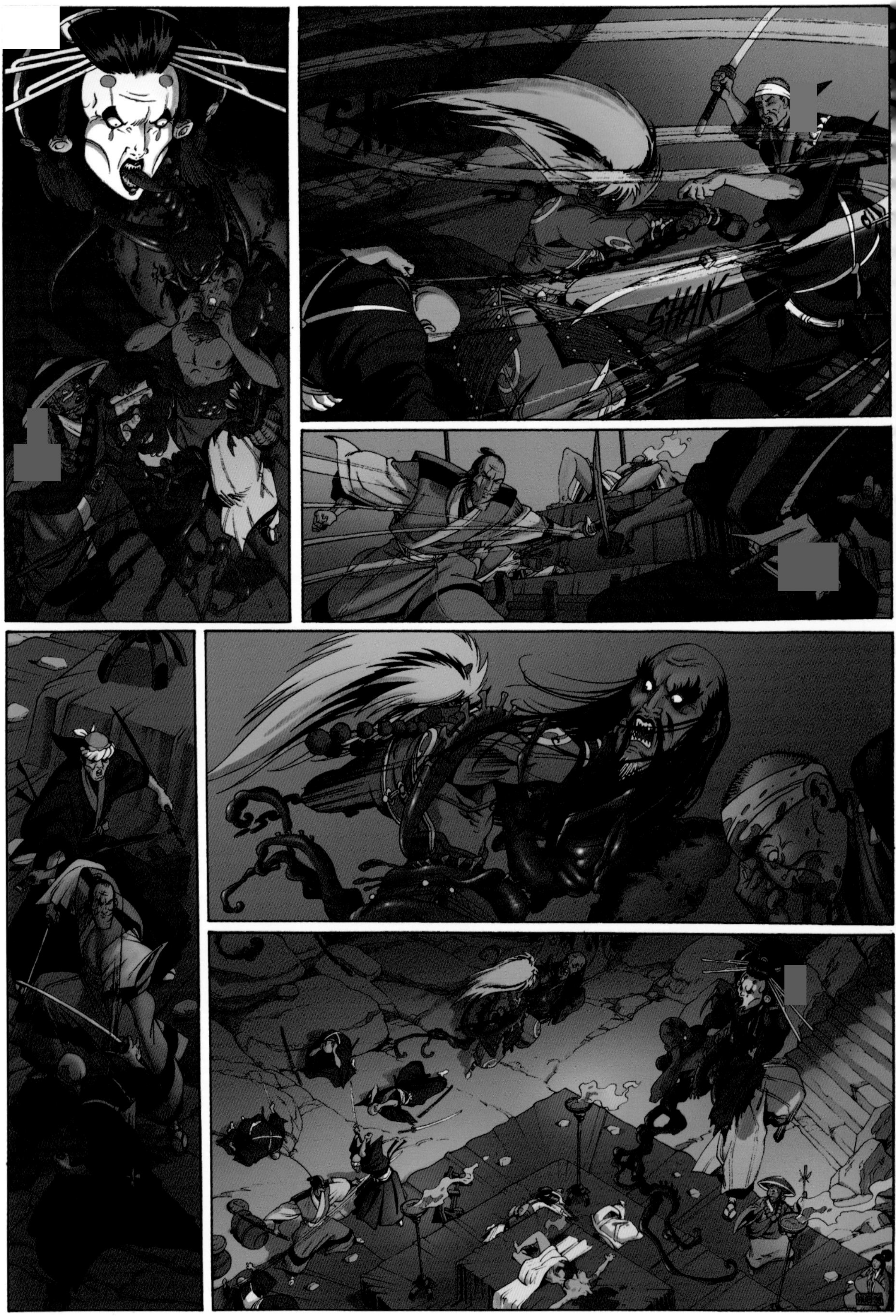
SHAK

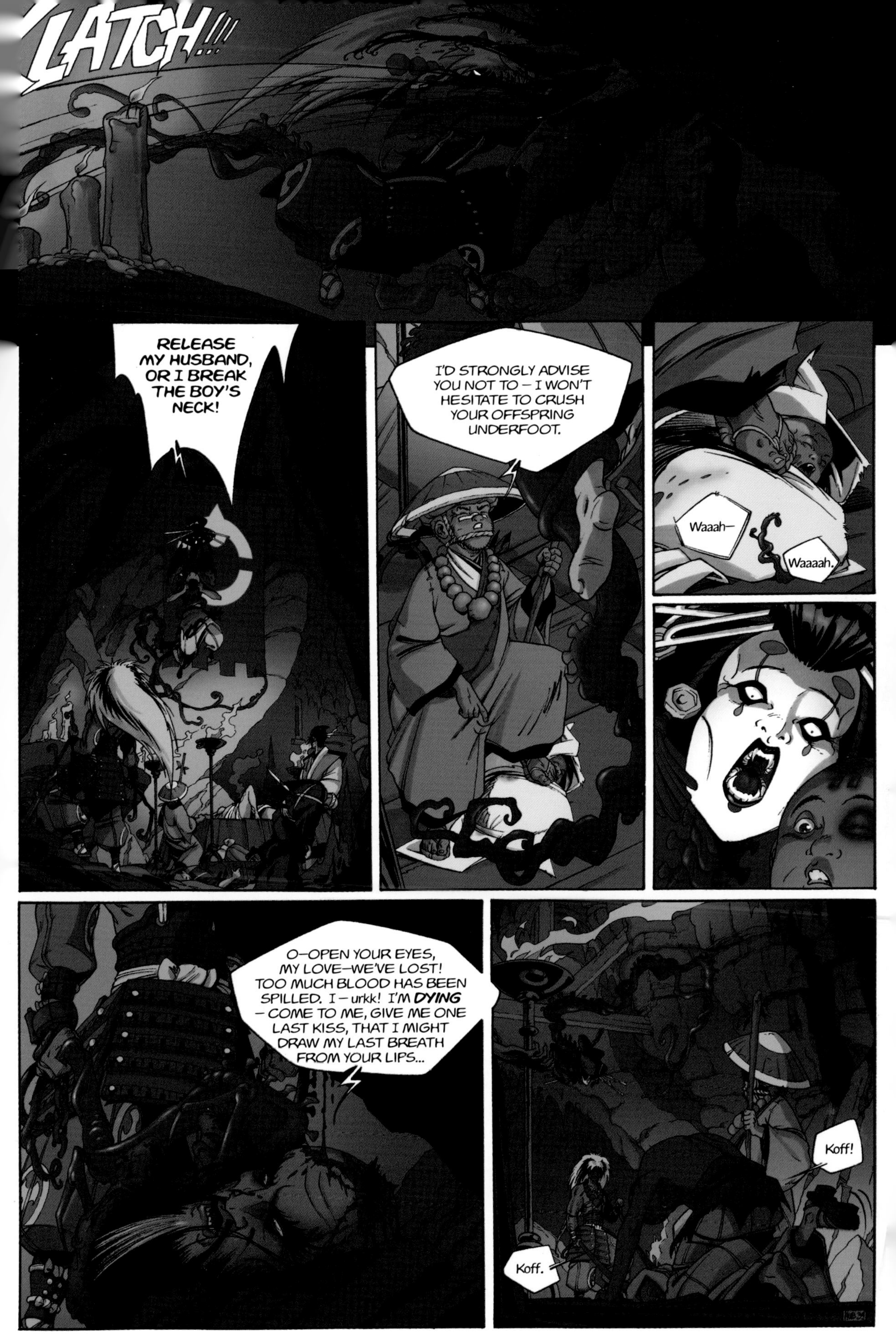
ZLATCH!!!
RELEASE MY HUSBAND, OR I BREAK THE BOY'S NECK!
I'D STRONGLY ADVISE YOU NOT TO – I WON'T HESITATE TO CRUSH YOUR OFFSPRING UNDERFOOT.
Waaah–
Waaaah.
O–OPEN YOUR EYES, MY LOVE–WE'VE LOST! TOO MUCH BLOOD HAS BEEN SPILLED. I – urkk! I'M *DYING* – COME TO ME, GIVE ME ONE LAST KISS, THAT I MIGHT DRAW MY LAST BREATH FROM YOUR LIPS...
Koff!
Koff.

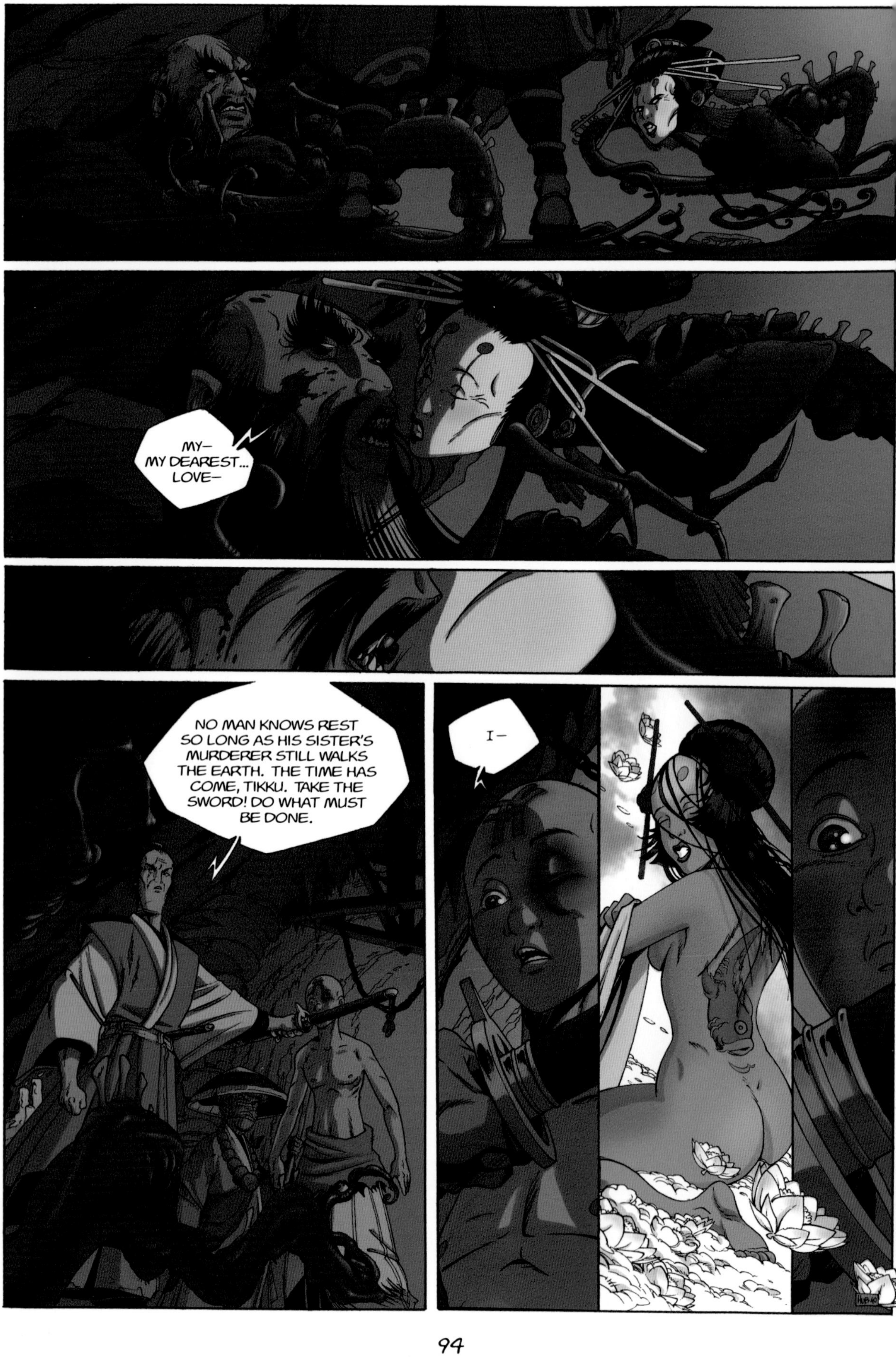
MY—
MY DEAREST...
LOVE—
NO MAN KNOWS REST SO LONG AS HIS SISTER'S MURDERER STILL WALKS THE EARTH. THE TIME HAS COME, TIKKU. TAKE THE SWORD! DO WHAT MUST BE DONE.
I—

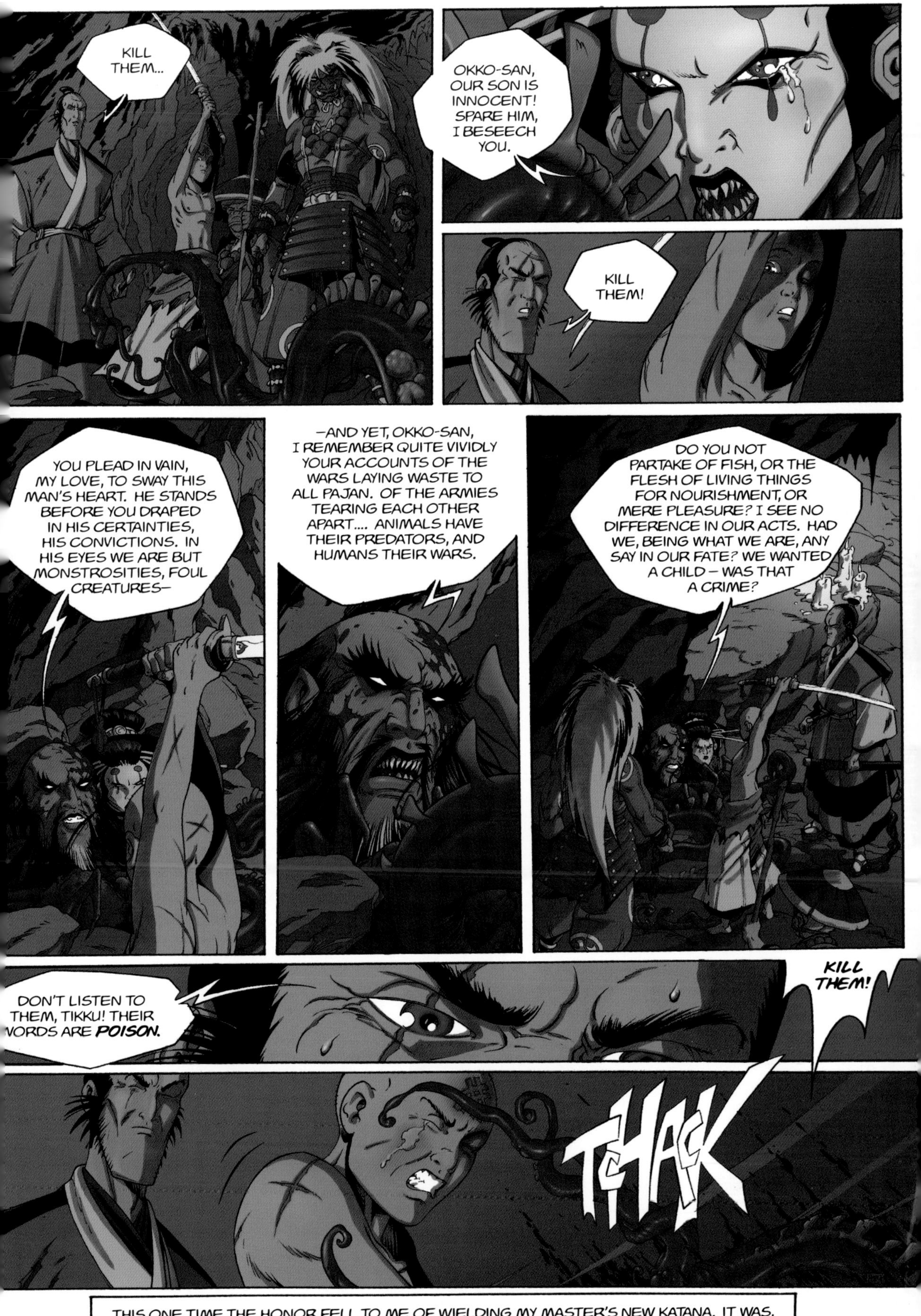
KILL THEM...
OKKO-SAN, OUR SON IS INNOCENT! SPARE HIM, I BESEECH YOU.
KILL THEM!
YOU PLEAD IN VAIN, MY LOVE, TO SWAY THIS MAN'S HEART. HE STANDS BEFORE YOU DRAPED IN HIS CERTAINTIES, HIS CONVICTIONS. IN HIS EYES WE ARE BUT MONSTROSITIES, FOUL CREATURES–
–AND YET, OKKO-SAN, I REMEMBER QUITE VIVIDLY YOUR ACCOUNTS OF THE WARS LAYING WASTE TO ALL PAJAN. OF THE ARMIES TEARING EACH OTHER APART.... ANIMALS HAVE THEIR PREDATORS, AND HUMANS THEIR WARS.
DO YOU NOT PARTAKE OF FISH, OR THE FLESH OF LIVING THINGS FOR NOURISHMENT, OR MERE PLEASURE? I SEE NO DIFFERENCE IN OUR ACTS. HAD WE, BEING WHAT WE ARE, ANY SAY IN OUR FATE? WE WANTED A CHILD – WAS THAT A CRIME?
DON'T LISTEN TO THEM, TIKKU! THEIR WORDS ARE POISON.
KILL THEM!
TCHACK

THIS ONE TIME THE HONOR FELL TO ME OF WIELDING MY MASTER'S NEW KATANA. IT WAS, FOR ITS PART, ABOUT TO WRITE IN BLOOD THE GREATEST PAGES OF ITS OWN LEGEND.

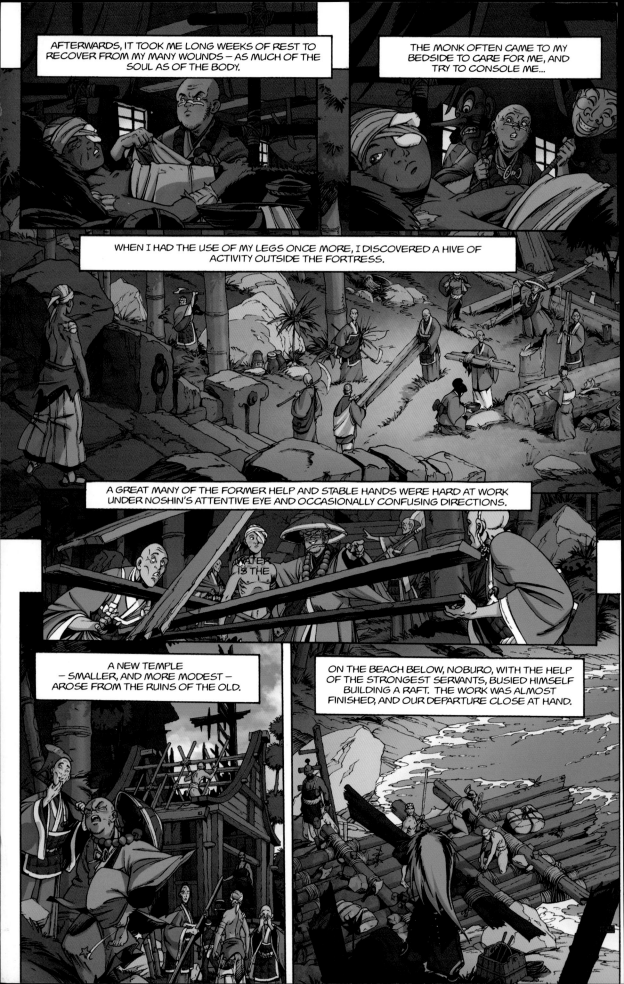

AFTERWARDS, IT TOOK ME LONG WEEKS OF REST TO RECOVER FROM MY MANY WOUNDS – AS MUCH OF THE SOUL AS OF THE BODY.

THE MONK OFTEN CAME TO MY BEDSIDE TO CARE FOR ME, AND TRY TO CONSOLE ME...

WHEN I HAD THE USE OF MY LEGS ONCE MORE, I DISCOVERED A HIVE OF ACTIVITY OUTSIDE THE FORTRESS.

A GREAT MANY OF THE FORMER HELP AND STABLE HANDS WERE HARD AT WORK UNDER NOSHIN'S ATTENTIVE EYE AND OCCASIONALLY CONFUSING DIRECTIONS.

A NEW TEMPLE – SMALLER, AND MORE MODEST – AROSE FROM THE RUINS OF THE OLD.

ON THE BEACH BELOW, NOBURO, WITH THE HELP OF THE STRONGEST SERVANTS, BUSIED HIMSELF BUILDING A RAFT. THE WORK WAS ALMOST FINISHED, AND OUR DEPARTURE CLOSE AT HAND.

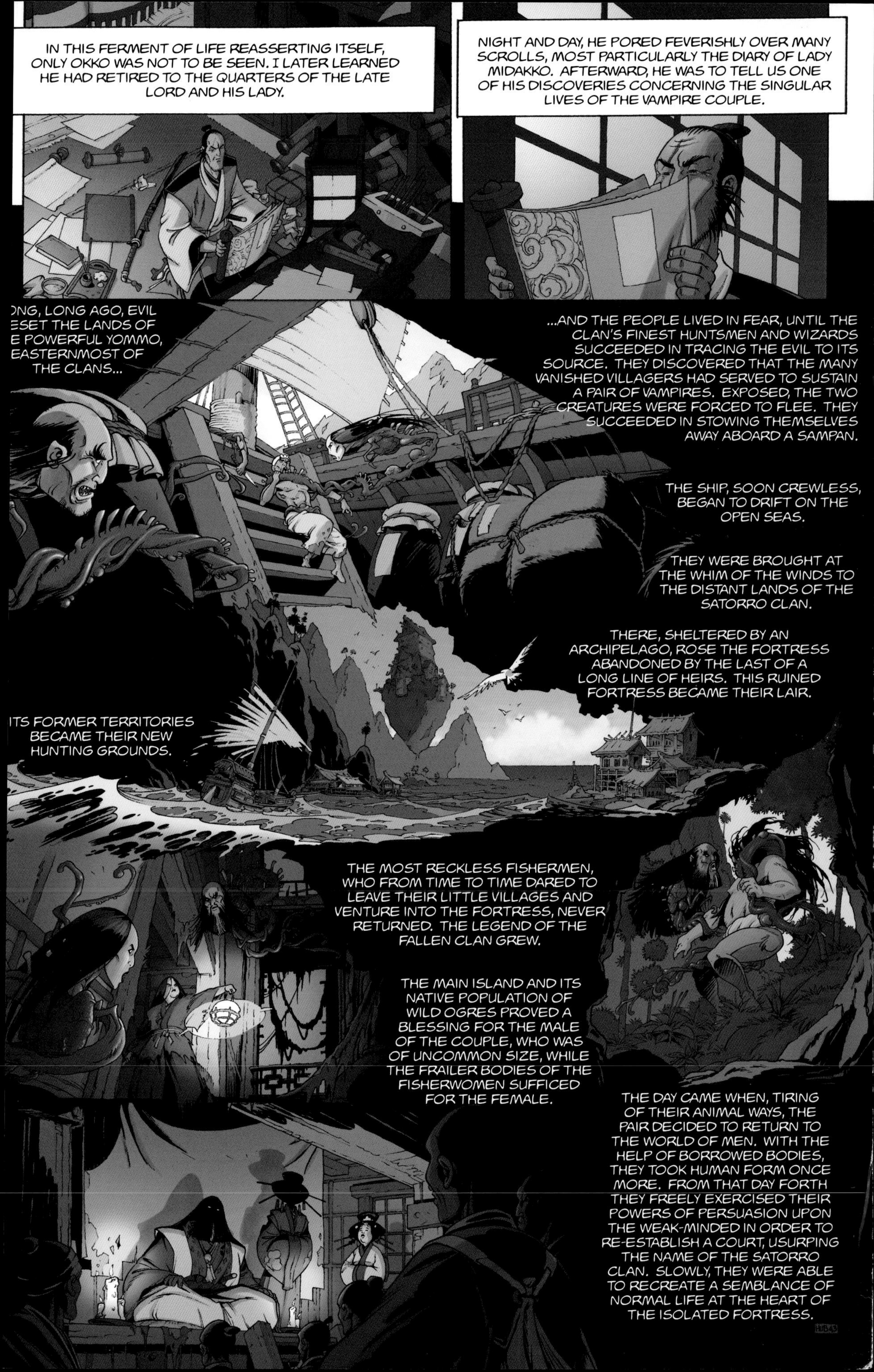

IN THIS FERMENT OF LIFE REASSERTING ITSELF, ONLY OKKO WAS NOT TO BE SEEN. I LATER LEARNED HE HAD RETIRED TO THE QUARTERS OF THE LATE LORD AND HIS LADY.
NIGHT AND DAY, HE PORED FEVERISHLY OVER MANY SCROLLS, MOST PARTICULARLY THE DIARY OF LADY MIDAKKO. AFTERWARD, HE WAS TO TELL US ONE OF HIS DISCOVERIES CONCERNING THE SINGULAR LIVES OF THE VAMPIRE COUPLE.
ONG, LONG AGO, EVIL ESET THE LANDS OF E POWERFUL YOMMO, EASTERNMOST OF THE CLANS...
...AND THE PEOPLE LIVED IN FEAR, UNTIL THE CLAN'S FINEST HUNTSMEN AND WIZARDS SUCCEEDED IN TRACING THE EVIL TO ITS SOURCE. THEY DISCOVERED THAT THE MANY VANISHED VILLAGERS HAD SERVED TO SUSTAIN A PAIR OF VAMPIRES. EXPOSED, THE TWO CREATURES WERE FORCED TO FLEE. THEY SUCCEEDED IN STOWING THEMSELVES AWAY ABOARD A SAMPAN.
THE SHIP, SOON CREWLESS, BEGAN TO DRIFT ON THE OPEN SEAS.
THEY WERE BROUGHT AT THE WHIM OF THE WINDS TO THE DISTANT LANDS OF THE SATORRO CLAN.
THERE, SHELTERED BY AN ARCHIPELAGO, ROSE THE FORTRESS ABANDONED BY THE LAST OF A LONG LINE OF HEIRS. THIS RUINED FORTRESS BECAME THEIR LAIR.
ITS FORMER TERRITORIES BECAME THEIR NEW HUNTING GROUNDS.
THE MOST RECKLESS FISHERMEN, WHO FROM TIME TO TIME DARED TO LEAVE THEIR LITTLE VILLAGES AND VENTURE INTO THE FORTRESS, NEVER RETURNED. THE LEGEND OF THE FALLEN CLAN GREW.
THE MAIN ISLAND AND ITS NATIVE POPULATION OF WILD OGRES PROVED A BLESSING FOR THE MALE OF THE COUPLE, WHO WAS OF UNCOMMON SIZE, WHILE THE FRAILER BODIES OF THE FISHERWOMEN SUFFICED FOR THE FEMALE.
THE DAY CAME WHEN, TIRING OF THEIR ANIMAL WAYS, THE PAIR DECIDED TO RETURN TO THE WORLD OF MEN. WITH THE HELP OF BORROWED BODIES, THEY TOOK HUMAN FORM ONCE MORE. FROM THAT DAY FORTH THEY FREELY EXERCISED THEIR POWERS OF PERSUASION UPON THE WEAK-MINDED IN ORDER TO RE-ESTABLISH A COURT, USURPING THE NAME OF THE SATORRO CLAN. SLOWLY, THEY WERE ABLE TO RECREATE A SEMBLANCE OF NORMAL LIFE AT THE HEART OF THE ISOLATED FORTRESS.

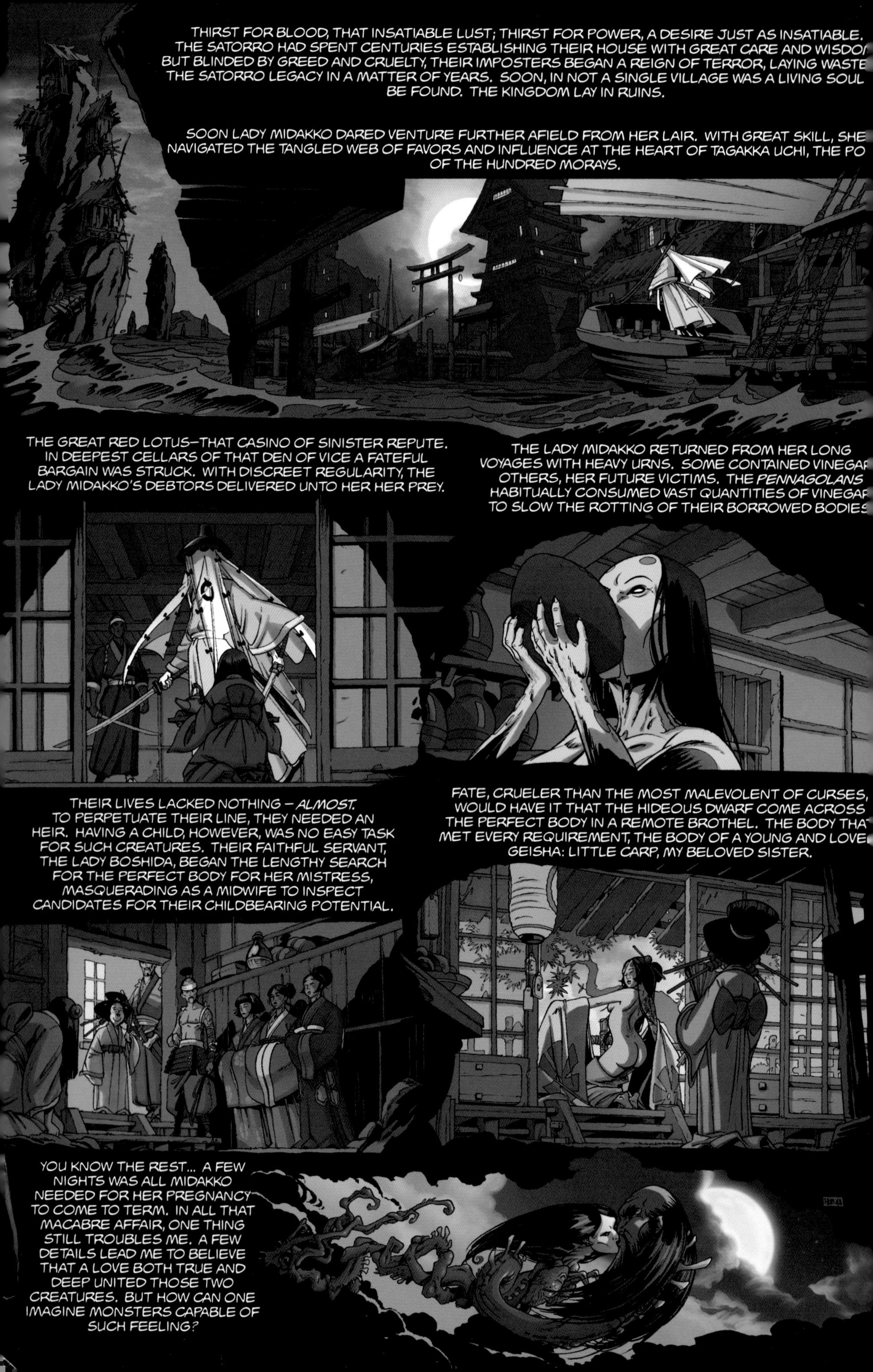
THIRST FOR BLOOD, THAT INSATIABLE LUST; THIRST FOR POWER, A DESIRE JUST AS INSATIABLE. THE SATORRO HAD SPENT CENTURIES ESTABLISHING THEIR HOUSE WITH GREAT CARE AND WISDO BUT BLINDED BY GREED AND CRUELTY, THEIR IMPOSTERS BEGAN A REIGN OF TERROR, LAYING WASTE THE SATORRO LEGACY IN A MATTER OF YEARS. SOON, IN NOT A SINGLE VILLAGE WAS A LIVING SOUL BE FOUND. THE KINGDOM LAY IN RUINS.
SOON LADY MIDAKKO DARED VENTURE FURTHER AFIELD FROM HER LAIR. WITH GREAT SKILL, SHE NAVIGATED THE TANGLED WEB OF FAVORS AND INFLUENCE AT THE HEART OF TAGAKKA UCHI, THE PO OF THE HUNDRED MORAYS.
THE GREAT RED LOTUS—THAT CASINO OF SINISTER REPUTE. IN DEEPEST CELLARS OF THAT DEN OF VICE A FATEFUL BARGAIN WAS STRUCK. WITH DISCREET REGULARITY, THE LADY MIDAKKO'S DEBTORS DELIVERED UNTO HER HER PREY.
THE LADY MIDAKKO RETURNED FROM HER LONG VOYAGES WITH HEAVY URNS. SOME CONTAINED VINEGA OTHERS, HER FUTURE VICTIMS. THE *PENNAGOLANS* HABITUALLY CONSUMED VAST QUANTITIES OF VINEGA TO SLOW THE ROTTING OF THEIR BORROWED BODIES
THEIR LIVES LACKED NOTHING – *ALMOST.* TO PERPETUATE THEIR LINE, THEY NEEDED AN HEIR. HAVING A CHILD, HOWEVER, WAS NO EASY TASK FOR SUCH CREATURES. THEIR FAITHFUL SERVANT, THE LADY BOSHIDA, BEGAN THE LENGTHY SEARCH FOR THE PERFECT BODY FOR HER MISTRESS, MASQUERADING AS A MIDWIFE TO INSPECT CANDIDATES FOR THEIR CHILDBEARING POTENTIAL.
FATE, CRUELER THAN THE MOST MALEVOLENT OF CURSES, WOULD HAVE IT THAT THE HIDEOUS DWARF COME ACROSS THE PERFECT BODY IN A REMOTE BROTHEL. THE BODY THA MET EVERY REQUIREMENT, THE BODY OF A YOUNG AND LOVE GEISHA: LITTLE CARP, MY BELOVED SISTER.
YOU KNOW THE REST... A FEW NIGHTS WAS ALL MIDAKKO NEEDED FOR HER PREGNANCY TO COME TO TERM. IN ALL THAT MACABRE AFFAIR, ONE THING STILL TROUBLES ME. A FEW DETAILS LEAD ME TO BELIEVE THAT A LOVE BOTH TRUE AND DEEP UNITED THOSE TWO CREATURES. BUT HOW CAN ONE IMAGINE MONSTERS CAPABLE OF SUCH FEELING?

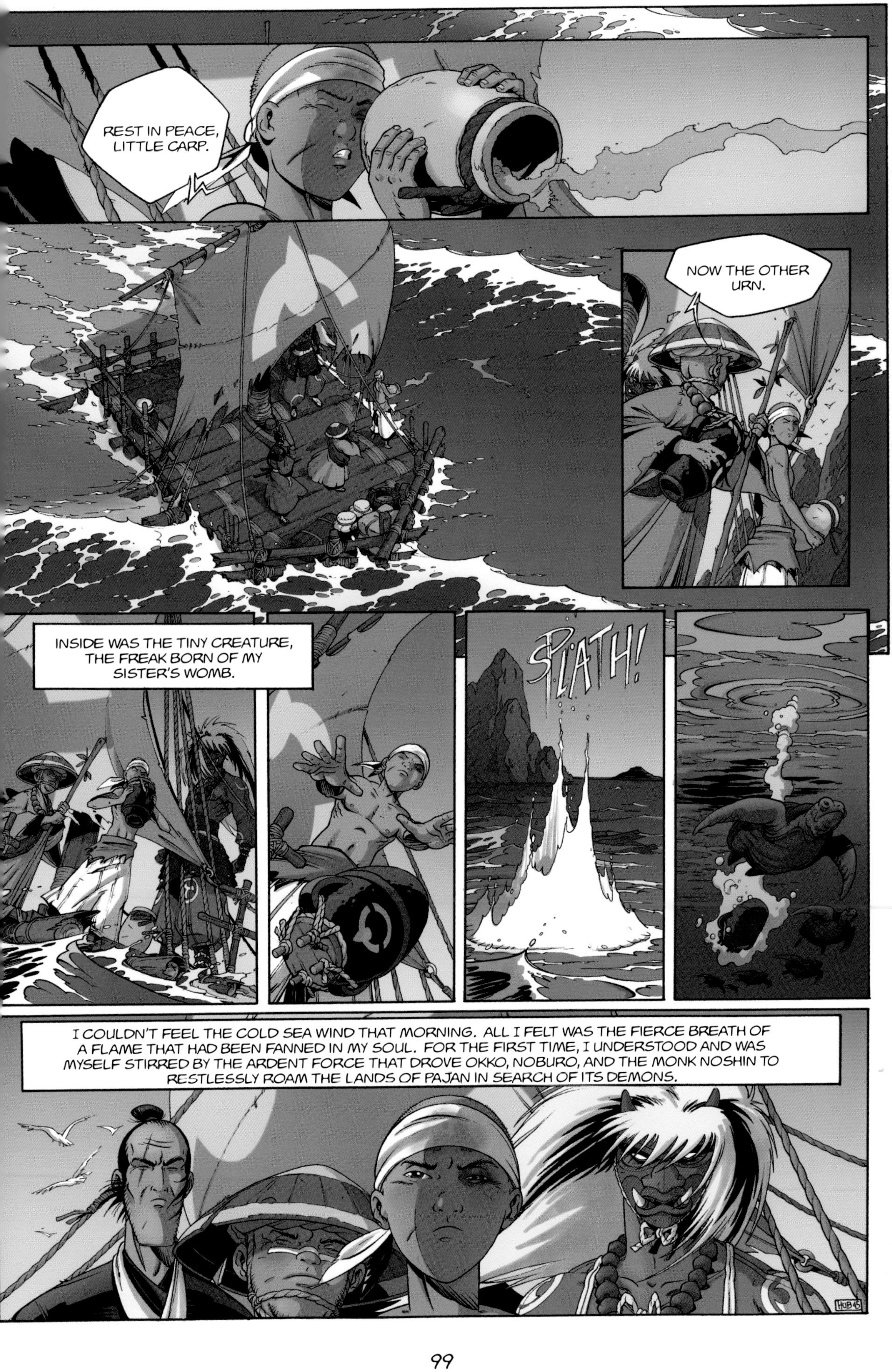
REST IN PEACE, LITTLE CARP.
NOW THE OTHER URN.
INSIDE WAS THE TINY CREATURE, THE FREAK BORN OF MY SISTER'S WOMB.
SPLATH!
I COULDN'T FEEL THE COLD SEA WIND THAT MORNING. ALL I FELT WAS THE FIERCE BREATH OF A FLAME THAT HAD BEEN FANNED IN MY SOUL. FOR THE FIRST TIME, I UNDERSTOOD AND WAS MYSELF STIRRED BY THE ARDENT FORCE THAT DROVE OKKO, NOBURO, AND THE MONK NOSHIN TO RESTLESSLY ROAM THE LANDS OF PAJAN IN SEARCH OF ITS DEMONS.
HUB 05

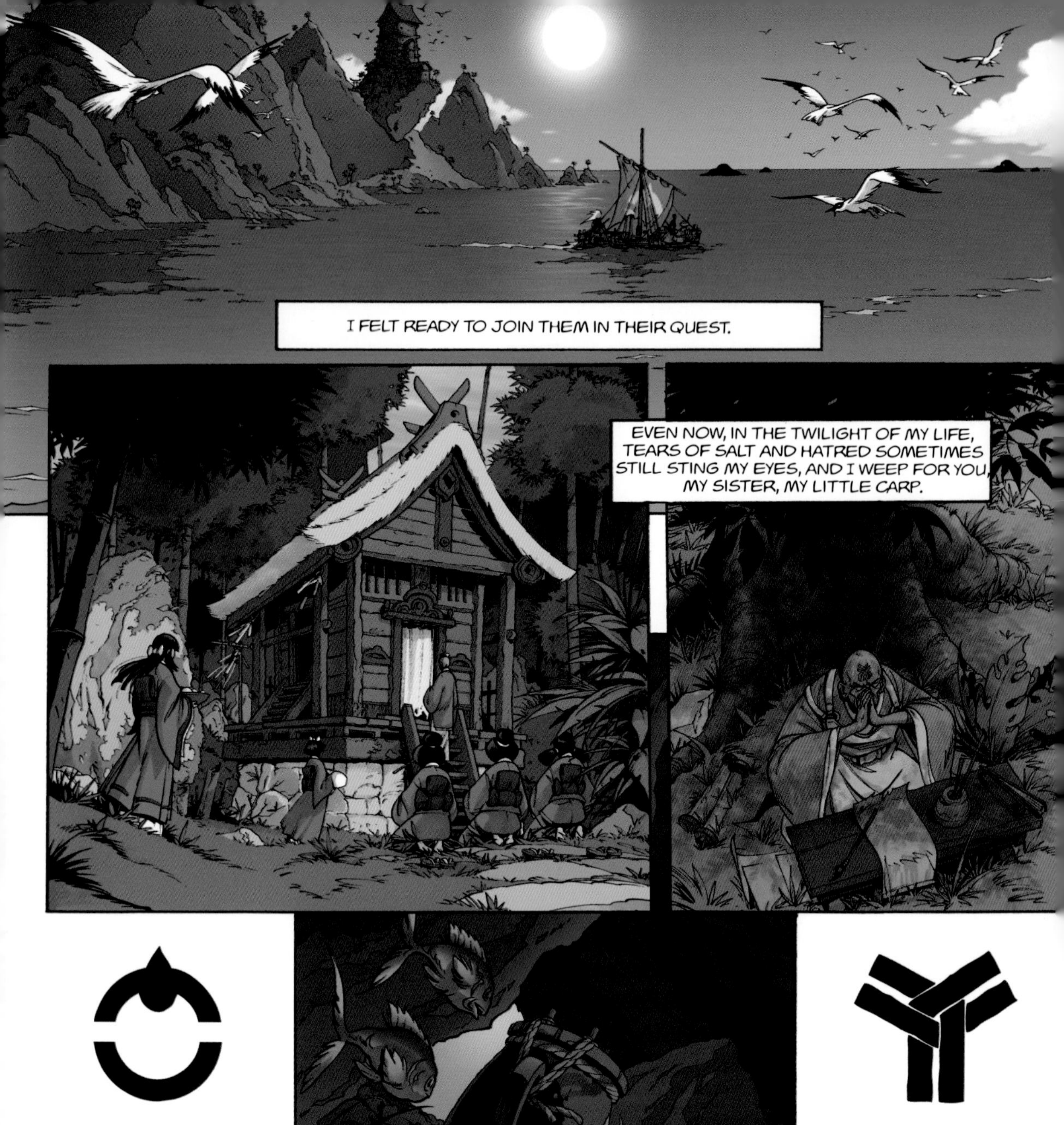
I FELT READY TO JOIN THEM IN THEIR QUEST.
EVEN NOW, IN THE TWILIGHT OF MY LIFE, TEARS OF SALT AND HATRED SOMETIMES STILL STING MY EYES, AND I WEEP FOR YOU, MY SISTER, MY LITTLE CARP.

THE END OF THE CYCLE OF WATER

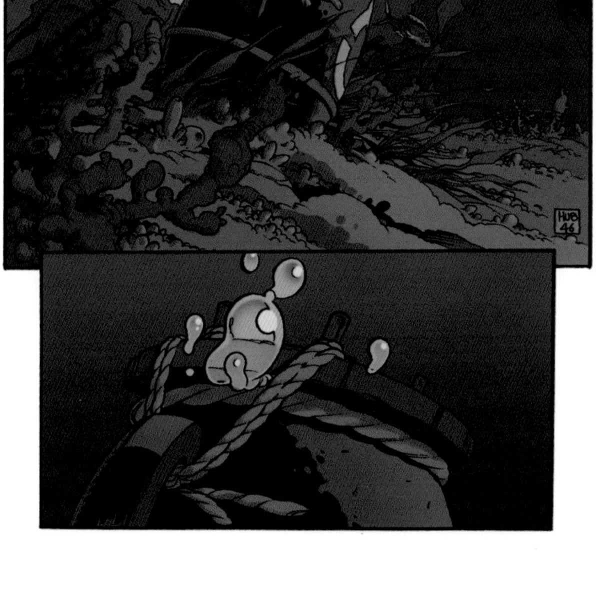

NEXT: THE CYCLE OF EARTH

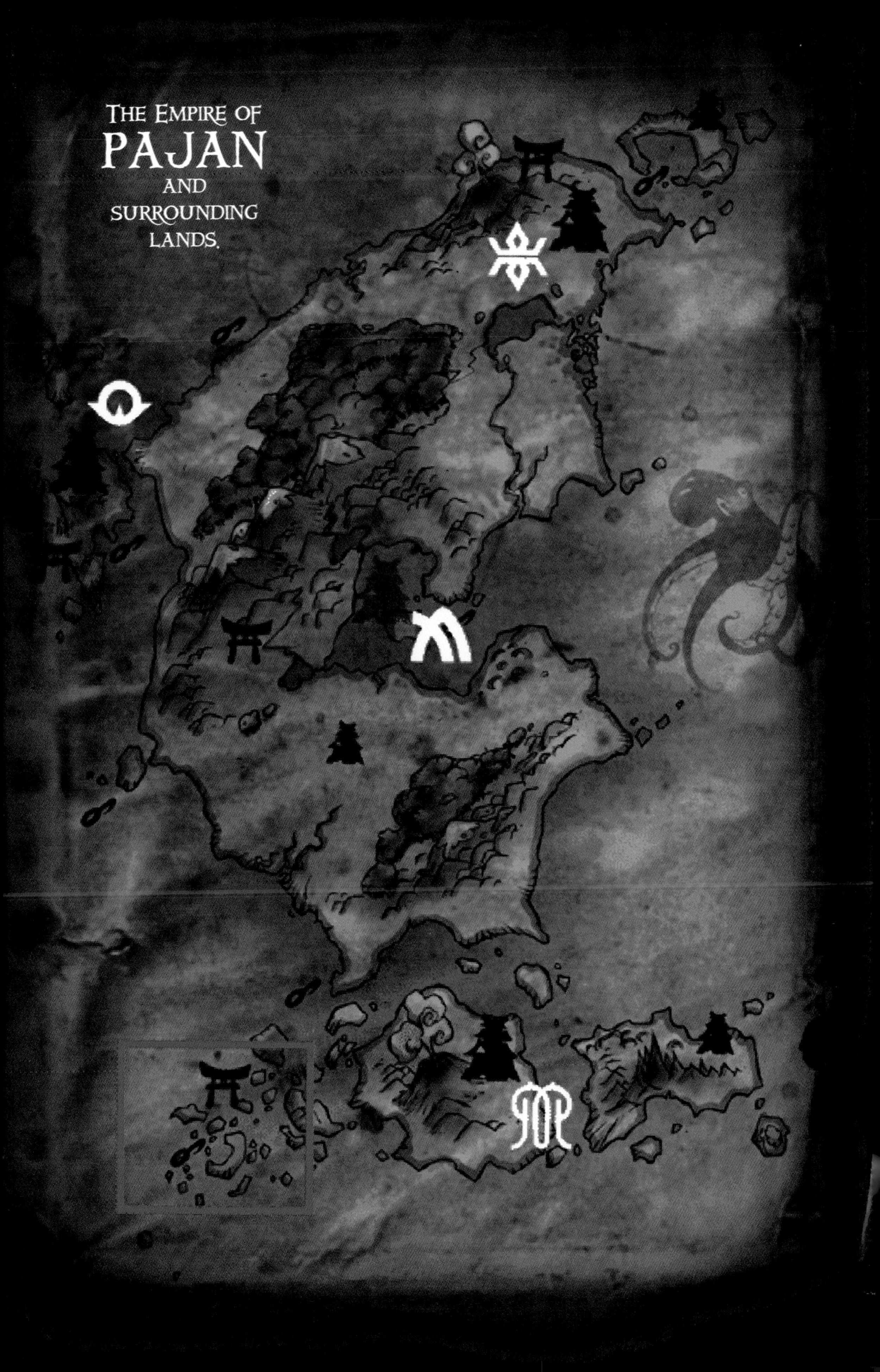

THE EMPIRE OF
PAJAN
AND
SURROUNDING
LANDS.

Map Key

Territory of the
Ataku clan

Territory of the
Boshimon clan

Capital of Pajan

Territory of the
Pajan Empire

Major Cities
and Palaces

Temples

Territory of the
Yommo clan

Major Ports

General region
of the events of
this book

A Brief History

The action of the first cycle of OKKO takes place at the far end of the known lands of the **Empire of Pajan**. Pajan itself is a vast and diversified island, surrounded by a multitude of archipelagoes. Its name is derived from that of its Imperial Family. Though the Pajans have reigned for a millennium, in the last few decades three major families - the *Ataku*, the *Boshimon*, and the *Yommo* - have called into question their legitimacy and now refuse to cease their battles against the Imperial Family. These power struggles have destabilized the Empire, and famine and catastrophes follow one another. This period of chaos is commonly called the *Era of Asagiri* (the *Time of Mists*). The OKKO series takes place in the middle of this tumultuous period, in the year 1108 of official calendar. The way of life and various habits of the inhabitants of the Empire of Pajan are rather close to those of medieval Japan. However, one major difference is a great technological revolution that appeared a few centuries ago: the *exo banraku*, colossal combat armors handled from within by marionettists. Their use has radically changed the ancestral art of war in the Pajan Empire. The Ataku family has taken the lead in the construction and the handling of these frightening machines of war.

The following is a brief description of the four major clans attempting to assert their power over the Empire of Pajan.

The Family Pajan

The ancestral clan of the Imperial family. Placing great value on the warrior's code of honor, their dojos have the reputation of producing the Empire's most valiant samurai. Their peerless tacticians defend the Imperial family's interests, stopping at nothing to restore its power.

The Family Ataku

In the last few decades, this family has gained a clear political advantage, winning many celebrated battles with the help of their *"Exo-bunrakus"*. The clan are masters of the construction and operation of these formidable war machines.

The Family Yommo

This mystical clan comprises the Empire's greatest sorcerers. On the battlefield, its elementalists can, with their powerful spells, sway the tide of the encounter in their favor.

The Family Bashimon

A cunning and mysterious clan composed of calculating diplomats, widely feared and dreaded. They are masters of Machiavellian manipulation, pursuing every secret or scrap of information that might further their interests. They prefer to work in the shadows and have the habit of employing ninjas for certain more... *delicate* missions.

PLAINFIELD PUBLIC LIBRARY
15025 S. Illinois Street
Plainfield, IL 60544